MW01283747

Summer 2011
Pacifica
Graduate
Institute

Transformation of the Psyche

Transformation of the Psyche

The Symbolic Alchemy of the *Splendor Solis*

**Joseph L. Henderson
and
Dyane N. Sherwood**

Routledge
Taylor & Francis Group

LONDON AND NEW YORK

First published 2003 by Routledge
27 Church Road, Hove, East Sussex,
BN3 2FA

Simultaneously published in the USA
and Canada
by Routledge
270 Madison Avenue, New York,
NY 10016

Reprinted 2004 and 2005

*Routledge is an imprint of the
Taylor & Francis Group*

© 2003 Joseph L. Henderson and
Dyane N. Sherwood

Typeset in Century Old Style by
RefineCatch Limited, Bungay, Suffolk
Jacket design by Sandra Heath
Index compiled by Lewis Derrick
Printed and bound in Italy by
Conti Tipocolor S.p.A.

All rights reserved. No part of this
book may be reprinted or reproduced
or utilized in any form or by any
electronic, mechanical, or other means,
now known or hereafter invented,
including photocopying and recording,
or in any information storage or
retrieval system, without permission
in writing from the publishers.

*British Library Cataloguing in
Publication Data*
A catalogue record for this book is
available from the British Library

ISBN 1–58391–950–3

This book was made possible in
part by a grant from the Life
Balance Institute

CONTENTS

LIST OF ILLUSTRATIONS

Plates

All 22 plates are from the illuminated manuscript of the *Splendor Solis* (Harley 3469), 1582, belonging to the British Library. (The numbering and titles are not in the original manuscript but have been added for ease of reference.)

Figures

Introduction

The First Series

The Second Series

Table

FOREWORD

It is an honor and a pleasure to write a foreword for this psychological study of the *Splendor Solis* by Drs. Joseph Henderson and Dyane Sherwood. The authors, both active members of the Society of Jungian Analysts of Northern California, together span the generations of analysts who have lived and worked in that mainstay of Jungian thought, the San Francisco Bay Area – the reader will readily feel the collective wisdom of this community distilled into the present volume. The authors each bring their own unique approach to the alchemical manuscript and images under study yet what emerges is a smooth synthesis that in turn demonstrates the power of the *Splendor Solis* to impact the psyches of its serious students. Dichotomies such as clinical versus symbolic perspectives melt as we are skillfully shown the intimate interplay between alchemical images and contemporary states of mind and soul, whether in the consulting office or in the larger world.

Having a background in chemistry and an interest in the history of science, I had briefly encountered several images from the *Splendor Solis* prior to my analytic training, though it was not until I viewed the videotape of Dr. Henderson's 1987 lecture on this manuscript that deciphering its psychological relevance became important to me. Given this key to the symbolism, I became especially interested in pursuing my own line of inquiry focused on the seven plates that accompany the Fourth Treatise of the text. These are displayed in Plate II–1 through Plate II–7 of the book you are about to read. They show a succession of scenes in flasks within alcoves which in turn are surrounded by depictions from life of those times (the sixteenth century). These scenes portraying various human activities provide a kind of cultural amplification that corresponds to the archetypal influence imagined to be constellated at that moment in the alchemical process. The archetypal designations are brought to our attention explicitly as the astrological 'god(s)' in the chariots at the top of the frame. In studying this aspect of the plates, I have found it worthwhile to reflect further upon the figures pulling the chariots. These figures are in effect images of the libido whose energy must be harnessed to allow particular archetypal expressions to unfold during the corresponding phase of the work. Thus while two dragons pull the chariot of Mercurius Senex in the first, Plate II–1, it is a pair of peacocks that are the motive force for the second chariot, that of Jupiter, Plate II–2. In passing I suggest this represents a shift from the efforts to exert control over the imagination that is reactively driven by unconscious, somatic processes, to a focus on employing various dimensions of narcissism that will be required for an expanded view of the Self that is to come. Perhaps the most compelling of these yoked beings is the final pair, Plate II–7: two human female figures pulling the chariot of the moon. Since the manuscript is the product of a patriarchal culture, these figures most likely represent the *anima*, or soul of the culture. It is the harnessing of this that provides the motive passion needed to bring the potential of the lunar realm, the true imagination, to bear in the *rubedo* and so bring this phase of the work to its full conclusion.

Over the years in preparing my own lectures on this series, I have wrestled with many aspects of these images but none more than the attempt to imagine what might have been occurring in the flasks in conjunction and in interaction with whatever processes were active in the psyches of the alchemists, the author of the text and especially the artist who rendered these exquisite images. As an example, consider the images in the third and fourth flask (see Plates II–3 and II–4): the three-headed eagle that is ascending would probably have been a white sublimate rising as a mist out of the material at the bottom when sufficiently heated; this sublimate would then have condensed against the cooler sides of the upper part of the flask (n.b.: chemically this is a method of purification for substances capable of sublimation). The three-headed dragon in the following flask would have been in turn the material remaining at the bottom now beginning to show signs of internal movement, e.g., bubbling, perhaps with some viscous, colored oils swirling within it. The sublimate could readily be interpreted as a physical analogue of the experience of gaining insight when clarity arises through transforming intuitions into differentiated thought, symbolized as the eagle, rising out of an activated muddle of confused feelings and sensation. This latter residue remains below, symbolized by the multicolored dragon, which as we know from parallels in analytic work will fall into problematic repression if not valued and attended to; hence flask four brings a return to the affective energies now activated in the soma. Though too limited to do justice to the images, this sampling of a more physically oriented approach is complementary to the reading of the present authors.

The aesthetic quality of the illuminated manuscript images of the *Splendor Solis* is unmatched in the whole of alchemy. It is difficult not to be captivated by their sheer beauty, yet this also adds a layer of complexity, for as Drs. Henderson and Sherwood tell us, the artist and 'Salomon Trismosin' could not have known one another; their lives were too separated in time for that to have been possible. The ability to portray what in modern analytical parlance we could term an individuation process through these images is apparent, but what was the role of the text and previous (inferior) images in fostering such a development? For a comprehensive understanding of this, beyond the important synthesis of available materials presented by the authors in this book, we must await additional historical studies that would provide us detailed biographical insights about the artist and author as well as to trace out a more complete history of the entire manuscript. In addition I have heard, perhaps apocryphally, that Jung felt the *Splendor Solis* was second only to the *Rosarium Philosophorum* in psychological import.

While analysts may debate the relative psychological worth of the various alchemical manuscripts, it does seem that these two are especially significant for Jungians. Both the *Rosarium* and the *Splendor Solis* depict a trajectory of processes that involve somatic and psychological transformations. The arrangement of images in each of these not only leads to the natural consideration of their representing a set of evolving processes but when each series is taken together we can get a glimpse of the operations of a larger whole, what Jung would have referred to as the Self. As processes described in contemporary scientific language, these could be termed 'emergent' – that is, they have components which interact on one scale while producing effects on a scale above that of the components. Thus the flask-images associated with the Fourth Treatise not only culminate in a *rubedo*, the golden state pictured in the seventh image of the series, but with the emergence of the archetypal figures in the chariots presiding over each 'step', we may surmise that they collectively interact to generate a cosmos that is itself embedded within the body of the whole work. Without further elaboration here we can still entertain the possibility that the *Splendor Solis* is constructed in a manner compatible with the edges of contemporary multidisciplinary thought. I would even be so bold as to suggest that in some ways it may supercede the *Rosarium*, not in worth but in its compensatory relevance to the current Zeitgeist (in the same way that I believe the *Rosarium* epitomized the spirit of the therapeutic world of Jung's time), which is part of the importance of the appearance of Drs. Henderson and Sherwood's book at this moment of complexity.

In reading the present text, I was gratified to find the close parallels between the authors' and my own understandings of the symbolism and its clinical applications, before we had any substantive discussions. The feeling of profound recognition as well as agreement rang out repeatedly as I reflected on their text and reengaged with the power of the images. A case that I have recently published exemplifies the impact that working with these images can have clinically.[1] In that therapy the following dream 'coincidence' occurred. In a moment of silence within a session in which painful affects had been touched on, I recalled a dream of my own from the previous night. At the time I was intensely involved in studying the psychological significance of the *Splendor Solis* and in my dream I had been puzzling over the second flask associated with the Fourth Treatise (Plate II–2), the one containing a black, a white, and a red bird lying at the bottom which has been interpreted as the birds either fighting or being dead – there was no reference or evident connection in the dream to this case. As the dream returned to consciousness I was curious as to how it might be tied to the present moment and observed my patient carefully, discerning a slightly glazed look about him. When asked about this, he sheepishly reported having 'left the room.' Treating this as a field phenomenon, I remarked that I had been reflecting on my own imagings and was wondering about the diffuse state that seemed present. The shared uncertainty reduced his felt shame and exposure, allowing him to go further into his 'disappearance.' We subsequently discovered an unconscious attempt at self-destruction he had made when as a child he had fallen into an open pit and had been rendered unconscious. This had occurred in a moment of abject loneliness but had never been consciously acknowledged as an internal assault. It was as if 'my' dream were being redreamt within the hour, amplifying the state of the field with its intensifying abandonment and loneliness unleashing unconscious rage that was knocking out consciousness through dissociation. The shared use of this coincidence, though not made explicit, helped to shift the therapy into a more emotionally nuanced phase.

After reading this book I had separate discussions, first with Dr. Sherwood and then with Dr. Henderson. In these I was struck by how each of our labors with the manuscript had brought us to similar experiences and conclusions. It was as if through this material we discovered a shared psychological appreciation of various aspects of Jungian psychology, some beyond the immediate scope of these images and text, for example, views on the range of intensities and frequencies of synchronistic phenomena in clinical practice. Perhaps we already shared certain features in our psychological make-up but it struck me more as a kind of kinship libido among us that had developed from our individual protracted considerations of this material. It is this animated quality of relationship to the *Splendor Solis* itself that gave me the sense of fit to join them by writing this foreword. It is my hope that readers will be similarly moved to join this emergent community of the psyche through their own deep encounters with this living material.

Joe Cambray

PREFACE

My first encounter with the plates of the *Splendor Solis* was in 1937, while I was completing medical school in England and still in analysis part-time with Jung. In those days, I was aware that Jung was making a study of alchemy, but I didn't know much about what he was writing. He had published nothing about alchemy in English except the commentary to Wilhelm's *Secret of the Golden Flower* (CW 13).[1]

At that time I began to dream of colors and color sequences. I was fascinated, but I didn't understand the dreams until I thought of Jung's comments on alchemy in seminars that I had attended in Zürich and that color sequences might refer to something alchemical. Although by this time I was strongly influenced by Jung's psychology, this upsurge of alchemical material in my psyche occurred spontaneously.

I do not remember how I happened to discover the beautiful illuminated manuscript by Salomon Trismosin called the *Splendor Solis*,[2] but there it was in the library of the British Museum, near where I was studying for my final examinations for graduation from medical school. I was permitted to look at this magnificent alchemical treatise, and in it I found many of the same colors and color sequences I had seen in my dreams. There was also a strangely synchronistic correspondence between my dreams and the text. It did not seem at all surprising: I reacted as if it were the most natural thing in the world. One's interest is attracted to what one needs. Does that also mean that what is called forth is attracted to one's interest? If so, that *is* surprising! Edward Edinger referred to this possibility when he wrote:

> The gods we have lost are descending on us, demanding reconnection. Like Baucis and Philemon, modern individuals are being visited by and asked to provide hospitality for transpersonal factors with which they have lost connection.[3]

After I had passed my medical examinations, I decided to give hospitality to alchemy by drawing with colored pencils what appeared to be a medieval stained-glass window in which the basic alchemical colors – black, white, yellow, green, and red – appeared in association with certain symbolic elements surrounding a central sun colored red and gold. I suspected myself of having contrived this design until I showed it to Jung, who said, 'Oh yes, this is eleventh-century alchemy.' How easy it is for us to doubt the messages that come from the deep unconscious! Apparently my conscious awareness of the alchemical images from the *Splendor Solis*, which was painted in the sixteenth century, had already deepened in the unconscious, and I had unwittingly descended to a much earlier period, when alchemy was more simply symbolized. I could no longer doubt the authority of this message that I was more subjectively receptive to alchemy than I had thought.

The deeper meaning of my psyche's turn to alchemy did not become known to me for a very long time. Eventually, it took an important place in my life and in work. While the three series of plates in the *Splendor Solis* were originally intended to illustrate the symbolism of alchemy, I found that they could express significant stages in any deep process of self-discovery.

In 1968, I was able to acquire transparencies of the whole series of the *Splendor Solis* paintings from the British Library, and I have used the slides for teaching at the C. G. Jung Institute in San Francisco ever since. I always find that the analysts-in-training respond especially well to them. These images seem to help them to understand the symbolism of the unconscious.

I usually conduct seminars of this kind by starting with what I call theory. The Latin term *theoria* – derived from the Greek word *thea*, meaning 'a view' – in this context can refer to *ideas* that arise from archetypal imagery. *Theoria* contrasts with practice (in Latin, *practica*, meaning 'capable of being used'). In the sense that we use this term in analytical psychology, it involves the psychological *application* of the imagery of the unconscious – in this instance, images from alchemy – to our work with individuals in psychotherapy. Our psychological point of view is not just a rational, scientific procedure but one that evokes the nature of the unconscious and its corresponding imagery.

Joseph L. Henderson

My interest in the images of the *Splendor Solis*[4] began in 1993 during my analytic training, after Mary Jo Spencer suggested to our seminar group that we view a videotape of a 1987 lecture by Dr. Henderson on the paintings contained in the *Splendor Solis*.[5] I was deeply impressed both with the images and with the clarity of Dr. Henderson's commentary.

I obtained color photocopies of the images[6] and also transcribed Dr. Henderson's remarks on the first eleven images. My classmate, Ellen Garfinkle, Ph.D., transcribed his commentary on the remaining eleven images. With Dr. Henderson's permission, we placed copies of our transcriptions in the library of the C. G. Jung Institute of San Francisco.

After completing my analytic training, my attention in consultation with Dr. Henderson focused from time to time on the relationship between the dreams of some of my patients and the images from the *Splendor Solis*. Specifically, I wanted to see if the images of the *Splendor Solis* helped me to understand the therapeutic process in a deeper way. Over time, the images became even more fascinating to me and took on a life of their own.

During the summer of 1998, after Dr. Henderson celebrated his ninety-fifth birthday, I proposed to him that his 1987 *Splendor Solis* videotape might serve as the basis for a small book.[7] He was delighted with this idea. Initially, my role was that of editor of the lecture notes and provider of clinical examples. As we refined the text and amplified the images and their symbolism, our appreciation of these images deepened and the project grew beyond our original expectations.

The 1987 lecture was concerned primarily with the first eleven images, comprising what we refer to as the First Series. During my editing of Dr. Henderson's remarks on the Second Series, I began to contribute to the work in more substantial ways, including a way of conceptualizing that series. I was hesitant to insert myself too much into the project, but Dr. Henderson welcomed my contribution. At that point, it became clear to us both that I had become a co-author, rather than an editor. My contribution expanded to include commentary on all the images and the writing of the Introduction. Over the course of many discussions, revisions, and additions, the book grew to its current size. I have spent several years waking in the morning with some new connection or meaning to be added. Research on the symbols and references in the paintings led me into many areas where I had little expertise, and I spent months reading with pleasure literary or historical material to help me understand a context or reference. Our collaboration felt not only effortless but also, I believe, a true joy to us both.

On a more personal note, when I first viewed the beautiful paintings contained in the *Splendor Solis*, I felt a special connection with images in the First Series that appear to be situated in Venice. When I was eight years old, my mother took me (and my younger sister and brother) along as she traveled from port to port in the Mediterranean to meet the aircraft carrier on which my father was stationed. In Italy, for the first time, I experienced real art, as well as a sensuous and emotionally expressive ordinary life. That experience allowed me to connect with parts of myself that felt entirely alone and unrecognized in my family and in my culturally bleak childhood surroundings of post-World War II housing developments near naval bases. For the rest of my childhood, I dreamt of Italy and hoped one day to revisit Venice. To my amazement, twenty years later I was able to walk from San Marco to the Hotel Luna, where I had stayed with my parents, without consulting a map.

Venice is a city of human proportions, where one can move from place to place by foot or boat. It faces the sea, looking east toward Istanbul, opening to the sea via canals that bring water into the heart of the city itself. For me, Venice is a symbol and a living experience of a good relationship between consciousness, civilization, and the unknown of both the watery depths and the world beyond one's own culture.

Many people have contributed to this book, both directly and indirectly. Jacques Rutzky, my husband, has given me his wholehearted support. Andrew Samuels took an early interest in our project and challenged me to expand Dr. Henderson's lecture into a full-sized book. John Beebe and Mary Jo Spencer both read an early draft and made many valuable suggestions. My sister, Aleta Neilson, read the Introduction and made comments that were both sensitive and substantive. Jean Kirsch graced the manuscript with deft and perceptive editing and commentary as I readied it for publication. Joe Cambray generously gave me feedback and suggestions when he read the manuscript in preparation for writing the Foreword. Tom Kirsch has helped me in countless ways for many years, and for this project he facilitated crucial contacts regarding publication and shared his valuable insights into my own process as I wrote. The staff of the British Library were gracious and helpful, both over a long distance and when I visited London to view the manuscript of the Harley *Splendor Solis*. That trip to London was made possible by a grant from the Scholarship Fund of the C. G. Jung Institute of San Francisco. Several of my colleagues have either contributed their own material or received permission from a patient to include material. The beautiful color images in this book would not have been possible without the generous and timely financial support of Phillip Moffitt and the Life Balance Institute. Robin Jaqua made a substantial contribution towards expenses incurred in the final preparation and initial promotion of the book. Finally, I am most grateful to my colleagues at Brunner-Routledge – Kate Hawes, Mandy Collison, and Helen Pritt – who have shared with me both the aesthetic vision and the attention to detail required of this project. It has been a pleasure to work with them.

If alchemy teaches us anything, it teaches us that concepts in isolation are sterile and that matter is essential. The matter of therapy is found in the material brought by the patient and in the relationship between the therapist and the patient. Many of my patients over the years have given me permission to use their clinical material – with their names withheld – in my teaching and writing. Their material has complex, profound, and intimate meanings that cannot be conveyed here. And this is as it should be: as alchemy also teaches us, the way of transformation cannot be revealed by the telling but only through the experience.

Dyane N. Sherwood

ACKNOWLEDGEMENTS

The authors and publishers are grateful to the British Library, for permission to reproduce images from the *Splendor Solis* (MS Harley 3469); 'Apollo Inducing a Healing Trance' (MS Sloane 6 f.175); 'Fifteenth Century Alchemical Apparatus' (MS Sloane 3548 f.25); 'A Medieval Apothecary's Shop' (MS Sloane 1977 f.49v); 'Alexander Being Lowered from a Ship in a Barrel to View the Wonders of the Sea' (MS Roy. 15 E VI f.20); 'Astrologers and Geomancers' (MS Add. 24189 f.15); and 'Zodiac Man' (MS Arundel 251 f.46). Also to Beinecke Rare Book and Manuscript Library, Yale University, for 'Tree with Flames at Its Base'; and 'Mercurius as a Three-Headed Dragon'; to Penelope Etnier, for 'Big Bang'; and 'Dark Matter'; to Glasgow University Library, Department of Special Collections, for 'Projection of the Tincture from the Heart of the King onto the Base Metals' (Ferguson MS 208, f.73^r); to The Hilma af Klint Foundation, for 'Swan' (nr. 24); to Städtische Galerie im Lenbachhaus, Münich, for 'Improvisation Sinflut' by Wassily Kandinsky; to Procuratoria di San Marco, Venezia, for 'The Baptism of Christ'; to Rare Books Division, The New York Public Library, for 'The Stag and the Unicorn in the Forest'; to Réunion des Musées Nationaux / Art Resource, NY, for 'The Golden Apple of the Hesperides, Guarded by a Snake'; to Sacro Convento, Assisi, for 'St Francis Preaching to the Birds'; to Dr Jean Schellenberg, for 'Torture'; 'Freed'; 'Baby Girl'; 'Facing It'; 'Honey Girl'; and 'Opening the Chakras'; to Studio Böhm, for 'St George and the Dragon'; to Thames & Hudson Ltd., for 'Saturn' (from *Astrology: The Celestial Mirror* by Kenton, published by Thames & Hudson Ltd, London and New York, 1989); and 'Kundalini Yoga, Showing the Chakras' (private collection from *Kundalini: The Arousal of the Inner Energy* by A. Mookerjee, published by Thames & Hudson Ltd., London, 1982); and to Zentralbibliothek Zürich, for 'Virgin's Milk' (MS Rh. 172 f.13v); 'Sophia Reveals her Mercurial Nature' (MS Rh. 172 f.11r); and 'The Signs of the Zodiac in Relation to the Alchemical *Opus*' (MS Rh. 172 f.29v). We are grateful to Taylor & Francis Books Ltd and to Princeton University Press for permission to reproduce extracts from *The Collected Works of C. G. Jung*, by C. G. Jung, 1953–79.

    This book was made possible in part by a grant from the Life Balance Institute.

INTRODUCTION

Alchemy and modern depth psychology

TO THE READER UNFAMILIAR with the work of C. G. Jung, it might at first seem puzzling that in the twenty-first century a book on psychological transformation should concern itself with images from a sixteenth-century illuminated manuscript, which in turn was based on a fifteenth-century alchemical treatise. In the seventeenth and eighteenth centuries, alchemical theories about the nature of matter and its transformation were discredited and replaced by modern physics and chemistry. The alchemists' obscure and convoluted way of talking about the transformation of matter was so obviously misguided that it was of interest only to a few mystics and to scholars of the history of science. By the twentieth century, the vestiges of alchemy were found in a handful of books and in the footnotes of textbooks, where the alchemists of medieval and Renaissance Europe might be acknowledged for their practical contributions to laboratory techniques. As alchemy in Europe had not been part of established centers of learning, many of its texts were lost. The surviving manuscripts were written in an arcane, symbolic language that made them nearly impossible to understand. However, in the early twentieth century the emerging field of depth psychology (called 'analytical psychology' by C. G. Jung) introduced an entirely new way of understanding the nature of alchemical pursuits.

Historically, the link between analytical psychology and alchemy began in 1928, when Richard Wilhelm sent C. G. Jung his translation of a Chinese Taoist text, *The Secret of the Golden Flower*. Jung has recounted how his investigations into the nature of the unconscious over the previous fifteen years had 'confronted' him 'with an extensive phenomenology to which hitherto known categories and methods could no longer be applied.'[1] In his search for some comparative material against which he could test the generality of his findings, he had studied Gnostic texts. However, he was frustrated by the lack of adequate sources and historical information. As it turned out, *The Secret of the Golden Flower* contained alchemical symbolism, and as Jung wrote, 'that put me on the right track.'[2]

Jung began to study medieval European alchemy, not for its chemical operations but as a source of information about human psychology. He reasoned that the alchemists, while trying to understand the unknown in matter, would project onto matter the images and categories of the unconscious. In this context, the concept of projection is used in a broad sense to include the way in which the mind shapes our experience of the world and also the way certain things in the outer world, which mirror an inner dilemma, become objects of fascination. Thus, we may translate an internal problem that would be hopelessly obscure and confusing into one we can interact with and reflect upon.

According to this rationale, a study of alchemical sources might reveal more about the structure and function of the psyche than about the 'objective' nature of the metals the alchemists believed they were studying. Jung wrote:

> The real nature of matter was unknown to the alchemist: he knew it only in hints. In seeking to explore it he projected the unconscious into the darkness of matter in order to illuminate it. In order to explain the mystery of matter he projected yet another mystery – his own unknown psychic background – into what was to be explained . . . This procedure was not, of course, intentional; it was an involuntary occurrence.
>
> Strictly speaking, projection is never made; it happens, it is simply there. In the darkness of anything external to me I find, without recognizing it as such, an interior or psychic life that is my own. . . . Such projections repeat themselves whenever man tries to explore an empty darkness and involuntarily fills it with living form.[3]

The results of his study must have been more than Jung could have hoped for: he even found remarkable similarities between medieval alchemical imagery and the dream images of his twentieth-century patients: 'Between such images and those spontaneously produced by patients undergoing psychological treatment there is, for the expert, a striking similarity both in form and in content . . .'[4] Examples of these parallels are found in many of his works from the late 1930s on, including his essay, 'Individual Dream Symbolism in Relation to Alchemy.'[5] To underline this point: the psyches of modern Europeans were producing imaginal, symbolic images that had much in common with symbols used by alchemists hundreds of years earlier.

In retrospect, perhaps it is not so surprising that alchemical imagery provided a window into the unconscious, in a way similar to dreams. As Jung pointed out, dreams were one source of alchemical symbolism: 'the alchemists themselves testify to the occurrence of dreams and visions during the opus.'[6] Jung saw that alchemy was a particularly rich source of projected psychological material, because alchemists had developed a *symbolic* way of expressing their ideas about the nature of matter and its transformation. In addition, the alchemists' observations were made with the senses, because they were personally witnessing the transformations of matter in the laboratory.[7]

Jung also believed that the study of alchemy might help us better understand the psychology of contemporary culture, because we can achieve perspective on our current situation 'when we can reach a point outside our own time from which to observe it.'[8]

The symbolism of alchemy evolved in both the East and the West over many centuries, crossing back and forth across cultural divides. Therefore it reflects ways of imagining ourselves that are not specifically conditioned by individual personal experience or by the presuppositions of a particular culture. Jung called these transpersonal categories or forms of imagination and perception 'archetypes' (from the Greek *arkhe-*, meaning 'original' and *tupos*, meaning 'model' or 'stamp'), borrowing the Platonic term for essential and authentic forms that underlie experience.[9] Because Jung's concept of the archetypes is so often misunderstood as reflecting a Lamarckian view of inherited images or ideas, it is worthwhile to let Jung speak for himself at some length:

> There is an *a priori* factor in all human activities, namely the inborn, preconscious and unconscious individual structure of the psyche. The pre-conscious psyche – for example, that of a new-born infant – is not an empty vessel into which, under favourable conditions, practically anything can be poured. On the contrary, it is a tremendously complicated, sharply defined individual entity which appears indeterminate to us only because we cannot see it directly. But the moment the first visible manifestations of psychic life begin to appear, one would have to be blind not to recognize their individual character, that is, the unique personality behind them. It is hardly possible to suppose that all these details come into being only at the moment in which they appear . . . [10]

> Again and again I encounter the mistaken notion that an archetype is determined in regard to its content, in other words that it is a kind of unconscious idea (if such an expression be admissible). It is necessary to point out once more that archetypes are not determined as regards their content, but only as regards their form and then only to a very limited degree. A primordial image is determined as to its content only when it has become conscious and is therefore filled out with material of conscious experience. Its form, however, as I have explained elsewhere, might perhaps be compared to the axial system of a crystal, which, as it were preforms the crystalline structure in the mother liquid, although it has no material existence of its own. . . . [11]

At a concrete level, the alchemists concerned themselves specifically with the transmutation of base metals into gold and with the search for the philosopher's stone, or *lapis*. The alchemists often used images to illustrate their work to transform and redeem matter. As Jung noted, 'symbolical images belong to the very essence of the alchemists' mentality. What the written word could express only imperfectly, or not at all, the alchemist pressed into his images; and strange as these are, they often speak a more intelligible language than is found in his clumsy philosophical concepts.'[12] If we hypothesize that the alchemists unconsciously projected their internal experiences of transformation into their work with matter, their images are most relevant to the work of psychological growth and healing. In fact, the alchemists themselves were quite often aware that they were using a symbolic language to talk about the phenomenology of inner experience.

In 'The Psychology of the Transference,'[13] Jung referred to a series of alchemical images to elucidate the nature of projections within the analyst–patient relationship. That series, known as the *Rosarium Philosophorum*, consisted of woodblock illustrations from a Renaissance manuscript, and its psychological interpretation has been extensively discussed since Jung's original article demonstrated its relevance to the analysis of the transference. Jung was also familiar with the *Splendor Solis*. In his works, he reproduced several images and quoted the text,[14] but he did not consider its images in detail, either separately or as a series.

The twenty-two illuminated paintings in the manuscript of the *Splendor Solis* belonging to the British Library (Harley 3469) are the most beautiful and accessible images of late medieval–early Renaissance European alchemy, and they provide us with a process in images that can touch us at a very deep level without our being scholars of alchemy. We have divided the images into three series, which we find compatible with our psychological interpretation.[15] As preparation for viewing these images, we will briefly examine the historic and symbolic underpinnings of late medieval–early Renaissance alchemy. We will then focus on the context in which the images of the *Splendor Solis* were made.

The ancient roots of alchemy[16]

If we consider alchemy in its broadest sense, as the human longing to transform ordinary matter into matter of value, purity, and beauty, then it must be very old indeed. Across many cultures, this wish to transform matter had as its ultimate goal the making of gold from common metals.

The wish to create gold seems naive to the contemporary mind because, according to atomic theory, gold is an element, a basic constituent, of matter. It has been generally accepted that gold can be purified when found mixed with other materials, but it cannot be created *de novo*. Yet how many of us know this from our own experience? In our modern culture, the transformation of metals is a process used in manufacturing, which few of us witness first-hand. If we also consider that we are surrounded by many synthesized materials that bear little resemblance to their raw ingredients, we might sympathize with the alchemists and begin to see how mysterious matter can be.

The closest most of us come to an alchemist's laboratory is in the kitchen, where we see rust form on iron implements and silver tarnish. We combine ingredients and use instruments to change the flavor and character of foods – for example, using heat and some cream of tartar to thicken a sauce, or a copper bowl and a whisk to transform egg whites from a dull, somewhat slimy mass into a light and stiff foam. How many of us understand the underlying properties of matter that allow these transformations? What if we decided to study these transformations for ourselves, using our senses of smelling, tasting, touching, and seeing while applying heat or adding other ingredients? Don't we also have an emotional reaction to each substance, its smell, taste, appearance, texture, temperature – as well as memories and associative images? How would that affect the names we gave to the new substances we created? With this in mind, we are better prepared to enter the world of the alchemist.

To help us envision the human experience in the time when alchemy was developing, we turn to *The Forge and the Crucible*, Mircea Eliade's scholarly account of the roots of alchemy in ancient metallurgy. Imagine the awe that human beings felt when they first discovered how to make fire, mine ores, intensify the fire's heat with a furnace, or when they learned how to smelt and combine metals and then forge metal tools. The early metallurgists believed that each step in the process crossed a sacred boundary between man and the supernatural. They prized, even venerated, the instruments of their craft, and they infused their operations with rituals and symbols to propitiate the gods.

The development of metallurgy has had such profound cultural repercussions that historians have named different mythological and historical ages according to the kinds of metals that a culture used for making tools (e.g., 'The Bronze Age,' 'The Iron Age'). Based on archaeological evidence, we know that there were skilled metallurgists in

Sumeria by at least 3500 BCE and in Egypt in 3000 BCE. Primitive metallurgy is even more ancient. Metal tools (copper and/or bronze) were widespread in the Fertile Crescent by 4000 BCE and in China and the Britannic Isles by 2000 BCE. Iron tools came much later and were widespread in the Fertile Crescent only by 900 BCE, in the British Isles by about 650 BCE, and in China about 500 BCE.[17] However, meteoric iron was used even earlier to fashion iron tools.[18]

The itinerant smith, a stranger who used fire to transform metals, evoked both fear and veneration and spread culture as well as tools.[19] His role went beyond the shoeing of horses (first used by the nomads of Central Asia), and he played an integral role in male societies centering on the horse cult.[20] The smith as arms-maker was of great importance to warriors, and he is interwoven into heroic mythologies.

In urban settings, the metalworker was initiated into the secrets of a craft. For example, in ancient Greece there were secret guilds associated with both metallurgy and the Mysteries, under the 'sponsorship' of mythical anthropomorphic creatures, such as the Cabiri and Dactyls.[21] The Cabiri are also just one example of mythic dwarves associated with work in mines.[22]

Miners and metallurgists spoke in a language of living metaphor, one that was similar across diverse cultures. Metals were believed to develop in the earth over time, becoming more perfect with age. This belief in the natural metamorphosis of metals is found – to choose widely ranging examples – in the Chinese text, the *Huai-nan tzu* (122 BCE) and in Ben Jonson's play, *The Alchemist* (first performed in London in 1610). The earth was the mother, and caves were her womb. We see this in the name of the sanctuary of Delphi ('delph' means 'uterus') and in the caves of the Sybils of Greek myth, where the blood-red earth evokes the menstrual blood of the goddess. A mine was like a cave, and so the mining of an ore involved the audacious act of entering the womb of the Earth Mother to take an embryo. In *The Alchemist*, lead and other metals are seen as embryonic gold growing in the earth, just as an egg is a chicken *in potentia*.[23] In European alchemy, it was said that the alchemical fire must burn for forty weeks, the time of gestation of a human embryo.[24]

The growth of metals in the earth was also likened to the growth of plants. The alchemists saw a parallel between the cultivation of plants and the heating of metals in the furnace. Human work using fire, such as cooking and forging, was used as a metaphor for the artificial acceleration of the 'ripening' process, and the furnace was likened to a womb. Gold was called the 'most mature fruit.' (This gives us an insight into the symbolism of the golden apples in the garden of the Hesperides, which will be discussed in the commentary to Plate I–7.) The metallurgist or smith, then, believed he was doing the same work that nature did – but using fire to accelerate the process.

Later, the work of the metallurgist was compared to the grafting of male and female fruit trees. Metals, and even tools and stones, were divided into male and female categories. The combining of metals was then referred to as their 'marriage.'

Another ancient idea associated with alchemy is the wish for long, even eternal life. Alchemy's two goals – the transformation of base metals into gold and the making of an elixir of immortality – coalesced in ancient China with the belief that gold was a magic medicine that could reverse the decline of the body and mind:

Gold by nature does not rot or decay;
Therefore it is of all things most precious.

When the artist (i.e., alchemist) includes it in his diet,
The duration of his life becomes everlasting.
When the golden powder enters the five-entrails,
A fog is dispelled, like rain-clouds scattered by the wind.
Fragrant exhalations pervade the four limbs;
The Countenance beams with joy and well-being.
Hairs that were white all turn to black;
Teeth that had fallen grow in their former place.
The old dotard is again a lusty youth.
The decrepit crone is a young girl once more.
He whose form is changed and has escaped the perils of life,
Has for his title the Name of True Man.

(*Ts'an T'ung Ch'l*, 142 AD)[25]

Likewise, in India, the *Arthavaveda* (*c.*1000 BCE) refers to ingestion of gold to increase longevity.[26]

Although eternal life was certainly their most ambitious goal, many alchemists were concerned with healing and medicine generally. Eliade cited evidence that early smiths, as masters of fire, were healers. For example, in the Congo, smiths were grouped into guilds and were often healers, priests, and/or kings.[27] A Yakut proverb said, 'Smiths and shamans come from the same nest.'[28]

In ancient China, India, Greece, and the Fertile Crescent, alchemists were working within cosmologies that related the earth and the heavens as macrocosm to the human body as microcosm. In China, the belief that there were five basic agents (often translated as 'elements'[29]) in the universe – water, fire, wood, gold or metal, and earth – was also held to be true of the human body, with particular agents associated with specific organs. It then followed that the secret of human regeneration could be discovered by studying the transmutation of the body's basic constituents as they appear elsewhere in nature. In other mythologies, metals were said to originate in the body of a god, as in the *Shatapatha Brahmana*, which tells of an excess of the body substance of Indra flowing out and becoming every plant, animal, and metal: 'From his navel, his life-breath flowed out and became lead, not iron, not silver; from his seed his form flowed out and became gold.'[30] This myth also conveys the way in which metals were experienced as animated.

From ancient times up to the seventeenth century, it was believed that the development of metals within the earth was influenced by the heavens, with certain planets said to govern the growth of particular metals. Just as the cultivation of plants was done in accord with solar and lunar cycles, the processes of mining and metallurgy were also performed in accord with these cycles. Each process had certain favorable and unfavorable astrological indications.

Astrology had developed into a highly complex and powerful explanatory system linking the movements of the sun, moon, planets, and stars to natural processes as well as human nature and events. It was used to explain the differences among periods of history, as well as human temperament and destiny. A person's astrological chart was used in medical diagnoses and for deciding upon treatment. In our discussion of the Second Series of images of the *Splendor Solis*, we will examine more closely the relationship between astrology, alchemy, and the healing arts.

From early times, alchemists also experienced their art in a philosophical or spiritual way. In other words, the attempt to transform matter was not only an attempt to gain wealth or to live a long life but also an attempt to improve human beings themselves. In this regard, alchemy was often one aspect of a spiritual discipline, as in ancient China where alchemy was associated with Taoism. For example, Ko Hung, a fourth-century Chinese Taoist philosopher, was also a poet, a medical writer, and an alchemist.[31] According to the *Huai-nan Tzu* (122 BCE), gold was believed to be at the center of the earth. The search for a method to make gold was explicitly considered a spiritual quest; it was mystically connected to sulfur, yellow mercury, and life in the hereafter.[32] Meditation was thought to allow the adept to return to a primordial state of chaos to discover the secret of creation and thus regeneration.[33]

By the end of the ninth century, certain Chinese alchemists began to divide alchemy between esoteric (using the 'souls' of substances) and exoteric (using concrete materials). In India, alchemy included both the exoteric and the esoteric: precise observations, such as the importance of the color of the flame for the analysis of metals,[34] and a mystical or tantric aspect, which emphasized different planes of experience.[35] In esoteric alchemy, the alchemical processes were within the body and consciousness, not in the laboratory.[36] In the Tantric system, matter was thought to have three qualities: *tamas*, the descending quality or inertia, represented as black; *sattva*, the ascending quality, represented as white; and the *rajas*, or dynamic qualities, represented as red.[37]

However, the art of alchemy was most often what today we might categorize as both external and internal, embodied and spiritual, practical and abstract. The language of alchemy is one that combines sensory observations of materials and processes with a language for the phenomenology of inner experience. The concrete and the symbolic are interfused, eluding a clear distinction.

Although there is debate as to whether alchemy as a formal discipline appeared earlier in the Near East than in China,[38] it is generally agreed that alchemy first came to Europe in the twelfth century from the Middle East and North Africa via Spain and southern Italy.[39] Arabian alchemists had assimilated aspects of Egyptian, Babylonian, Indian, and Chinese alchemy[40] and were influenced by Greek thought, particularly Aristotelian ideas, which came into Egypt at the time of the Alexandrian conquest. Alexandria, founded in 332 BCE by Alexander the Great, became the most important cultural center in the Western world and remained so for nearly a millennium. Its academies and library, which had acquired Aristotle's personal collection, attracted scholars from around the Greek world.

Alchemy in classical Greece and post-classical Alexandria

Many of the fundamental and enduring ideas of European alchemy originated in the writings of the ancient Greeks, first brought to Europe by the Arabs and later, in the Renaissance, translated directly from the Greek.[41] Empedocles (*c.*450 BCE) had theorized that matter was formed by four elements: earth, air, fire, and water. Plato (*c.*400 BCE) believed that matter existed prior to the creation of its qualities, and so alchemists thought that they must begin their process with a substance devoid of distinguishing characteristics. Aristotle (384–322 BCE) theorized that the four elements were formed by combinations of basic properties or qualities of matter (hot–cold, wet–dry), and therefore they could be converted into one another (Figure 1).[42] Undifferentiated matter, or

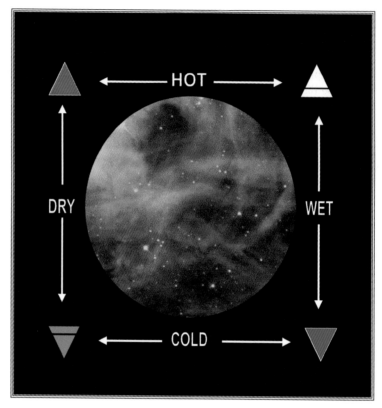

FIGURE 1   Aristotle's Four Elements and Their Qualities. Aristotle hypothesized that the four basic elements arose from the initial chaos under the influence of four fundamental qualities of matter: hot, cold, wet, and dry. The central image representing the initial chaos is taken from a United States National Aeronautics and Space Administration (NASA) photograph of the heart of the Crab Nebula, as viewed by the Hubble Telescope in 1995. The Crab Nebula was first viewed from earth in the year 1054, as recorded by Chinese astronomers. Rock paintings by Native Americans show that they also observed its appearance. Actually, the Crab Nebula was a giant star that exploded as a supernova. The variations in color are caused by chemical elements, created during the life and the explosion of the star. Modern-day astronomers believe that the chemical elements in the earth and in our bodies were made by the explosion of stars billions of years ago. ▼: Earth. △: Air. ▲: Fire. ▼: Water. (D. N. Sherwood)

chaos (shown in the center), becomes differentiated into the four elements when two of the four qualities of matter combine.

Early in the Alexandrian period (*c.*200 BCE), a scholar in nearby Mendes, Bolos Democritos, became interested in the transmutation of matter, which he believed to be shown by changes in the color of metals. (Color continued to play an important role for alchemists.) Democritos began to research the formulas used by metallurgists, glass-makers, and dyers in Egypt, Persia, Babylonia, and Syria, and he collected his recipes in a book entitled *Physika*. His goal was not to make actual gold but rather to make one metal resemble another through processes of alloying, dyeing, varnishing, or tinting.[43] Many later alchemists, with little practical experience and primarily philosophical or spiritual goals, were more gullible than trained metallurgists or goldsmiths, and so they could actually believe that a substance with a gold luster was gold itself.

Zosimos, a Gnostic who lived in Panopolis (Akhmim) in Egypt (*c.*300 CE), wrote a 28-volume encyclopedia of alchemy, compiling earlier (now lost) texts and original observations.[44] He believed that imitative silver and gold were superior to the metals themselves: imitative gold was yellower than ordinary gold and could impart yellowness to other metals. This may be the origin of the idea that a special gold could transform other metals into gold, and it may also be behind the idea that the philosopher's stone or tincture can multiply itself.

The writings of Zosimos indicate that for him alchemy was both the art of transforming substances and an inner experience in which dreams and visions played an important role: 'And as I spoke thus I fell asleep, and I saw a "sacrificer" standing before me. . . .'[45] In his visions Zosimos witnessed the intensely felt suffering that can accompany profound inner transformation:

> [The 'sacrificer' speaks to him:] I am Ion, the priest of the inner sanctuaries, and I submit myself to an unendurable torment. For there came one in haste at early morning, who overpowered me, and pierced me through with the sword, and dismembered me. . . . And he drew off the skin of my head with the sword, which he wielded with strength, and mingled the bones with the pieces of flesh, and caused them to be burned upon the fire of the art, till I perceived by the transformation of the body that I had become spirit.[46]

Within his dreams and visions, Zosimos was able to ask questions of the figures who appeared, and they gave him instruction about the meaning of the actions and symbols within the visions. C. G. Jung studied these visions and wrote a commentary entitled, 'The Visions of Zosimos,' which includes the text of the visions.[47]

All of late Alexandrian-Greek alchemy used the transmutation of base metals into gold as a symbol of human regeneration and transformation.[48] For example, Stephanos of Alexandria (seventh century) was a highly respected scholar who gave public lectures on the philosophies of Plato and Aristotle and on mathematics, astronomy, and music. He wrote two books on alchemy, which he viewed as an inner process, and his work is imbued with the poetry of mystical experience. In the following excerpt, we see that he is talking about a quality of experience, using light and color as metaphors for the intangible:

> O moon clad in white and vehemently shining abroad whiteness, let us learn what is the lunar radiance that we may not miss what is doubtful. For the same is the whitening snow, the brilliant eye of whiteness, the bridal procession-robe . . ., the mind-constructed beauty of fair form, the whitest composition of the perfection, the coagulated milk of fulfillment, the Moon-froth of the sea at dawn, . . . the many-named matter of the good work, that which lulls the All to sleep, that which

bears the One which is the All, that which fulfils the wondrous work. What is this emanation of the same Moon? ... For it is white as seen, but yellow as apprehended, the bridegroom to the allotted moon, the golden drop from it, the glorious emanation from it, the unchangeable embrace, the indelible orbit, the god-given work, the marvelous making of gold.[49]

Probably the oldest and certainly one of the most famous alchemical documents, the *Emerald Tablet* of Hermes, or the *Tabula Smaragdina*, is believed to have been written originally in Greek but to have come through Syria into the Arab world by about 800 CE. Its legendary author, Hermes Trismegistos, was often considered to be the father of alchemy. Many quotations in alchemical texts are attributed to him, although they undoubtedly were written much later than his alleged date of about 3400 BCE. According to legend, the *Tablet* of Hermes was an emerald slab with Phoenician characters, discovered in the tomb of Hermes by Alexander the Great. The *Emerald Tablet* contains thirteen precepts:

1. I speak not fictitious things, but that which is certain and true.
2. What is below is like that which is above, and what is above is like that which is below, to accomplish the miracles of one thing.
3. And as all things were produced by the one word of one Being, so all things were produced from this one thing by adaptation.
4. Its father is the sun, its mother the moon; the wind carries it in its belly, its nurse is the earth.
5. It is the father of perfection throughout the world.
6. The power is vigorous if it be changed into earth.
7. Separate the earth from the fire, the subtle from the gross, acting prudently and with judgment.
8. Ascend with the greatest sagacity from the earth to heaven, and then again descend to the earth, and unite together the powers of things superior and things inferior. Thus you will obtain the glory of the whole world, and obscurity will fly far away from you.
9. This has more fortitude than fortitude itself; because it conquers every subtle thing and can penetrate every solid.
10. Thus was the world formed.
11. Hence proceed wonders, which are here established.
12. Therefore I am called Hermes Trismegistos, having three parts of the philosophy of the whole world.
13. That which I had to say concerning the operation of the sun is completed.[50]

Islamic alchemy

While Europe struggled through the Middle Ages, culture and learning were flourishing in the Middle East.[51] By the eighth century, less than 100 years after the founding of Islam, a vast Islamic empire stretched from Spain to northern India. Although many cultures lived within this region, Arabic became the common language of educated discourse. An attitude of open curiosity and inquiry, rather than a reliance on authority, fostered important intellectual advances. In the eighth and ninth centuries, many academies and observatories were founded. Arab scholars employed Nestorian[52] Christians and Syrian pagans to translate from Greek into Arabic many important works on philosophy, mathematics, astronomy, and medicine.

From the seventh through the thirteenth centuries, the study of alchemy flourished openly in the Islamic world. The first Muslim with an interest in alchemy may have been Khalid Ibn Yazid (d. 704), a Umayyad prince. He reputedly was tutored in alchemy by a student of Stephanos, Morienus of Alexandria (who is quoted by the author of the *Splendor Solis*). Whether or not this account is accurate, it is clear that Alexandria was the primary influence on Islamic alchemy. The Islamic alchemists quoted Zosimos, Democritos, and Stephanos, as well as other Alexandrian alchemists such as Ostanes and Maria Prophetissa (second to third century, often referred to as 'Mary, the Jewess'). In addition, the Muslim alchemists also absorbed influences from Persia and Syria.

The work of four Muslim alchemists became well-known in the West: Jabir ibn Hayyan (eighth century), al-Razi (ninth century), Muhammad ibn Umail at-Tamini (tenth century) and Ibn Sina (eleventh century). They were responsible for many of the practical observations and laboratory techniques, adopted by European alchemists, that led eventually to modern chemistry and medicine. Their philosophical and mystical writings were also highly developed.

Jabir ibn Hayyan, known in the West as 'Geber,' was a Shiite Muslim. This branch of Islam was known for valuing direct, inner experience of the spiritual and for its symbolic interpretation of the Qur'an, in contrast to the Sunnis who interpreted the Qur'an literally as truth to be obeyed.[53] Geber belonged to a branch of the Azd tribe from south Arabia that lived in Kufa, on the banks of the Euphrates, and practiced Sufism. He may have known Greek and was a well-read scholar who authored original works in diverse subjects, including mathematics, astronomy, and alchemy.

Geber expanded upon Aristotle's theory of the four elements and qualities. He postulated that the union of two natures with substance produced the four basic elements, as in Aristotelian theory. However, Geber held that metals had two *internal* natures and two *external* natures, which were the opposites of one another. According to this scheme, gold is hot and moist externally but cold and dry internally. This theory did not prove helpful in explaining the observable properties of metals, but it might remind us of Jung's theory of complexes: the outwardly manifest attitude constellates its opposite in the unconscious. For example, someone with an inferiority complex (an overt feeling of inferiority) might be expected unconsciously to have an attitude of superiority.

Geber also introduced a new theory of metals, the sulfur–mercury theory, which remained highly influential for nearly a thousand years, up to the end of the seventeenth century (see Figure 2). According to this theory, metals are formed in the earth under the influence of the planets by the union of sulfur and mercury. Base metals were formed because the sulfur and mercury were not always pure or in the right combination (balance). He believed that metals could be purified by treatment with an elixir and that the right balance could be found.

While other alchemists used only minerals in the preparation of elixirs, Geber pioneered the use of animal and vegetable products. He experimented with a variety of laboratory processes and made careful observations, thereby making contributions to practical chemistry. There is less certainty about his real views on the more philosophical aspects of alchemy, since works attributed to him are not available in the original. The

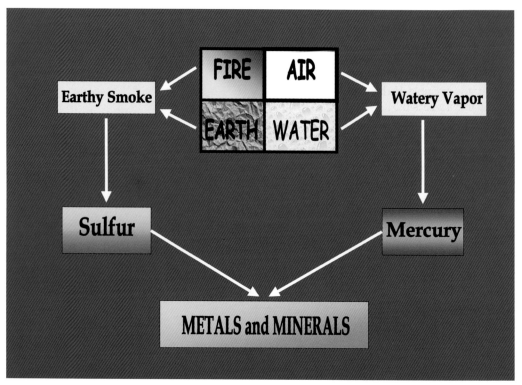

FIGURE 2   Geber's Sulfur–Mercury Theory. (D. N. Sherwood)

earliest available copies are those transcribed in the tenth century by the Isma'ilite sect, who believed that Muhammad is not the last prophet (as Geber had believed) and that all religions have elements of truth. It is therefore hard to know whether some of the more philosophical aspects of his works were originated by or were only modified by the transcribers.

Abu Bakr Muhammad ibn Zakariyya or Al-Razi ('Rhazes' in the West) was born near Tehran in 825 or 826 and lived to the age of one hundred. He has been said to be on an intellectual level with Galileo. Al-Razi was highly educated in philosophy, mathematics, metaphysics, poetry, and music (authoring an encyclopedia of music). He was also the originator of the classification of things into animal, vegetable, and mineral. His most notable contribution was to medicine: he was the first to distinguish between smallpox and measles, and some of his books were still read by medical students in Europe in the seventeenth century. He designed a new hospital in Baghdad, which he later headed, sitting in the courtyard to teach his many pupils. His medical researches led him to alchemy, and he accepted Geber's sulfur–mercury theory of metals but suggested that there was a third constituent of a salty nature. Although he was primarily interested in practical chemistry and medicines, he did believe that base metals could be changed into gold and that ordinary stones or glass could be transformed into gemstones. He described distillation, calcination, solution, evaporation, crystallization, sublimation, filtration, amalgamation, and ceration (conversion to a waxy condition), and his work is known for accurate descriptions of chemical operations and their products.[54]

Abu Ali ibn Sina (980–1037), known in the West as 'Avicenna,' was a Persian who grew up in a village near Bukhara (now in Turkistan). Avicenna was a man with extraordinary capacities for observation and rationality, coupled with a sensitive awareness of the ineffable. He has been described as the greatest genius of the Muslim world, on a par with Aristotle. By the time he was sixteen, physicians were coming to study with him and he was appointed physician to a prince before he was seventeen. Although he lived only to the age of fifty-six or fifty-seven, he authored over a hundred tracts on medical, philosophical, literary, musical, and scientific subjects. He wrote a treatise in Arabic entitled *The Bird*, a first-person narrative in which the bird represents the human soul. Other birds free the bird from its cage, and they fly over eight mountain peaks in search of the 'Great King.'[55]

Avicenna's studies of music theory were more advanced than anything in Europe at the time, and his studies in physics included the suggestion that light travels at a finite velocity. He also invented a kind of vernier scale (showing his interest in accurate, quantitative measurements) and made astronomical observations. His contribution to medicine was highly original. He was far ahead of his time in his views on disease transmission, and his encyclopedia of medicine included 760 drugs. In his work as an alchemist, he adhered to the sulfur–mercury theory of Geber but differed with his contemporaries in that he was extremely skeptical that metals could be transmuted. He was of the opinion that metals might be made to appear like one another, but that the properties of metals observed by the senses were probably not the actual basis of their differences. He is known for having written, 'Three things are necessary, namely: patience, deliberation, and the instruments,' which was modified in the thirteenth century *Aurora Consurgens* to, '. . . and skill with the instruments.'[56]

During the tenth century, there were a number of distinguished Spanish-Arab alchemists, but none comparable to Geber or Avicenna. Muhammad ibn Umail at-Tamini (*c*.900–60, known in the West as 'Senior') was a mystic who led a secluded life, writing *A Book of the Silvery Water and Starry Earth*, known in Latin as *De chemia*. The lectures by Marie-Louise von Franz on this work are well worth reading.[57] One of the last noteworthy Arab alchemists was Aidamur al-Jildaki, who lived in Cairo in the second half of the fourteenth century, traveled widely in search of alchemical knowledge, and preserved a large number of quotes from original sources which have now been lost.

Alchemy in medieval and Renaissance Europe

While culture was flourishing in the Islamic world, Europe experienced hundreds of years of unusually frigid weather, storms, floods, famines, war, plague, and epidemics. Murder and kidnap-for-ransom were common, and many crimes involving property were punishable by death. Most people lived in tiny communities and seldom ventured away; they tilled their fields by hand. The Christian Church persecuted pagans but persecuted Christian threats to its hegemony with even more vehemence. More Christians died at the hands of the Church than had died during the persecution by the pagan Romans prior to Constantine's conversion. The Crusades took some of the warfare out of Europe, but as late as 1204, when the Fourth Crusade failed to reach the Holy Land, its army sacked

Constantinople and massacred its citizens. Such was the state of disorder that in the year 1500, the Roman roads, built 1000 years before, had not been improved upon.[58] The only significant inventions were waterwheels in the ninth century and windmills in the twelfth.

Alchemy was apparently unknown in Europe until it was introduced through contacts with Islam in the twelfth century. Jews who spoke Arabic played a role in the transmission and translation of texts from the Arabic, and Jewish texts were also influential, particularly with regard to the magic properties of words and letters. Perhaps the earliest surviving translation that includes illustrations is the *Tractatus de herbis*, made in Apulia in southern Italy and dating from the early fourteenth century.[59] One of its illustrations is an early example of a return to the observation of nature and interest in landscape in the Middle Ages (probably sparked by the influx of Persian-influenced paintings and illuminated manuscripts from the East). This rudimentary illustration shows a man using an ax to cut sulfurous rock from a volcanic landscape. Sulfurous fires or smoke rise from a volcano behind the village. In addition to its importance to alchemical processes, refined sulfur was used medicinally as a laxative and to induce sweating.[60]

At the time of the Renaissance, Greek sources became more directly available. For example, the *Hermetic Corpus* of the legendary Greek alchemist, Hermes Trismegistus (already known through translations from the Arabic), was translated from the Greek by the Neoplatonist philosopher Marcilio Ficino (1433–99) at the behest of Cosimo de' Medici.[61]

Medieval European alchemists seem to have added little of practical value to alchemical theories or methods, with a few exceptions. Roger Bacon was the most notable creative mind and the first to propose the inductive method that became fundamental to modern science. In the thirteenth century, Albertus Magnus, who lived and taught in Cologne, was a scholar of Greek philosophy and Islamic alchemy. He was a small, agile man with an engaging and dynamic personality, who is thought to have had an important formative influence on his pupil, Thomas Aquinas. Albertus Magnus believed that chemical *analysis* had a physical basis but that *synthesis* required the influence of the soul, which in turn was influenced by God's instruments, the stars.[62]

A thirteenth-century alchemical text, *Aurora Consurgens*, has been attributed to Thomas Aquinas though it has many inconsistencies with his other works. Marie-Louise Von Franz, who was a colleague of Jung, translated *Aurora Consurgens* from the Latin and wrote an extensive commentary on its symbolism.[63] *Aurora* is of a revelatory, mystical nature and its text mixes biblical and alchemical imagery in seven parables outlining the opus. After a careful study of Aquinas's life and writings, von Franz considers it quite possible that the *Aurora* was a breakthrough of unconscious material (compensatory to his conscious attitude) dictated to a companion during an ecstatic state in Aquinas's final illness.

Let us now turn to the steps in the alchemical opus that became well-known in medieval Europe, keeping in mind the many variations in choice of substances and the importance of color dating back at least a millennium. In order to start with a substance without distinguishing characteristics, alchemists fused together the four base metals – lead, tin, copper, and iron. This fusion produced a substance with a black surface color. This first stage was called the *nigredo*. Another version of the first step, attributed to Maria Prophetissa, was to make a lead–copper alloy with sulfur. The second step was to heat the black alloy with a small amount of silver and then mercury (including arsenic and antimony) or tin, which caused a white color, *albedo*, to appear. In the third step, yellowing or *citrinatis*, gold and sulfur waters were added. In the early days of alchemy, the fourth and final step produced a violet color that sometimes had a striking iridescence.

The result of combining mercury and sulfur,[64] mercuric sulfide or cinnabar, came to replace the final violet stage in the color sequence. Because cinnabar was blood red, this stage was called the *rubedo*. Although the process was usually much more complex than four steps, this color sequence – *nigredo, albedo, citrinatis, rubedo* – black, white, yellow, red – played an important part in alchemical symbolism beginning with the Greeks and Arabs, and it is found throughout the *Splendor Solis*. Von Franz[65] has applied the symbolism of the *nigredo* and *albedo* to the psychological process of working through a complex: the *nigredo* represents the disturbance, usually projected outwardly onto a person or persons. After 'a long process of inner development and realization,' the projection is withdrawn, and '... a sort of peace establishes itself – one becomes quiet and can look at the thing from an objective angle ... that corresponds to the albedo.'[66] The *rubedo* would then refer to the new life that appears spontaneously after libido is freed from the complex.

According to Mircea Eliade, two streams influenced the European alchemy in late medieval times, the first a learned tradition going back to ancient Mesopotamia (and Greece) and the other to be found in primitive myth which worked its way into the imagery of alchemy. Local traditions of metallurgy also influenced the alchemists, as can be seen in the *Bergbuchlein* (1505),[67] a work that was contemporary with the original *Splendor Solis*. It was also the earliest German book published showing the 'symbiosis' of the metallurgical and alchemical traditions in late medieval Europe. Attributed to a distinguished physician, who lived among miners in Freiburg, the *Bergbuchlein* was written in the form of a discussion between a teacher and apprentice. In it, we find the sulfur–mercury theory. Their combination was likened to the union of male (sulfur) and female (mercury) 'seeds' at conception. However, another scheme is also mentioned, where sulfur is combined with 'a humid, cold and mucous matter ... extracted from the earth.'[68] Heavenly bodies – associated with Greco-Roman deities – were believed to influence the growth of metals, with the growth of silver most strongly influenced by the moon, copper by Venus, lead by Saturn, and iron by Mars. Gold was influenced by the Sun:

> According to the opinions of the Sages, gold is engendered from a sulphur, the clearest possible, and properly rectified and purified in the earth, by the action of the sky, principally of the sun, so that it contains no further humour which might be destroyed or burnt by fire nor any liquid humidity which might be evaporated by fire.[69]

In some alchemical works of that time, the planets were associated with colors as well as metals. Gold and silver were of course associated with the sun and moon. Saturn was represented by brown, Venus by green, Jupiter by blue, and Mars by red.[70]

In medieval and Renaissance Europe, the art of alchemy was often practiced surreptitiously or by individuals who lived at the fringes of the dominant culture. Texts seldom were signed with their authors' real names, and it was a common practice either to ascribe writings to famous alchemists of the past (many early medieval texts were ascribed to Geber) or to use a Greek or Latin pseudonym. At that time, in the regions of Europe dominated by the Church of Rome, an open inquiry into the nature of matter and the nature of inner experience was an activity that could lead to a summons from the Inquisition, followed by torture, imprisonment, and even death. This was true although there are also indications that alchemy was practiced in monasteries and by well-known clerics, such as Albertus Magnus.

Although somewhat later than the writing of the *Splendor Solis*, two of the many cases brought by the Inquisition in northern Italy may convey a flavor of the authority that the Church exercised. The first is the well-known case of Galileo, who was forced to repudiate his astronomical findings, which supported a heliocentric rather than geo-centric view of the orbits of the sun and planets. Galileo was a devout, believing Catholic with close ties to the Vatican, and he was careful to check with his Vatican contacts before he published his findings. When he did finally publish his work, it was in the form of a debate between fictional figures, rather than a direct exposition. Nevertheless, he was summoned by the Inquisition. Confined by the Vatican and in ill-health, he agreed to the Vatican's terms and repudiated the heliocentric theory.[71]

The other case is found in Carlo Ginsburg's fascinating study of the trials of a sixteenth-century Italian peasant, a village miller who was executed by the Roman Church for expounding heresies.[72] The miller believed that there was validity to the different religions, as they had all come from God, and that if he had been born an Arab he might well have believed in the Muslim religion. Ginsburg made a careful study of the possible sources for the miller's beliefs but did not consider alchemy as a possible basis for the miller's heresies, either directly or indirectly, through the infusion of alchemical symbols into folk culture. However, a number the miller's heresies were quite similar to alchemical ideas of the time. Like the alchemists, he espoused a cosmology that began with chaos, out of which the four elements emerged. He claimed that matter coagulated 'like a cheese,' suggesting that he might have heard the famous alchemical dictum, 'solve et coagula' (dissolve and coagulate).[73] The miller argued at times that spirit came out of matter, a heresy that is expressed symbolically in the *Splendor Solis* paintings. Ginsburg quotes a passage from one book, known to have been read by the miller, which talks about the parts of an egg as symbolic of the four elements, an idea well-known to alchemists (cf. Plate I–9). Perhaps the level of scrutiny by the Church directed to the case of a simple village miller could explain in part the obscure language used by European alchemists, even when talking about straightforward procedures, as well as their preference for pseudonyms when publishing their texts.

Those alchemists who did announce their claims in public were often charlatans and swindlers. Their claims could lead to generous financing from rulers eager to increase their own wealth. Their tales end either with a timely escape or with the imprisonment or death of the charlatan.[74]

Paracelsus and the nature of the soul

Born Theophrastus Bombastus von Hohenheim in 1493 near Zürich,[75] Paracelsus[76] was the most famous of the late medieval–early Renaissance alchemists. He has often been credited with being the father of modern medicine and chemistry, although his legacy remains the subject of debate.[77]

In his own time, Paracelsus was a controversial figure, who was always ready to proclaim his successes and to rail against the stupidity of others. The historian of alchemy, E. J. Holmyard, put it this way: 'Paracelsus had virtues but modesty was not one of them, and he would have had no need for a publicity agent.'[78] In 1929, Jung was invited to give a lecture on Paracelsus in the house where Paracelsus was born.[79] Noting Paracelsus' reliance on astrology as a diagnostic instrument, Jung began his lecture with the comment that Paracelsus was born in Scorpio,

> a sign that, according to ancient tradition, was favourable to physicians, the ministers of poisons and of healing. The ruler of Scorpio is the proud and bellicose Mars, who endows the strong with warlike courage and the weak with a quarrelsome and irascible disposition. The course of Paracelsus's life certainly did not belie his nativity.[80]

Paracelsus was an only child, and his mother died when he was born. He was brought up by his father, who was a physician in Villach, and he remained a devout Catholic all his life. He studied medicine and alchemy with his father, and he probably studied medicine at the university in Basel. When he was about twenty-one, he went to the Tyrol to study mining and metallurgy with an alchemist. Afterwards, he traveled through Germany, France, Belgium, England, Scandinavia, and Italy, where he earned a medical degree from the University of Ferrara. He may also have been an army surgeon, and it is thought that he visited Venice, Russia, and the East during various campaigns.

Unlike most educated men of his time, Paracelsus was interested in folk medicine, and he enjoyed the company of gypsies, astrologers, apothecaries, miners, and peasants. He began to practice medicine in Strasbourg in 1526 but was summoned to Basel to the bedside of an important citizen, whom he cured quickly and completely. It happened that the Dutch scholar Erasmus was a house-guest, and he was so impressed with Paracelsus that he recommended him to be the City Physician and a Professor of Medicine at the University of Basel. This appointment lasted only two years, as Paracelsus seemed to take every possible opportunity to insult the professional competence of members of the medical elite and to further offend their sense of propriety by writing and lecturing in German instead of Latin. He spent much of the rest of his life wandering through Germany and Austria, and he died in Salzburg in 1541 at the age of 48.

It is difficult to give an overview of Paracelsus' beliefs and work, as they contain so many contradictions. His theory of illness depended upon astrology and his theory of cure upon the restoration of harmony between man and nature. He believed that the way in which medicines were prepared influenced their healing powers, and he also emphasized careful chemical processes. As he put it,

> The purpose of alchemy is not, as it is said, to make gold and silver, but in this instance to make arcana [secret remedies] and direct them against diseases . . . For all these things conform to the instruction and test of nature. Hence nature and man, in health and sickness, need to be joined together, and to be brought into mutual agreement. This is the way to heal and restore to health.[81]

C. G. Jung has written about Paracelsus' spiritual beliefs and about his work as a physician.[82] According to Jung, 'The driving force behind Paracelsus was his compassion. "Compassion," he exclaims, "is the physician's schoolmaster." '[83]

It was Paracelsus' outspoken view that chemistry should play an important role in medicine, including the use of metals as medicines. This was an affront to the medical establishment of his time, but Paracelsus has been credited with helping to introduce chemistry into medical curricula. He accepted the Aristotelian theory of the four elements, but he extended the sulfur–mercury theory and applied his theory to all substances, not just metals. He did this by adding a third basic constituent, salt, as Rhazes had done seven hundred years previously. For Paracelsus, salt represented the principle of incombustibility and non-volatility. This theory, which became known as *tria prima*, referred to three basic *qualities*, not to ordinary mercury, sulfur, and salt:

> You should know that all seven metals originate from three materials, namely from mercury, sulphur, and salt, though with different colours. Therefore Hermes has said not incorrectly that all seven metals are born and composed from three substances, similarly also the tinctures and Philosphers' stone. He calls these three substances spirit, soul, and body. But he has not indicated how this is to be understood nor what he means by it ... you should know that they mean not other than the three *principia*, that is mercury, sulphur, and salt, out of which all seven metals originate. Mercury is the spirit, sulphur is the soul, salt the body.[84]

According to the theory of *tria prima*,[85] mercury (spirit) was associated with water and characterized by its fusibility and by being volatile yet unchanged by fire. Sulfur (soul) was associated with air and characterized by its inflammability and being volatile and changed by fire. Salt (body) was associated with earth and was characterized by its not being vaporized by fire and so being found in the ashes. If this theory is kept in mind, it is most helpful in understanding both text and image in alchemical works:

1. mercury–spirit–water–fusible–volatile–unchanged by fire;
2. sulfur–soul–air–inflammable–volatile–changed by fire;
3. salt–body–earth–not flammable–ashes.

Explicitly stated, the triadic theory of the basic qualities of substances – particularly when these qualities are directly associated with spirit, soul, and body[86] – was daring for its time. The medieval European Christian might be allowed to have a body and a soul, but not a spirit. The Roman Church held that only God had spirit and that only the Church and its ordained had the authority to mediate the spiritual relationship between God and mankind. The Church enforced its authority by prosecuting and punishing challenges to its teachings.

The Church's view that only God possesses a spirit had not been a fundamental tenet of Christianity. In fact, the early Christians believed that the Holy Spirit descended from heaven after Christ's resurrection to help his disciples continue Christ's mission to the world. For a period, the Holy Spirit was referred to as feminine, the divine Mother. Richard Tarnas has explained:

> The New Testament described the Spirit as like a wind that blows 'where it wills.' But as such, the Spirit possessed inherently spontaneous and revolutionary qualities that placed it, by definition, beyond any control ... [The] principle of the

Holy Spirit ... threaten[ed] the traditional separation between Creator and creature ...[87]

The Christian movement became allied with the Roman Empire after the conversion of Constantine (fourth century). Rome not only became Christian, but Christianity became Roman, organizing itself into a centralized hierarchy with a supreme ruler (the Pope), control over the content and meaning of rituals, and a complex legal system dictating what its citizens must believe. Wherever the Roman Empire went, the Roman Church spread its message and forcibly suppressed local 'pagan' religions and folk beliefs. After the fall of the Roman Empire, the Church used its own army to conquer and rule over territories. In medieval and Renaissance Europe, even in regions where the Church did not have secular sovereignty, its power to prosecute heresy was often conceded. Over time, it further consolidated its power through strong hierarchical control over what ecclesiastics and lay people could believe or discuss, and this required a suppression of spontaneous spiritual experience or any rational inquiry that threatened Church dogma or cosmology. To quote Tarnas again,

> The charismatic and irrational expressions of the Spirit – spontaneous spiritual ecstasies, miraculous healings, speaking in tongues, prophecies, new assertions of divine revelation – were increasingly discouraged in favor of more ordered, rational manifestations, such as sermons, organized religious services and rituals, institutional authority, and doctrinal orthodoxy. A fixed canon of specific apostolic writings was carefully selected and permanently established with no new revelations recognized as God's infallible Word ... The notion of the Holy Spirit as a divine principle of revolutionary spiritual power, immanent in the human community and moving it toward deification, diminished in Christian belief in favor of a notion of the Holy Spirit as solely invested in the authority and activities of the institutional Church. The stability and continuity of the Church were thereby maintained, though at the expense of more individualistic forms of religious experience and revolutionary spiritual impulses.[88]

The Church, then, discouraged practices like that shown in Figure 3, where the legendary founder of medicine, Apollo, is shown putting three patients into a trance state.

The Roman Church had formally asserted its exclusive right to interpret or mediate the Holy Spirit at the time of the schism between the Eastern and the Western (Roman) Churches, at the Eighth Ecumenical Council of Constantinople (869–70). Canon 11 stated:

> While the Old and New Testaments teach that man has one rational and intellectual soul, and this is the teaching also of all the fathers and doctors of the Church, some persons, nevertheless, blasphemously maintain that he has two souls. This holy and general council, therefore, anathematizes the authors and adherents of that false teaching. Anyone presuming to act contrary to the decision of this great council, shall be anathematized and cut off from the faith and society of Christians.

From that time on, according to the Roman Church, man has a soul (giving form and intellectual faculties) and a body, but not a spirit or a second soul.

FIGURE 3   Apollo Inducing a Healing Trance. (Sloane MS 6, f. 175, by permission of the British Library)

In the late Middle Ages and early Renaissance, with the resurgence of interest in classical Greek ideas, the Aristotelian concept of soul as the principle of life – rather than the Platonic idea that the person is a soul within a body – entered into discussions. This blurred the distinction between the body and soul, and it also opened the possibility that humans could have both a rational, God-given soul and a life-giving soul that could be transformed and expressed through life. The influx of Arab ideas, especially the works of Avicenna, spawned the idea that spirit might be some kind of mediating third between soul and body.[89] Nevertheless, in sixteenth-century Italy, eight centuries after the ecumenical council in Constantinople, the Inquisitorial interrogations of the ill-fated Italian miller revisited this controversy. The miller wavered between claiming that 'soul and spirit are one thing,' and 'When the body dies the soul also dies but the spirit remains.'[90] He explained that the soul was the intellectual faculties, while the spirit was something that came from God and gave us will and inspiration, a view that shocked his priestly inquisitors.[91]

Paracelsus recognized that there were contradictions between his Catholic faith and his beliefs as an alchemist and physician: 'I also confess that I write like a pagan and yet am a Christian.'[92] Paracelsus believed that everything in the universe was alive and that there was an intermediate state between the material and the immaterial consisting of entities that have a body and spirit but not a soul. In doing this, he acknowledged what we might call the imaginal world as a third alternative to the world of literalism or the world of abstraction. He further argued for a distinction between the domain of theology and that of medicine. In his view, the former came from revelation, while the latter depended on the *lumen naturae* or light of nature:

> Look at Adam and Moses and others. They sought in themselves what was in man and have revealed it and all kabbalistic arts and they knew nothing alien to man neither from the Devil nor from the spirits, but derived their knowledge from the Light of Nature. This they nurtured in themselves . . . it comes from nature which contains its manner of activity within itself. It is active during sleep and hence things must be used when dormant and not awake – sleep is waking for such arts – for things have a spirit which is active for them in sleep. . . . for it is the Light of Nature which is at work during sleep and is the invisible body and was nevertheless born like the visible and natural body. But there is more to be known than the mere flesh, for from this very innate spirit comes that which is visible . . . the Light of Nature which is man's mentor dwells in this innate spirit.[93]

This idea of the light or spirit to be found in nature had been embodied in the life of Francis of Assisi (1182–1226), who lived as an ascetic in a cave and expressed his awe of nature in his 'Canticle of the Sun.' In Figure 4, we see a fresco (1236) of St. Francis preaching to the birds, who listen with rapt attention. (He did not go so far as to listen to the birds and learn from them.) The look of concern on the face of his companion is a good reflection of the consternation of church officials about Francis's ascetic life. However, as depicted in a beautiful fresco by Giotto, the pope decided not to persecute

FIGURE 4 'St. Francis Preaching to the Birds.' Maestro di S. Francesco, Basilica di S. Francesco, Assisi. (By permission of Sacro Convento, Assisi)

Francis after he had a dream that Francis would help to hold up the Church rather than destroy it. Although the message of St. Francis, that the sacred can be found by living a simple life in the natural world, did not become a dominant theme of Christianity or of European culture, its spirit has survived in the Catholic order bearing his name.

Paracelsus made conscious and explicit an important psychological undercurrent that had been manifest in medieval alchemy but had not been openly discussed: the spirit in nature, or the notion of spirit coming not only from above but also from below. We shall see this theme in the *Splendor Solis*, even though the images (if they originated around 1500) predate Paracelsus' writings.

The enduring metaphors used in alchemy have to do with creation and destruction – initial chaos and lack of differentiation, conception, the womb or matrix, embryos, gestation, milk, marriage as a union of opposites, the growth and cultivation of plants, and dismemberment, decay, and death. The alchemists ask, 'How is it possible to speed up processes which happen only very slowly in nature?' We might say that alchemists attempted to master the capacity of nature to animate, renew, and multiply itself, that they were studying the mysterious and miraculous qualities of the life force. This may be taken in a very literal modern way as a problem of biology. However, from a psychological point of view, alchemy is concerned with the mysterious human capacity for renewal and change and the symbols that our psyches use to communicate to us about that experience.

The Harley *Splendor Solis*

There are many unanswered questions surrounding the provenance and antecedents of the beautiful illuminated manuscript in the Harley Collection of the British Library. (The title page is shown in Figure 5.)

Our interest is in the paintings, but some clues about the context for the images may be found by an examination of the text. Although most medieval texts were written in Latin, this manuscript is in German. (For an English translation, see the Appendix.[94]) It is divided into seven treatises, each replete with quotes from famous alchemists, apparently selected and arranged to convey the author's view of the essentials of the alchemical process. The authorities quoted in the text include: Alexander, Alphidius, Aristotle, Avicenna, Calid, Farrarius, Galenus, Geber, Hali, Hermes, Menaldus, Morienus, Ovid, Rhases, Rosinos, Senior, Socrates, and Virgil.[95] According to Marie-Louise Von Franz, the *Splendor Solis* contains many passages taken from the *Aurora Consurgens* (thirteenth century); her scholarly research into the sources of that work provides valuable background to the *Splendor Solis*. Von Franz dates the original version of the *Splendor Solis* as 1490 but doesn't state her rationale or source.[96] However, a date of 1490–1500 is plausible based on the purported autobiography of the author, Salomon Trismosin (see below). Unlike *Aurora Consurgens*, the text of the *Splendor Solis* makes no specific biblical or Christian references (although it does refer to 'God, the creator'). Neither does the *Splendor Solis* text contain any accounts of original visionary or mystical experiences.

The author in historical context

We do not know the identity of the author of the *Splendor Solis*, who used the pseudonym Salomon Trismosin.[97] The *Aureum Vellus* (Rorschach, 1598), a collection of

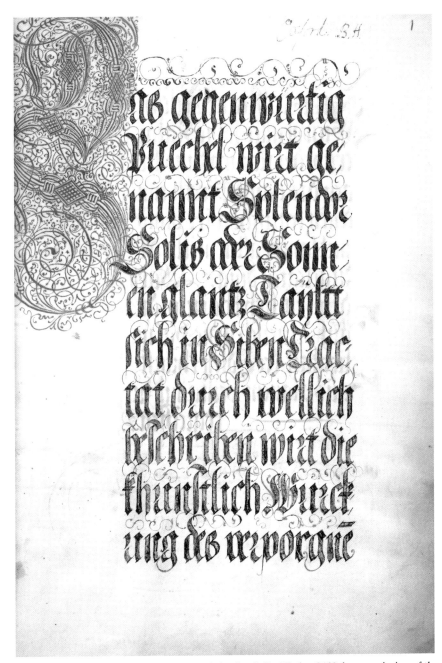

FIGURE 5 The Title Page of the Harley *Splendor Solis*. (Harley 3469, by permission of the British Library)

alchemical works, contains a brief and colorful account of a young man's travels in search of alchemical secrets that is attributed to Salomon Trismosin (reprinted in the Appendix[98]). It is an odd amalgam of youthful gullibility and particulars that make it plausible as a true account by some individual, perhaps the author of the text – but its character is not consistent with the depth conveyed through the illuminated paintings.

The account does give an interesting glimpse into the times, and Italy, particularly Venice, was a popular destination for those in search of a cosmopolitan and innovative environment. From various details we can surmise that the author was a literate German-speaking layman, also able to read, understand, and perhaps speak Latin, but without considerable personal means. His alchemical quest began after he observed a miner-alchemist making silver and gold from lead. He was eager to learn the miner's secret, but the miner refused to reveal it; shortly thereafter, the miner fell down a mineshaft!

Believing that it was indeed possible to make gold and silver from lead, 'Trismosin' set out in 1473 on a journey to discover the secret of this art. After traveling for eighteen months, he spent a year in a monastery near Milan, attending lectures and serving as an assistant. He then traveled 'up and down Italy,' where he met an Italian and a Jew, who worked together making silver. He worked for them, tending the fire and working with 'corrosive and poisonous materials,' and he claimed that in fourteen weeks, he learned how to 'make English tin look like silver.' He then traveled to Venice, where he had the 'silver' assayed and learned it was definitely 'false silver.' However, his conversation with the assayist led to an apprenticeship in a large alchemical laboratory belonging to a Venetian nobleman. The laboratory had a chief chemist, a German named Tauler, and each assistant had his own room. Although 'Trismosin' did not describe the details of the laboratory, we might imagine the instruments at his disposal by viewing an illustration from a fifteenth-century alchemical manuscript (Figure 6). 'Trismosin' claims that while in the nobleman's laboratory, he used several different formulas for making gold, with success.

According to this account, 'Trismosin' arrived in Venice sometime after 1476. While he did not describe his impressions of the city, at that time Venice was one of the three largest cities in the world (the others being Paris and Naples) with a population of 150,000.[99] Venice was also the most powerful, magnificent, and cultured city in that part of the world. The metalworking trades, which served as a basis for practical alchemy, had been honed in the fabrication of weapons and armor, as well as in the minting of gold currency. At that time, Venice was an important trading center and, through its many ties with the East, an excellent place to acquire alchemical texts. In his account, 'Trismosin' reports that the nobleman who employed him bought and studied alchemical books in many languages.

The atmosphere in Venice at that time supported innovation and intellectual freedom. It had been governed under a constitution for two centuries, and, along with nearby Padua, had been a cultural and academic center for five hundred years. Marco Polo had returned from China a hundred years before, and Dante's *Commedia* had been widely known for nearly two hundred years. The mosaics in the cathedral of San Marco, with their brilliant golden background, were accessible to all. 'Trismosin' could also have viewed the paintings of the Venezianos, the Bellinis, Mantegna, and Titian.

If he had remained in Venice into the first decade of the sixteenth century, he might also have viewed Carpaccio's *Healing of the Madman* (c.1496) and his

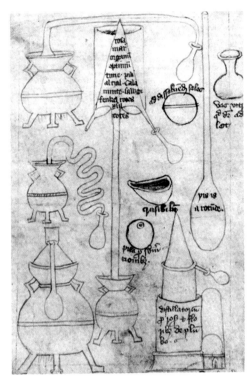

FIGURE 6 Fifteenth-Century Alchemical Apparatus. These were also used for the distillation of spirits and herbal infusions. From a fifteenth-century English MS. (Sloane MS 3548, f. 25, by permission of the British Library)

magnificent friezes of St. George and the Dragon in the Scuola di San Giorgio degli Schiavoni. His stay in Venice was cut short by the death of his employer, who was drowned in the Adriatic when his 'grand pleasure ship' sank in a hurricane. He then went to 'a still better place,' where he had access to cabalistic books in Egyptian, which he had translated first into Greek, and then from Greek to Latin. He claimed he found a tincture of 'such a beautiful red colour as no scarlet can compare with . . .'

Despite the unlikely claim of success in making gold, this account also indicates skepticism and wariness of being taken in by tricks that could make a substance appear as silver or gold. This reminds us of alchemy's important role as a proto-science, bringing together the practical and the theoretical, in contrast to 'truths' about the nature of the universe and matter held sacrosanct by the medieval Christian Church.

It would be more than a century before Galileo, appointed a professor of mathematics at the University of Padua in 1592, began to use careful observation and mathematical reasoning to understand the natural world. He produced immediate and indisputable practical results: Galileo consulted to shipbuilders about the physics of their craft, studied the tides, observed the movement of heavenly bodies so important for navigation, and introduced the telescope as a useful military instrument to the astounded Venetian Assembly. As noted previously, he showed later in his life that the movements of heavenly bodies as observed from the earth was consistent with a Copernican, sun-centered planetary system.[100] So we need to remind ourselves that in Trismosin's time, the sun, which brought light and life, was believed to revolve around the earth. As William Manchester has written:

> Everything was as it had been for as long as the oldest European could remember. The center of the Ptolemaic universe was the known world – Europe, with the Holy Land and North Africa on its fringes. The sun moved round it every day. Heaven was above the immovable earth, somewhere in the overarching sky; hell seethed far beneath their feet. . . .
> When the cartographers of the Middle Ages came to the end of the world as they knew it, they wrote: *Beware, Dragons Lurk Beyond Here.* . . . [101]

With the same certainty that the earth was the center of the universe, medieval Europeans, knowing nothing about Aristotle's spherical theory, believed that the earth was flat:

> [The Church endorsed] the absurd geographical dicta of *Topographia Christiana*, a treatise by the sixth-century monk Cosmas. Cosmas, who had traveled to India and should have known better, held that the world was a flat, rectangular plane, . . . Jerusalem was at the center of the rectangle, and nearby lay the Garden of Eden, irrigated by the four Rivers of Paradise. The sun, much smaller than the earth, revolved around a conical mountain to the north.[102]

From a psychological point of view, we can see Cosmas' map as a mandala and wonder whether the medieval psyche, faced with a world of conflict and much misery, might have needed the reassurance that the earth itself did have a basic order. (In our commentary on Plate II–4, we shall discuss mandala symbolism in relation to individual psychology.)

A simplicity of thinking held that two opposites, *A* and *not-A*, could not both be true at the same time. Alongside this rigidity of thinking, the medieval mind was filled with myth, allegories, and richly symbolic imagery. This reminds us that Jung wrote about 'what takes place between light and darkness,'[103] concluding that,

> Here only the symbol helps, for, in accordance with its paradoxical nature, it represents the 'tertium' [the third] that in logic does not exist, but which in reality is the living truth.[104]

In the 1930s multivalent logic was formulated, and more recently, we have seen the development of systems theory, chaos theory, and emergence theory. The clinical practice of psychotherapy, not to mention our personal experience, shows us that our consciousness as human beings has not caught up with these intellectual developments. As Jung has stated, 'Experience of the opposites has nothing whatever to do with intellectual insight or with empathy.'[105]

The illuminated paintings

The beautiful illuminated paintings of the Harley *Splendor Solis* reflect great subtlety and originality, as well as familiarity with Greek and Roman mythology and literature. The Harley images are assumed to date from 1582, which appears on two of the paintings. If von Franz is correct in her dating of the original text (supra), then the Harley manuscript was made eighty to ninety years after the original. In that case, the Harley painter could not have known the author of the text. There are several older versions of the *Splendor Solis*, and one of the earliest, dated 1532–5, is held in the Staatsbibliothek Preussischer Kulturbesitz, Berlin.[106] It contains the same series of pictures, although they are technically inferior and differ in their details. (Compare Figures 7A and 7B.) It is tempting to speculate that the images were developed over time rather than being created in all their sophistication by a single artist and then simply copied thereafter. According to Adam McLean,

> Trismosin's works, which were published at the end of the 16th century, had a profound influence upon the alchemical tradition. They are obviously the products of a particular alchemical esoteric school which had worked extensively with symbolism. Students of this school prepared for their own use manuscript copies of the various series of symbols, such as the *Splendor Solis* and the *Spiegel* (or *The Mirror of Philosophy*), also ascribed to Trismosin.[107]

However, documentation of this very plausible assertion has not yet been published.

In contrast to the illuminated paintings, later printed versions of the *Splendor Solis*, illustrated with engravings,[108] are simplified and vary somewhat in content from the Harley version in ways that could imply a different interpretation of their symbolism. For example, the 1708 Hamburg edition includes only the central images and also lacks the subtlety and complexity of the illuminated paintings. (Compare Figures 7A and 7B with Figure 7C.)

We do not know if the artist who painted the images of the *Splendor Solis* might also have been an alchemist or working under the guidance of an alchemist.[109] However, we do know that in medieval and Renaissance times the apothecary, the alchemist, and the artist were all connected in very practical ways: the grinding of stones and the preparation of plant extracts were essential to all these arts. Further, the alchemist or artist might acquire materials at an apothecary's shop (see Figure 8).[110] Gold was used for medicinal purposes, and gold leaf and powdered gold were used in illuminated manuscripts.[111] (The British Library manuscript of the *Splendor Solis* includes gold in the elaborate first letters of paragraphs, as decorative flourishes on otherwise blank sections of pages, and within the paintings themselves, as shown in Figure 5.)

In the Renaissance, the illuminator's reds included cinnabar (mercuric sulfide), a substance well-known to alchemists. Vermilion red was extracted from Brazilwood, and a purplish red was derived from the root of the madder plant.[112] The sap of the shrub *Pterocarpus draco* produced a popular red called 'dragon's blood.' Yarn had it that 'dragon's blood' was the co-mingled blood of an elephant and a dragon who had slain one another in battle.[113] Blues were obtained from stones (azurite, lapis lazuli) and from

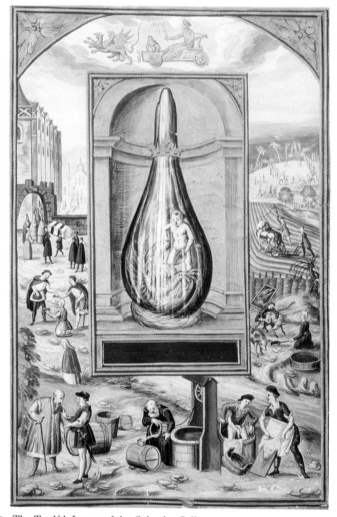

FIGURE 7 The Twelfth Image of the *Splendor Solis*.
A. Illuminated painting from MS Germ. Fol. 42, *c*. 1532–5. (By permission of Staatsbibliothek
    zu Berlin – Preussischer Kulturbesitz)

plants (the seeds of turnsole or *Crozophora* in alkaline solution).[114] Lapis lazuli must
have seemed nearly as mysterious and difficult to obtain as 'dragon's blood,' since at
that time it was found only in a mine in north-east Afghanistan.

 The importance of color in alchemy[115] has its counterpart in the importance of
color to artistic expression and the capacity of color to convey and evoke emotion. The
importance of color to inner experience was expressed by a woman with a degenerative
illness, who entered analysis in her thirties in order to prepare for a premature death. To
her first session she brought something she had written as a senior in college: 'I love
color because it symbolizes a living spirit. I am feeling color, feeling alive. My inner

B. Illuminated painting from Harley 3469, dated 1582. (By permission of the British Library)

senses speak more loudly every day, telling me I am alive. Slowly, I am beginning to believe in myself.'

The Harley *Splendor Solis* is a rather late example of an illuminated manuscript, since it was made after the advent of printing. When alchemical works began to be printed, they were illustrated with woodblock prints and later with engraving – and they lost their color. Another, less obvious, aspect of the illuminated painting also disappeared. The painter of illuminated manuscripts worked with great care and focus, sometimes using a single hair as a brush. The paintings convey this care, with details at the limit of what the human eye can perceive. The viewer is transported into a unique and sacred space. The impressions induced by an illuminated painting – the intensity

C. Engraving from the 1708 Hamburg Printed Edition. (Salomon Trismosin, *Aureum Vellus, oder Guldin Schatz und Kunstkammer*, Hamburg)

and subtlety of feeling communicated by the colors, the meditative quality conveyed by the great care with which it was created – were easily lost in reproduction.

Recently, the connection between alchemy and art has been rediscovered, with images and processes of alchemy used consciously by artists in their art and as metaphors for the creative process.[116] James Elkins of the Chicago Art Institute has written evocatively about what has been lost to the process of painting now that artists no longer make their own colors from natural materials.[117] He also describes the artistic process itself as alchemy, asserting that, 'One of the crucial traits of alchemy, that makes it an apposite metaphor for artistic creation, is the "involvement" of the observer in the process.'[118]

FIGURE 8 A Medieval Apothecary's Shop. From an early fourteenth-century French manuscript. Hanging from a hook on the ceiling is the plate used for mixing ingredients. (Sloane MS 1977, f. 49v, by permission of the British Library)

The intense involvement of the alchemist, even a feeling of inner devotion, also characterizes the work of analysis. Psychology is a very young discipline – perhaps as naive in its way as European alchemy was in the fifteenth and sixteenth centuries. Psychology, too, has struggled with the tensions between the exoteric and esoteric, between a scientific empiricism focused on behavior and an opposing approach that includes the embodied inner life of the individual and does not exclude mystical or spiritual experiences. Within psychoanalysis, concepts that once seemed so promising in the attempt to *define* and *explain*, like 'superego,' 'ego,' 'unconscious,' or 'self,' now seem as elusive as the 'mystical' religious symbolism they proudly tried to replace. Despite Jung's use of metapsychological language, in 1942 he clearly expressed his reservations:

... deeper insight into the problems of psychic development soon teaches us how much better it is to reserve judgement instead of prematurely announcing to all and sundry what's what. Of course we all have an understandable desire for crystal clarity but we are apt to forget that in psychic matters we are dealing with processes of experience, that is, with transformations which should never be given hard and fast names if their living movement is not to petrify into something static. The protean mythologem and the shimmering symbol express the processes of the psyche far more trenchantly and, in the end, far more clearly than the clearest concept; for the symbol not only conveys a visualization of the process but – and this is perhaps just as important – it also brings a re-experiencing of it, of that twilight which we can learn to understand only through inoffensive empathy, but which too much clarity only dispels.[119]

The images of the *Splendor Solis* return us to a time when matter was animated, when there was no shame in believing that mysterious forces and qualities could transform the ordinary and the foul into something of value. The images you are about to encounter come from a period when alchemy was neither fully concretized nor fully philosophical. The alchemist was truly interested in transforming matter, and the origins of the imagery in concrete chemical operations can often be seen. The imagery also clearly conveys the recognition that, through his labor to transform matter, the alchemist was changed. This is not unlike our work as analysts: as Jung observed, 'When two chemical substances combine, both are altered. This is precisely what happens in the transference.'[120]

The twenty-two illuminated paintings of the *Splendor Solis* form three dramatically different sequences of images depicting the alchemical opus, or work.[121] Although we cannot know what they meant to the artist, we do approach them as expressions of their creator's capacity for self-reflection and psychological transformation. We can study them as we would images from dreams or active imagination, but without the advantage of knowing the personal associations and conscious attitudes of their creator. We can research their symbolism from a cultural perspective and explore the many mythological references contained in their complex symbolism. Indeed, these images are a valuable commentary on the cultural attitudes of Western European civilization, attitudes that still affect the psyches of individuals as well as the collective political life of groups and nations.[122]

The mercurial nature of symbols

We do not offer a definitive interpretation. A symbol by its very nature cannot be interpreted definitively, and it will evoke different associations and meanings in each person and in the same person at different times. To give but one example: early in his analytic work, a man reported an energy-filled dream from his youth, and he referred to it often as he recalled the suffering of his childhood. Later in his analysis, he wrote about the way its meaning for him had changed:

When I was twenty-seven years old, I had a very dramatic dream, which I felt contained profound meaning about a transformation and direction in my life. In the dream, Christ was standing within a circle of horses, and he addressed me saying, 'You are stuck between the hammer and the anvil.' As he spoke to me I saw an excruciating image of myself pinned between a huge hammer and anvil. Initially I thought that this dream pointed to a personal experience, the abuse during my childhood or the severe inner conflict I experienced almost continually. Nearly twenty years later, however, I was stunned to read a passage in which Jung wrote that between the hammer and anvil, the patient is forged into an indestructible whole, an individual. Reading this helped me to recognize that the symbol of the hammer and anvil also pointed to a universal process beyond my own personal experience. I now feel that the hammer and anvil symbolize a living fire that continues to burn, heal, and shape me.

Both interpretations were correct but were meaningful for the patient at different times in his life. This man's dream also gives us an image of the opus, of the suffering human being as the metal that is being forged between the hammer and the anvil. Its symbolism, containing processes known for thousands of years, seems to reach across time, suggesting that the dream of a twenty-first-century man in California could also have been the dream of a man from a different time and place.

The images of the *Splendor Solis* give us a rare opportunity to examine a symbolic process represented sequentially, and this includes the use of symbols in different contexts, in a way that enriches and develops their meanings across the series. We use examples from our work as Jungian analysts to demonstrate the value of alchemical imagery to the study of psychotherapeutic process[123] and the actual practice of depth analysis. Our intent is to open these beautiful paintings to the imagination of the viewer, to differing interpretations, and to further scholarly and clinical inquiry.

THE FIRST SERIES

Plate I–1 A Sick Sun and a Healthy Sun [1]

THE SYMBOLISM OF THE first painting of the *Splendor Solis*, which is the frontis-piece of the illuminated manuscript, informs us that this work does not concern itself with methods for the practical, concrete transformation of base metals into gold. For the author of the *Splendor Solis*, alchemy was a practice for the healing and transformation of the human soul.

The world of this beautiful painting is full of the unexpected and the paradoxical, challenging our ordinary assumptions: a coat-of-arms proclaims weakness and disinte-gration, animals play musical instruments and show generosity to other species, and a two-dimensional image on a banner becomes three-dimensional, swirling out into the scene. As we look at it carefully, we may begin to feel unsettled.

The large, golden *trompe-l'oeil* frame conveys the great value of the painting within. On the upper part of the frame, the words, 'Arma Artis,' are inscribed in gold letters on a crimson background. 'The Arms of the Art,' presumably tells us that the coat-of-arms in the banner below represents 'the art' of alchemy.

Within the painting, we see two men engaged in conversation, standing upon verdant ground just beyond a high archway. Presumably, one of the men is the alchem-ist, and the other is his adept or student: alchemy, like analysis, involved relationship and discourse. As he speaks, the man dressed in black gestures toward the right with his left hand, while the other man, dressed in red, faces in that direction and looks intently, as if anticipating something or seeing something for the first time. They are separated from the viewer by a waterway, in which rapidly flowing, turbulent water has risen nearly to the level of the pavement. Yet the two men do not seem alarmed.

Behind them lies a landscape with a town or fortress on a steep hillside in the distance, with a mountain still further away. They are standing just outside a gate to the city, implying that alchemy requires one to step outside the familiar structure of one's life and set out on a journey. Their relationship suggests that, although this journey will be solitary in the sense of being unique to the individual, it is undertaken with the counsel and companionship of one who has returned from his own journey.

This reminds us that the still-popular ideal of the solitary hero's quest of self-discovery – like the Greek Ulysses or the Neoplatonic solitary journey to the One – was challenged by Dante as long ago as the fourteenth century. In *The Inferno*, the poet fails

35

Arma Artis!

PLATE I–1[1]

in his attempt to climb up a mountain to reach the entrance to the underworld. He begins anew, this time assisted by Virgil:

> . . . my guide climbed up again
> And drew me up to pursue our lonely course.
> Without the hand the foot could not go on.[2]

The central area of the painting is dominated by a crimson banner. At first glance, the design appears to be a stereotypical coat-of-arms, but when we observe the lower part closely, we realize that it is a coat-of-arms in a process of falling apart. The design on the upper portion suggests the martial regalia of a king, with the helmet embellished by several waving plumes and a crest composed of three silvery crescent moons. Above the crown, brilliant against the darkened background, shines a golden sun with human features and a steady gaze. Its rays, alternating straight and sinuous, spread out in all directions. The lowest of its downward-pointing rays penetrates the concavity of the topmost crescent moon. The blue star-studded fabric attached to the helmet whirls out past the banner, as if it is transforming from two dimensions into three. Below the helmet, a shield rests on the pavement, tilting toward the viewer's left, so that the golden sun depicted upon it is askew. Moreover, the lower sun's human features are as horrifying as the upper sun's features are benign. The face of the lower sun is pock-marked and, from each eye and extended tongue, a tiny, demonic face peers forth. Instead of straight rays, the rays emanating from this sun are like hooks that bend back upon themselves.

The cultural symbols found in the illuminated paintings of the *Splendor Solis* reflect a radical change of attitude toward the ideals of medieval chivalry that was taking place in the late Middle Ages and early Renaissance. The knight, who had once seemed invincible in his heavy metal armor, was seen as weighed down and awkward:

> Knighthood, a pivotal medieval institution, was dying. At a time when its ceremonies had finally reached their fullest development, chivalry was obsolescent and would soon be obsolete. The knightly way of life was no longer practical. Chain mail had been replaced by plate, which, though more effective, was also much heavier; horses which were capable of carrying that much weight were hard to come by, and their expense, added to that of the costly new mail, was almost prohibitive. Worse still, the mounted knight no longer dominated the battlefield; he could be outmaneuvered and unhorsed by English bowmen, Genoese crossbowmen, and pikemen led by lightly armed men-at-arms, or sergeants.[3]

In the humanistic light of the Renaissance, the knight and his chivalric order seemed patronizing and, as Cervantes represented them, even ridiculous.

In this alchemical coat-of-arms, primordial elements are replacing the old cultural images. A king in his battle-armor is the incarnation of the principle of dominion through force, but here we see that his costume is empty, collapsed. Yet the upper sun shines steadfastly, its prominent lower ray pointing toward the three crescent moons below. To understand the symbolism here, it is important to remember that in European alchemy, the moon was usually associated with the Feminine Principle and the sun with the Masculine Principle. So this configuration suggests that help is needed from the restorative power of the feminine, a theme we shall encounter repeatedly in this series.

With regard to the presence of *three* crescent moons, a conjecture by Marie-Louise von Franz points to an underlying psychological theme: 'Threefold rhythms are most probably connected with processes in space and time or with their realization in consciousness.'[4]

Finally, we should remark on the position of the viewer in relation to the banner. We face it but cannot see how it is held up, and we are on the inside of the city looking out. This banner does not declare a worldly power backed by force-of-arms, promising protection for the viewer from danger without; rather, the viewer is faced with a failure and dissolution of an order that had once seemed impregnable.

This scene is analogous to the beginning of an analytic encounter between analyst and patient.[5] The analysand might have been trying very hard to sustain a heroic over-achievement, represented by the knight's helmet. The patient's psyche is divided, as represented by the healthy (upper) sun and the (lower) sick sun. The sick sun is isolated, distorted, cut off from relationship, and morbidly subjective, suggesting self-doubt and self-loathing – a true description of a neurosis. The person so afflicted also has a healthy side, which may be projected onto the analyst as healer and carrier of consciousness during the course of work on the less healthy part

An example of this painfully divided state of being is shown in Figure 9. A woman in analysis made this painting several years into the work, when her personality was in a profound state of upheaval. Her heroic defenses had failed her, and she was often in despair about how she could live her life. The sun is barely visible in the upper left-hand corner, and the earth is barren except for a snaking river. A jagged red line separates the darkness surrounding the earth from the blue sky above. This painting shows the way an inner state is often represented as something in the natural world, a felt correspondence of the personal (microcosm) and the outer world (macrocosm), which will be discussed further in relation to Plate I–9.

Thus, from a psychological point of view, the alchemical coat-of-arms might be viewed as the configuration of a certain schizoid condition that threatens to become paranoid and overshadow the personality. It might also refer to any defense which once served the individual (or was necessary for survival) but has outlasted its usefulness.

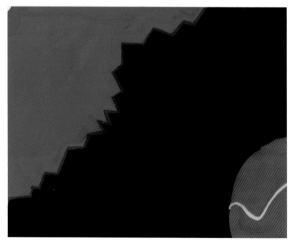

FIGURE 9 'Heaven and Earth are Far Apart.' (Painting by a woman in analysis)

The defense may be represented in dreams by attire, such as a uniform or helmet, or by an animal or human figure. For example, a woman in her twenties came into analysis in a depressed, withdrawn, and fearful state. This state contrasted with her usually enthusiastic and upbeat persona (represented in her dreams as a cheerleader), academic achievements, and tirelessness. Some months into therapy she dreamt that,

> I was bathing a tiny turtle in a bowl of water, and the turtle's shell came off. I attempted gently to support it with my hand because its interior skeleton was too weak to provide adequate support for it to keep its head above water. A woman of my acquaintance, who is demanding and insensitive, was with me, and she became angry at the turtle for slouching. I was afraid that she would cause it some permanent damage. I also saw that it would not be possible to replace the shell, because it had been damaged when it came off.

The shell of the turtle represents a defense against emotional lances and blows. The patient identified her true self as vulnerable, like the shell-less turtle, unable to support herself from within. She felt that the acquaintance in the dream represented a judgmental and self-scrutinizing part of herself who demanded performance and efficiency, and she was surprised that her dream ego was so caring and protective toward the turtle. She related this new sensitivity to the care of the analyst who had not judged her harshly for her difficulties, but we can also view it as coming from a deeper, wiser part of herself.

This dream was a moving image of a fundamental problem that the patient and the analyst would be addressing. In practical terms, the analyst used the image of the shell-less turtle to remind herself of the patient's underlying vulnerability and anxiety. This was especially helpful when the patient was in a hypomanic 'cheerleader' state. Those times were painful to the analyst because the patient's defense precluded authentic empathic contact. The image from the patient's dream helped the analyst to hold the patient's more vulnerable parts and to ask herself what might have happened between them or in the patient's life that had caused the shell to be put back in place during their session. This is an example of the way symbols in dreams are more than a reductive or a purely relational aspect of the transference–countertransference. They may symbolize the problem in a much broader and deeper way that will give both the therapist and the patient support and holding while the delicate process unfolds.

Understandably, the patient was reluctant to risk the uncovering process, nor was she ready to acknowledge consciously her transference fear of the analyst's judgments. Much careful work lay ahead to pave the way for those feelings to be openly acknowledged. (There is additional alchemical symbolism in this dream, including the *solutio* of the bath.[6] As throughout the book, we will not present an extended interpretation of dreams or clinical process; the focus will be on the symbolic connection to the *Splendor Solis* image under discussion.)

Another woman in analysis reflected on the defenses that had cut her off from herself, already in place by adolescence:

Patient: . . . which is where I was when I was twelve, like the way he was treating me last night.
Analyst: It took you back to that emotional field.

Patient: Where there is a heavy coat of armor. (long silence) . . .

Analyst: Can you speak as an adult about the twelve-year-old?

Patient: Yes, I'd say he doesn't get it.

Analyst: What doesn't he get?

Patient: The fact that she can't express her true self to him because she hasn't the language. That his demands for her performance harden her, so that all he or anyone else will know is the exterior like a shell. It may be a beautiful shell like a turtle but he will never know the inside of her. (silence) Or it may be a hideous shell, but again he won't know what's inside. He won't know that her core is being twisted in unspeakable ways, and even more damaged by not acknowledging what we – she and I – plainly see. I guess I would also point out that although her mind has appeared functionally adequate that we know nothing about her underbelly.

This hidden thing that we know nothing about is the *prima materia*. But what could motivate a person to face something unknown yet attended with emotions of horror and shame? The symbolism of the coat-of-arms may help us here: the steady and balanced upper sun can be seen to represent some larger and wiser aspect of the patient's personality, not necessarily conscious, which helps to balance paranoid anxieties with hope for healing. It may also represent the strength, integrity,[7] and perseverance necessary to gaze upon the unhealthy parts of herself. This aspect of the work is also supported by the analyst's steadiness. Note, however, that in the image, the healthy sun is not alone: although it shines by its own light, it exists in relation to the crescent moons below. This suggests an integrity that acknowledges the value of the changeable, related, vulnerable aspects of human life.

    The idea of the feminine as vessel is echoed by the golden frame, which is decorated with delicately rendered symbolic images of plant and animal life. These natural forms are in keeping with the first words of the text, 'The Philosopher's Stone is produced by means of Greening and Growing Nature.'[8] In medieval times, flowers were thought to be the earthly counterparts to stars. In Greek alchemy, flowers signified spirits or souls, and the lapis was called the 'blossom of metal' and the 'well-formed flower sprouting from four branches [or elements].'[9]

    On the left side of the frame, an owl, associated with the Greek goddess of wisdom, Athena (Minerva in Roman mythology) faces left. Two monkeys sit on a green ledge at the base of the frame. The monkey to the left reaches out and offers a fish to a heron, while another heron looks on from behind the monkey. This scene contains parallels to the work of the alchemist. Like Hermes, the patron and mythical founder of alchemy (the 'Hermetic art'), a heron can travel from the earth to realms both above and below. The heron's long neck evokes the long neck of a flask. A monkey is feeding the heron, just as the alchemist 'feeds' the *prima materia* to the retort, the *vas Hermetica*, and uses natural processes but in a conscious and deliberate way that both contains and intensifies them.

    We note that the animals' activities are not 'natural.' In fact, they are going against their usual nature. For example, monkeys do not offer food to other species. Here, the monkey has transcended his instinctual nature, as humans can when they become more conscious. Animals in dreams often represent negative or destructive aspects of human instinct (for example, a greedy, impulsive monkey) or they may evoke emotional reactions in the dreamer (e.g., fear of attack). But animals in dreams can also represent positive aspects of our nature that have been wounded or repressed. In both their positive and negative aspects, animal figures in dreams may initiate the dreamer into a relationship to the unconscious and to the natural world. They become inner guides if they are valued.[10]

The monkey facing toward the right is playing a lute. Music was important to the alchemists, both in theory and in practice. Theories of music employ mathematics and number symbolism, thus pointing toward an underlying, unseen order in the universe. In ancient Greece, the Pythagoreans discovered that, in a stringed instrument, there is a proportional relationship between the length of the string and the tone produced. They inferred that the motions of the planets produced sounds, and Plato later described a 'music' or 'harmony of the spheres.'[11] The alchemists believed that mathematical relationships based on musical ratios could be applied to relationships between elements and the planets to provide guidance about the ratios of ingredients in their preparations.[12] John Read, the eminent Scottish historian of alchemy, speculated that,

> in view of the alchemical belief in the beneficent influence of music, it is likely that the processes of the Great Work were sometimes performed to the accompaniment of musical chants or incantations. To the religious mystics among the alchemists, in particular, these processes partook of the nature of a religious ritual, and it would be natural for them to introduce music from one of these closely related activities to the other.[13]

A new attitude toward the natural world is also reflected in the paintings of the *Splendor Solis*. To the early medieval perception, nature was regarded as chaotic and unhealthy; there was very little of what we today refer to as the appreciation of nature's beauty.[14] However, in the golden *trompe-l'oeil* frame seen here, natural forms are at once generative, symbolic, and beautiful. They reflect the inquisitive and aesthetic spirit that had already begun to develop in the late Middle Ages, when poets like Dante and Petrarch began writing about nature and extolling its beauties. There is a suggestion of nature as a source of renewal and nourishment, especially signified by one monkey feeding a heron while the other monkey is playing music. Both monkeys look toward the right, as if looking toward the next picture, which will take us into a new stage of the transformation.

Before we leave this picture, however, we should reflect further on its depiction of an outworn persona, as represented by the helmet. This image of defended consciousness is about to be discarded, displaced, or transcended by the golden crown. The crown proclaims alchemy as the Kingly Art, but using the symbol of kingship in a different way, as a ruler with a broad view who considers his subjects rather than working solely to defend and promote his own interests. Psychologically, this refers to a perspective beyond keeping the ego safe: the larger view of transformation pertains to what Jung called the Self. The symbols in this painting tell us that the Self does not have a unified, conscious goal; it is shown here as an imaginal union of two complementary opposites, represented by solar strength and constancy willingly uniting with the lunar rhythm of change. This symbolism of the Self is compensatory to the lower image of self-doubt. It offers to both therapist and patient a promising image of the possibilities that might lie ahead if they can agree upon treatment.

PLATE I–2[15]

Plate I–2 Setting Out on a Journey

In the foreground, a bearded man clothed in a red robe and cap, with a purple outer cloak, is walking in a deliberate manner from left to right. His fine garments have golden threads along their borders, but his feet are bare. Beyond him a winding path leads past a tall, straight tree and through a beautiful natural setting down to the sea. The landscape includes valleys, forests, hills, and mountains, towns and open spaces. In his left hand he holds up a silvery, long-necked flask, or *cucurbit*, containing a transparent golden fluid. He directs his gaze toward the vessel and points to it with his right index finger. Upon a black ribbon encircling the neck of the vessel and spiraling upward, the words 'Eamus Quesitum Quatuor Elementorum Naturas,' or 'We are seeking the nature of the Four Elements,' are printed in gold letters. What does this mean? Presumably, the fluid within the vessel may be treated by the alchemical work to reveal the essential characteristics of the material world, in other words the Four Elements – Earth, Air, Fire, and Water. The psychological equivalent of such a procedure is what we might call the activation of the basic constituents of the psyche (or the primal self), with its four potential functions of consciousness,[16] in order to make their influence available for conscious development. It is a call for return to the ground of being so that the natural personality can be purged of influences which have distorted its expression.

Around the main picture is a large frame decorated with plants and animals. An owl appears on the right. At the bottom is a peacock with a long tail, or *cauda pavonis*, which will become important at a later stage of the work.[17] Nearby, a doe and a stag seem to look up toward the alchemist in the picture. From ancient times, the deer was used to represent a non-ordinary awareness or the capacity to communicate with the spirit world. The stag's antlers, which are lost and renewed annually, are symbols of death and rebirth. Their branching pattern of growth evokes the growth of plants – and when worn by a human represents the growth of consciousness. Prehistoric symbolic images of human skeletons wearing antlers have been found in England, France, Persia, Asia Minor, and China.[18] Painted statues of deer, with bodies carved from wood and real antlers, were placed in tombs in ancient China,[19] possibly to help the deceased make the transition to the next world. In Siberia and in North America, shamans often wore headdresses with reindeer antlers or antlers made of iron.[20] Alchemists used the deer to represent *the spirit within matter*, also represented by *Mercurius*, the androgynous, changeable Roman god who was known as Hermes to the Greeks. In this plate, the mercurial spirit – in both its Feminine and Masculine forms – is aware of the alchemist as he begins his opus. Jung referred to the deer as a symbol of 'Mercurius, the essence, moisture, or principle behind or within the quicksilver . . . that indefinable, fascinating, irritating, elusive thing which attracts an unconscious projection. . . the *cervus fugitivus* . . . [fugitive stag . . .]'[21] With regard to analysis, this could represent the thing that brings the patient to therapy, the thing which his ego has not been able to contain or manage, and which has disrupted his psychological equilibrium – but it can also take the form of a compelling interest that seems to come out of the blue.

In the alchemical worldview, Mercury refers to the mercurial *quality* of matter rather than to the element we now call mercury. The alchemists believed that metals differed from one another because they contained greater or lesser amounts of particular *qualities*. According to Paracelsus' theory of *tria prima*, the three fundamental properties of matter were represented by mercury, sulfur, and salt.[22] Sulfur was associated with Sol, the sun, and thus with the Masculine Principle, while mercury was closely associated with silver, the Moon, and the Feminine Principle.[23] Salt – the fixed, immutable, quality of matter – was associated with body and earth.

Possibly the most important image from alchemy is the alchemical vessel itself, called the *vas*, *alembic*, or *cucurbit*, in which the transformations of the elements, or of metals, take place. In the practice of analytical psychology, it symbolizes the privacy of the encounter between therapist and patient and the need to keep this container[24] closed, i.e. confidential. It represents a space without 'leaks,' one without careless talk outside the therapy session that dissipates the focus and meaning of the work. This archetypal injunction to maintain confidentiality, as if in a hermetically sealed vessel, is more than the physician's Hippocratic Oath; otherwise, it would have little psychological value. The alchemist's insistence on keeping the alembic closed (and its contents therefore private) conveys a deeper meaning to the psychotherapist: it encourages the therapist to support a patient's efforts to use the material that arises in the course of transformation in an appropriately introverted way and to avoid betraying the integrity of the process either by recklessly acting it out or by fruitless theorizing (i.e. discussing it in an abstract and objectified way).

Dreams early in analysis often warn the patient about this need for containment. This is necessary because people are oriented to cultural values and expectations that may easily distract them from the task of self-reflection. This tendency may appear as a fear about what the outside world may think about therapy or analysis, represented in a dream where people come into the waiting room, possibly even into the consulting room, and interfere. Sometimes this intrusion is so disturbing that the whole room is taken over by a cacophony of externalized comments. The anxiety about 'what people might think' is also a reflection of the complexes or attitudes *within* the analysand, what *they* might think about the therapy.

There is another common fear that has nothing to do with cultural attitudes or with the impact that the therapy might have on important relationships and social adaptation. Warded-off energies and impulses, whether destructive or creative, may at first alarm the analysand when they press for conscious recognition and integration. This fear is illustrated by the dream of a woman patient early in analysis. She dreamt that she held a basket in her hand. She stood up and opened it, and a cobra jumped out! The patient dropped both the cobra and the basket on the floor in great alarm. The dream showed her inner fear of something getting out of control, or fear of breakdown, if she continued the analysis. Later she imagined putting the snake – no longer a cobra – back in the vessel and closing it. From then on the therapy went very well. In other words she was able to feel contained, and the unconscious responded by indicating that the snake, instead of being a poisonous reptile that would kill the process, could become the guardian spirit.

Plate I-3 The Inner Quest

From a strictly alchemical point of view, this stage is concerned with the separation of the two basic opposites and their subsequent recombination. In the painting, a knight wears gray armor ornamented with gold. He holds a drawn sword[25] in his right hand, and in his left he holds a red banner with an inscription in gold letters:

PLATE I–3[26]

> Ex duabus aqui unam facite, qui quaeritis Sole et Luna facere. Et date bibere inimico vino. Et videbitis cum mortuum. Dein de aquaterra facite. Et lapide multiplicastis.[27]

which may be translated as,

> From two waters make one, whereby seek to make the sun and moon. And prepare to drink the wine of the antagonists. And you shall see with the Dead. Thereupon, make watery-earth. And multiply the stone.

The knight faces toward the left and stands upon two fountains, with a foot on each. The fountain to the right is surmounted by a metal figure of a nude boy, who holds a stick in his raised right hand. He is urinating a gray fluid into a basin, which overflows via a conduit into the basin at the left. The left fountain is surmounted by a similar nude figure, probably a girl, with a stick resting on her left shoulder. She urinates a golden liquid into the receptacle below. The blending of the two streams produces a golden fluid, which overflows, flooding a well-tended countryside with fields bordered by rows of trees. Two villages can be seen in the valley, and another rests on the hillside to the right. Mountainous areas are indicated in the distance.

As in the previous paintings, the central image is surrounded by a beautiful golden frame, filled with plant and animal life. A peacock appears in the upper left, a butterfly on the right. An owl in the lower part of the frame, facing left, is heckled by two birds. This suggests the internal strife and ambivalence attending the wisdom of combining the opposites. However, two other birds more calmly face the owl, one on either side.

Here the knight symbolizes the ego strength that supports the individual in taking charge of the situation, making decisions, and initiating action. So, we see that, even though the first image of the series implied that the knight is no longer a satisfactory symbol of the whole personality, the strength of the hero is definitely required for this new and difficult task. Holding the sword upright suggests the heroic stance of the ego that says, 'Yes, I straddle the opposites, and with my sword I shall free the elements from this containment.'

The seven stars[28] over the knight's head are a symbolic reference to initiation. Seven is the traditional number associated with undergoing a complete process over time, as in the seven days of the week, and the alchemical opus was often described as having seven stages. The Stairway of the Seven Planets figured prominently in late Classical initiation rites, symbolizing the ascent of the soul to the sun-god, or the *solificatio*.[29] The author of *Aurora Consurgens* used seven parables, which alluded to the seven stages and to the seven planets. Seven stars were associated with the whitening, or purification, of the *prima materia*:

> After thou has made those seven (metals) which thou has distributed through the seven stars (and has appointed to the seven stars) (and) has purged them nine times until they appear as pearls (in likeness) – this is the Whitening.[30]

In her commentary, von Franz further noted that within each parable, the entire opus is described in miniature, thus creating a spiral.[31] We shall see that the symbolism of the number seven reappears in a variety of contexts in this series of paintings.

The knight has stripes of different colors on his breast-plate: black, white, yellow, and red. This is the first statement of the *stages* of the alchemical process, represented by colors. Black represents the *nigredo* or blackness – the initial chaos or undifferentiated state – which turns into white, or *albedo*, representing a rebirth or sense of renewal; yellow announces a transitional stage from the white, and the red, the *rubedo*, represents the final result of transformation. Throughout the paintings of the *Splendor Solis*, we shall encounter this color symbolism.

The stream of urine from the little boy is gray or silver, associated with spirit and with Luna, the changeable. Silver also denotes Mercurius at the beginning of the work. The girl's urine is a golden stream, which refers to soul, sulfur, and Sol. As we discussed previously, sulfur and mercury represented opposite qualities of matter, often thought of as masculine and feminine. According to John Read,

> In the operations of the Great Work, the union of masculine and feminine principles was associated with the process known as conjunction [*coniunctio*];. . . .Sulphur was said to bestow, and mercury to receive, the form assumed by the material resulting from their conjunction – just as wax takes and retains the impression of a seal. There were innumerable synonyms for each of these principles, many of which were used also to denote the Philosopher's Stone. Sophic sulphur was called Sol, king, male, brother, Osiris, lion, toad, wingless dragon, . . ., etc. Sophic mercury was disguised under such names as Luna, queen, female, sister, Isis, . . . serpent, eagle, winged dragon, . . . etc.[32]

Here the sulfur and mercury are represented as freely flowing essences, extracted from their original containment. Silver, like the moon, is associated with the dark, whereas sulfur is associated with the sun and is one with the light. The apparent paradox of the little girl's 'masculine' urine[33] is of the kind that runs throughout alchemy and will be seen in this entire series of alchemical paintings. The alchemists did not keep a fixed dichotomy of male and female.[34] They understood that there is femininity in men and masculinity in women, but we see here that the masculinity in the girl is expelled, as is the femininity in the boy. So the *separatio* is represented as a biological process. The alchemists wanted to join the opposites in a fluid way to form an ultimate unity, here represented outside of the human figures as the fluids in the two basins flow together.

Water symbolism having to do with this first stage of initiation into the process of transformation may be woven into dreams but personalized by individual experience, as in bathroom dreams. For example, a woman with a well-developed persona, who had chosen the security of patriarchal values at the expense of her deeper feelings, began treatment after her daughters' unhappiness forced her to question their conventional and affluent life. Early in her therapy, she dreamt that she was in her home city, with its very strict notions of propriety, sitting in full view on a toilet in the garden behind her home. It bordered a sidewalk, so she was exposed to anyone who happened to pass by. She found that, rather than feeling humiliated, she enjoyed something about her 'rudeness.' Following this dream, she recalled many childhood incidents of shaming, which stifled her natural playfulness and initiative. For a time, she experienced intense and troubling anger about the many expectations placed upon her by her husband, children, and social position. She also over-identified with her children's anger toward authority figures. All this gradually dissipated after she was able to differentiate and express her feelings rather than unconsciously conform to expected social roles. Analytic work released new energies, both for her inner life and for her relationships with her husband, children, and friends.

The fountain with its children, appearing early in the series of paintings, shows that self-purification is needed first of all. Urine is the natural way that the body rids itself of impure substances. Psychologically, this is the first stage of initiation,[35] which often involves a purification by water, as in baptism. This archetype, so often associated with the education of the young, may be activated in transitional phases at any age; as such, its symbols become a vehicle for individuation.

From a developmental point of view, urination is at first an involuntary act, completely natural and unconscious, but at a certain point physical and psychological development allow it to come under the voluntary control of the ego. So it is one of our earliest experiences of agency and independence. At the same time a child is being shaped by culture to repress aspects of the personality that are incompatible with expected gender identity. So we might see the urine as representing aspects of the primal self that, in the interests of adaptation, were sacrificed by being dissolved back into nature, into unconsciousness. This brings with it the notion that ego development requires a sacrifice of undifferentiated wholeness.

The urinary symbolism is also found in other traditions, such as Kundalini[36] yoga, where the second *chakra* refers to transformation taking place in the region of the bladder. The second *chakra* is seen as potentially both positive and negative, indicating that the process can go forward into a renewal or back regressively.

This is true as well in alchemy. The alchemists recognized what we too must recognize when we work with patients, that what comes up from the unconscious may be full of promise or full of meaning and then suddenly be devoured or go back again into the unconscious as if it didn't exist. The process can either go forward and become the next stage or undergo a regressive deconstruction.

One determinant of whether there is a forward movement is the therapist's ability to detect the patient's regressive tendencies and bring them into the open. The children of the fountain do remind us that the defense of regression may be expressed actively, as with the boy's upraised stick, or passively, as with the girl's stick resting on the shoulder. The mercury reminds us that the ever-changeable trickster, the *Spiritus Mercurius*, is likely to play a prominent role at this stage.

This initial stage in the work of transformation is still oriented downward rather than upward. In other words, it is *chthonic*, earth-oriented, and, like urine, flows outward toward everyday life. It is as if the person in therapy would say to himself or the therapist might say to him, 'Well, of course, what we are doing is to make your life more livable. And so, take your insight and go back and live better than you did before.' That is what we might call supportive psychotherapy or counseling. But the inner spiritual problem of the opposites has been stated. There is the question, 'Can the patient go back?' Maybe she has to go forward. And this is the point at which the initiation theme comes so strongly into play. The seven stars suggest that the patient will feel that the process *has* to go forward, whether her ego likes it or not.

Psychologically speaking, then, the individual in analysis is beginning to recognize the need for a thoroughgoing process of change, a process that can take him from one stage of development to another. The patient's psyche is beginning to participate in a more fundamental change than a relief from troublesome symptoms or the need to adapt to a life situation. As Jung put it, 'there is in the psyche a process that seeks its own goal independently of external factors . . .'[37]

In a dream from the early stage of my own (J. H.) analysis, two underground lakes were flowing together. They couldn't be seen but I knew they were there: it was a kind of abstract memory as if I had always known about these lakes but now they were flowing together. At a personal level, this image was associated with my sister, although she didn't appear in the dream. When I was a boy, my sister had been a kind of *anima* figure. She was eight years older, and I hadn't really known her very well – but she made a vivid impression on me nonetheless. She had red hair and a very fair, white complexion. Apparently, something about her coloring, red and white, influenced my unconscious. (A well-known alchemical image is the red king and the white queen.) The mixing or meeting of opposites here suggests an initiatory experience in which one could *imagine* a union of the opposites, male and female, that could take place at a later time. This is not a matter of thought-images or pure fantasy. The underground lakes symbolize a boyhood potential for growth and emotional development, something instinctual and embodied, a stirring of emotions that could not have been expressed in words. Just as alchemy always involves matter, real psychological transformation always involves embodied experiences, not just ideas. This dream, then, signaled a reactivation of the feminine potential represented by my sister, so long underground, so that it could become an integral part of my adult emotional reality and very being. In its outer form, it became the capacity to fall in love with a real woman.

Plate I–4 The King and the Queen

The fourth picture shows a verdant countryside, with the opposites represented as a king and queen standing on a path in the foreground. Almost everything about this picture emphasizes the polarity between the two. The queen's hair is carefully arranged while the king's hair is loose and somewhat disheveled, suggesting mental agitation. Two villages of differing architecture are shown in the background – but we can also see people walking toward a village that is shown directly between the king and queen, symbolizing that movement to reconcile the opposites begins once they have recognized each other.

The outer garments of the king and queen are of contrasting colors: the king wears a golden and red crown and red garments trimmed with gold; the queen wears a silver-gray crown and a dress of pale blue. One of her shoes is red and the other black. The silver-gray borders of her dress and of her crown match what might be seen as a silver-gray sun in the sky above her head. However, the lining of the king's garment is pale blue-gray – the color of the queen's garment; conversely, the lining of the queen's garment is red – the color of the king's garment. This implies that each contains the other inwardly, *in potentia*.

The king stands upon a blazing fire of orange and golden flames. The queen stands upon a dark gray sphere, which has a face at a slight slant. Whether this sphere represents the moon or the earth is not clear. According to the description by J[ulius] K[ohn], the English translator of the *Splendor Solis*,[39] the queen is standing upon a dark full moon.[40] However, in *Psychology and Alchemy*,[41] Jung indicated that she is standing on the earth, not the moon. (The moon, then, is represented as full and radiant above her head.) The sphere on which the queen stands is not only *earth*. According to Jung, this

PLATE I-4[38]

sphere is called the *rotundum* and represents 'the round nature of the *lapis* which arises from and constitutes the primal sphere, hence the *prima materia* is often called *lapis*.'[42] We could call this *prima materia* the experiential ground of being itself, which contrasts with the masculine demand to do or know something about one's existence.

The queen looks calmly toward the king, while his gaze is directed toward her with surprise and perhaps alarm. In the sky over her head, the silvery moon directs its eyes towards the king inquiringly. Above him, a golden-red sun directs its eyes towards the queen questioningly. The sky above is tinged with blue, pink, and yellow with fluffy gold-highlighted clouds. Clearly, there is a strong emotional tension between the two human figures.

In his hand, the king holds a scepter with a scroll, bearing an inscription in golden letters, 'Coagula Masculinum,'[43] or 'Coagulate the Masculine.' For the alchemists, the process of coagulation turned a fluid into a dry solid. The queen holds a blue scroll with 'Lac Virginis,'[44] or 'milk of the virgin' (spiritual food), also inscribed in gold letters. On a concrete level, the alchemists applied this term to a variety of white fluids.[45] In Figure 10, we see two alchemical images of virgin's milk. In one, the virgin sits atop

FIGURE 10 'Virgin's Milk'
A. A Sea of Milk (Stolcius de Stolenberg, Viridarium chymicum, 1624, reprinted in CW 12, Fig. 222)

B. The Alchemists taking in the spiritual nourishment from the virgin's breasts. (From a late
   fourteenth-century manuscript of *Aurora Consurgens* in the Zentralbibliotech Zürich,
   MS. Rh. 172, f. 13v)

a monstrous fish, and together they are spouting an ocean of milk. In the other, two
alchemists or philosophers drink from the breasts of a virgin.

The two scrolls – 'Coagulate the Masculine' and 'Virgin's Milk' – taken together
suggest a process that was central to alchemy: *solve et coagula*, dissolve and coagulate.
This instruction is found in an ancient manuscript of Maria Prophetissa.[46] The
alchemists repeated the *solve et coagula* many times in order to purify the coagulate.
This process is much like the repetitions that occur in analysis, where an unconscious
attitude or complex manifests itself in behavior and in symbolic material such as
dreams. The patient and analyst both reflect on the occurrence and are also affected
unconsciously; this happens repeatedly. If the treatment is successful, the problem will
be resolved, opening the way for new developments. Just as the word 'resolved' implies,
the new attitude or coagulate may then go back into solution in the unconscious, but in a
form better suited to the patient's personality as a whole at that point in time.

The alchemists associated the dissolving, or *solutio*, with the moon, moisture, cold,
and softness, and sometimes called it 'feeding the stone' with 'the virgin's milk.' The
coagulation was associated with sun, dryness, hardness, and heat (represented in this
image by the fire under the king). The alchemists believed that to make the philosopher's
stone, the hard substance had to be made soft or spiritual, and the soft substance had to
be made hard or given form.[47] This also is like the work of analysis, where inflexible or
hardened attitudes are softened, while too malleable or undeveloped aspects of the
personality are strengthened and differentiated.

This process is illustrated by the case of a teenage girl who was referred for therapy
because of her angry attitude toward her parents. In turn, she complained about their

yelling at her and not respecting her judgment. These roles were not simply a part of adolescent development: from both the patient's and the parents' points of view, the tensions had begun at an early age whenever she attempted to express her autonomy. During therapy, she spontaneously recalled a dream from the time she was five or six years old: A cow began giving milk and could not stop, so that her house was flooded and the family had to try to escape on a boat. In her dream, a positive, nurturing aspect of the feminine is taken to a boundless extreme that is life-threatening, symbolizing a danger to the development of an autonomous ego. We can also see that the qualities of hard and soft were connected with the presenting problem: the patient was in the rebellious role (hard, 'bad') while her mother sacrificed her own autonomy in an attempt to be all-giving (soft, 'good'). Not surprisingly, one area of conflict centered on food: the adolescent rejected her mother's cooking and dietary preferences. At a deeper level, her wish to have control over what she took in symbolized freedom from the projections she carried for the parents, which were a distorted reflection of her real nature. The hardened roles and attitudes in the family needed to be softened, while the too-permeable boundaries between the mother and daughter needed to find more form. In therapy, the patient experienced herself outside the family dynamic and began to see it more clearly, including her own part in the conflict. She became aware of her loving feelings towards her parents (softening). As she gained self-control, her parents escalated their attacks on her but later came to respect and even admire her – their attitude first hardened, then softened.

The dimensions of soft and hard have primal associations to the physical experience of contact with people and objects.[48] In analysis, this dimension of experience may become more conscious, especially in work with the transference. The alchemical dictum, *solve et coagula*, is of such relevance to depth psychotherapy that it is one vantage point from which to look at any clinical session. As the process of *solve et coagula* is repeated, it moves from unconscious, instinctual expectations and actions – as in the previous plate where the two children are urinating – to greater awareness and capacity to tolerate the opposites, as in the present image. In 'Psychology of the Transference,' Jung pointed out that,

> The instincts and their specific fantasy-contents are partly concrete, partly symbolical ... We know that it is possible to interpret the fantasy-contents of the instincts either as *signs*, as self-portraits of the instincts, i.e., reductively, or as *symbols*, as the spiritual meaning of the natural instinct ... In any particular case it is often impossible to say what is 'spirit' and what is 'instinct.'[49]

In the case of the adolescent, her inner life began to take new form as her conflict with her parents receded. From time to time she asked to make something in the sandtray[50] in the therapist's office. Then, she worked intently and silently, carefully molding the sand and arranging items from the therapist's collection. Her abstract sand sculptures suggested a deep communion with the archetypal feminine in its expressive and receptive aspects, as well as a sense of her emerging woman's body as sacred. Thus her psyche's image of becoming a woman was transformed from an undifferentiated instinctual outpouring (her dream of the cow) to a more spiritual yet also embodied, symbolic Mystery (see Figure 11). The design in the upper tray, two circles separated by an undulating line, is nearly identical to the ancient Tantric symbol of the goddess as protector. This same symbol also was used for Kama, the god of phallic love.[51] In the tray at the bottom (made six weeks later), there is also symmetry but the two sides do not mirror one another. Rather

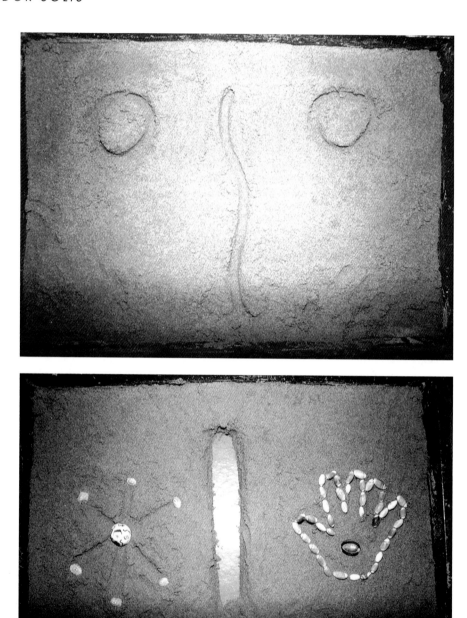

FIGURE 11   Two Sandtrays. (Made by an adolescent in psychotherapy)

we see on the left a six-pointed star. In its center is a tiny Native American clay vessel, and at the end of each ray is a shell. To the right, we see the outline of her hand, made with tiny shells, with a shell in the center of the palm. Down the midline of the tray, a wide line exposes its blue bottom, usually used to indicate water. The symbols in this tray show us the archetypal feminine on the left and the personal feminine on the right. Both sides contain spiral-shaped shells, symbolic of protected development, containing yet making room for growth. The imprint of her hand in the sand, delicately outlined by the shells, suggests the unique imprint she will make in her life.

Returning to the image of the king and queen, we see that this queen is in full command of herself. She represents the essence of a developed feminine consciousness with her own source of light, as represented by the radiant, silvery moon above her head. This contrasts with the more typical cultural representation of the feminine as *merely* lunar, often in the form of a crescent moon, subordinate to and reflective of a superior masculine rationality and consciousness.

The frame bordering the main picture contains flowers and birds on a golden background. This plate is the first in which the central picture rests on a solid, three-dimensional base.[52] Here the dark gray base contains three bas-reliefs. The one on the left (Figure 12) shows a battle scene labeled in gold letters, 'Achiles' [*sic*] and 'Hector.' This is the famous duel at the siege of Troy, when Achilles slew Hector to avenge his friend Patroklos, despite the prophecy of Achilles' mother, the sea nymph Thetis, that his own death would quickly follow. As Kerényi puts it, 'Thus he took death upon himself.'[53] His bones were mingled with those of his friend Patroklos, placed in a golden amphora, and buried on Cape Sigeion, at the entrance to the Hellespont. It became a pilgrimage site and was garlanded by Alexander the Great.[54] So we might see Achilles as embodying both intense loyalty and intense enmity, almost superhuman heroism and yet fatal vulnerability.

In the central bas-relief (Figure 13A) we see Alexander the Great as ruler and warrior. He sits upon a throne, his staff raised high, surrounded by his army. Across a turbulent river is a fortified castle and town. Above its battlements are written the words 'Basiliski Capsis' (shown in greater detail in Figure 13B). This can be translated as, 'the basilisk in an enclosure,' or 'the basilisk contained.' Below the final 'i' of 'Basiliski,' it is possible to discern a dragon-like figure, painted in gold, just above the city. This figure is the basilisk – the monstrous combination of a cock and a toad or snake, said to have hatched from a yokeless egg, which was laid by a cock and brooded by a toad on a bed of dung.[55] The basilisk, like the gorgon, could kill with a look and would die if it saw its own reflection. In Christian iconography, the basilisk was synonymous with the devil, its three-pointed crest and trifurcated tail the inverse of the Holy Trinity.[56] The origins of this symbol must be very old: a basilisk-like creature is found in the center of the 'Wheel of Existence' in East Indian and Tibetan iconography. The center of the wheel in Buddhist versions has a pig, cock, and snake, while one exemplar from the Tibetan Bon religion has a monster with the body of a cow, the tail of a snake, and three heads – of a cock, a pig, and a snake.[57] According to the Bon *Sutra of the Magic Production of Offspring*,

> From the circle of light of heaven, empty and infinite, a black light shone forth to the bottom of the sea; a vapour of black obscurity arose. From the obscurity a noxious body ripened – the cow of poison of living beings. On the cow three noxious heads appeared, four limbs and serpent's tail. As for the three noxious mouths of the three heads, hate was the mouth of the snake, delusion that of the

FIGURE 12   The Battle of Hector and Achilles. Bas-relief at the Base of Plate I–4, left. (Harley 3469, by permission of the British Library)

pig, and desire-passion that of the cock. Thus the three poisons ripened into visible bodily form.[58]

This interpretation fits well with alchemical symbolism, in which the basilisk represented the *prima materia*. Containing the basilisk/*prima materia* is essential for transformation; in other words, the passions must be restrained for psychological transformation to begin.

According to legend, Alexander the Great was educated by Aristotle (384–322 BCE), who developed a philosophical system based upon empirical observation and logic

FIGURE 13 Alexander the Great as Conqueror. (Harley 3469, by permission of the British Library) A. Bas-relief at the base of Plate I–4, center. B. Detail, showing the basilisk.

– the predominant world-view of Western civilization. The text of the *Splendor Solis* quotes a legend of Alexander in which Aristotle instructs him in alchemy: 'Choose for our Stone that wherewith kings are decorated and crowned,' referring to a subtle gold.[59] The presence of Alexander on this bas-relief reminds us that the alchemists were aware of the roots of their art in the fusion of Greek ideas about the nature of matter and Egyptian metallurgy in Alexandria, the great Egyptian center of learning, founded by Alexander.

Alexander, the most famous conqueror in Western history, epitomized the power of ruthless, strategic planning for successful aggression and domination – a combination of physical might and rationality. According to the historian Thomas Martin, 'The popularity of the legend of Alexander as a symbol of the height of achievement for a masculine warrior-hero served as one of his most persistent legacies to later ages. . . . When at Alexander's deathbed his commanders asked him to whom he bequeathed his kingdom, he replied, "To the most powerful." '[60]

Alexander was also known for his curiosity. The text for the British Library Special Exhibition in 1999 noted that:

Alexander's relentless energy and apparently limitless ambition drove him to explore remote parts of the world inhabited by strange peoples and monsters, investigate the wonders of the heavens and the depths of the sea and seek out the secrets of true wisdom and immortal life. It is these legendary journeys that are recounted in the *Romance of Alexander* that originated as a Greek text, but soon proved popular in innumerable versions and translations that were spawned across Western Europe, the Middle East and India.

These legends fed the curiosity of medieval European society about the distant reaches of the world. After encountering all sorts of monsters and monstrous peoples, ascending into the sky in a cage carried by griffins (and falling suddenly to the earth), Alexander descended to the depths of the sea, his final adventure. In Figure 14, we see an illustration of this episode, which appeared in a fifteenth-century French manuscript.

The basilisk, then, can be seen as the shadow side of Alexander: his rational and strategic abilities were used in the service of his greed for experience and need for power. In the painting, the 'basilisk contained' is separated from Alexander by the great divide of a wide and rapidly flowing river.

FIGURE 14   Alexander being lowered from a ship in a glass barrel to view the wonders of the sea. From The Old French Prose Alexander Romance manuscript, Rouen, 1445. (Roy 15E.V1 f.20v min, by permission of the British Library)

FIGURE 15 The Meeting of Alexander the Great and Diogenes. Bas-relief at the base of Plate I–4, right. (Harley 3469, by permission of the British Library)

The bas-relief to the right (Figure 15) again shows Alexander (with the sun in the sky behind him), now with his entourage visiting a man in a tub. The man, fully clothed, faces the king and holds his hands together in supplication. This image probably refers to the meeting between Alexander the Great and the Greek philosopher, Diogenes (412–323 BCE). Diogenes was an ascetic, who for a time lived out-of-doors in a tub belonging to the temple of Cybele. He taught the virtues of a simple life and recommended a return to nature. It is said that he taught at the Isthmian games, where he met Alexander, who offered him a boon. Diogenes asked only that Alexander not stand between him and the sun. Alexander replied, 'If I were not Alexander, I would be Diogenes.' Diogenes was said to have died in Corinth on the same day that Alexander died in Babylon.[61] This meeting of men of opposite life-paths suggests a wholeness *in potentia*, as does the encounter of the king and queen in the main image.

We can see a progression from left to right across the bas-relief – the passionate, impetuous heroism of Achilles; the planning, will-to-power, and curiosity of Alexander; and the meeting between Alexander and Diogenes, whose renunciation of worldly power was antithetical to the values by which Alexander lived his life. The pedestal or *basis*, then, shows us the paradoxical heritage of Greek civilization. As Richard Tarnas has summarized:

> Just when the Greek intellectual achievement had reached its climax during the fourth century BCE, Alexander the Great swept down from Macedonia through Greece and onward to Persia, conquering lands and peoples from Egypt to India and creating an empire that was to encompass most of the known world. The very qualities that had served Greece's brilliant evolution – restless individualism, proud humanism, critical rationalism – now helped precipitate its downfall, for the divisiveness, arrogance, and opportunism that shadowed the Greek's nobler qualities left them myopic and fatally unprepared for the Macedonia challenge. Yet the Hellenic achievement was not fated for extinction. . . . inspired by the Homeric epics and Athenian ideals, Alexander carried with him and disseminated the Greek culture and language through the vast world he conquered. Thus Greece fell just as it culminated, yet spread triumphantly just as it submitted.[62]

The three bas-reliefs suggest both the problem in the cultural unconscious and a possible new attitude. The two on the left show that Western culture had adopted rational and heroic values, identified as masculine, to the neglect of values identified as feminine. The centrality of this theme was clear in the first plate of the *Splendor Solis*, but it is developed more specifically here. The bas-relief on the right, the meeting of Alexander and Diogenes, represents a shift toward inner development rather than exclusive valuation of outer mastery and conquest. It also prefigures the final plate of the series (Plate I–11), where the alchemist has entered the alchemical bath. The alchemists' development beyond an overvaluation of worldly power and mastery (wanting actual gold) was made explicit by the author of the *Splendor Solis*, Salomon Trismosin, in a simple verse appended to his 'alchemical wanderings':[63]

> Study What Thou Art,
> Whereof Thou Art a Part,
> What Thou Knowest of This Art,
> This is Really What Thou Art.
> All that is Without Thee Also is Within,
> Thus Wrote Trismosin.[64]

Similarly, Jung wrote, 'It is in truth the inner man, . . . who passes through the stages that transform [base metals] . . . into gold, and who thus undergoes a gradual enhancement of value.'[65]

Now that the cultural background has been made explicit, we may return to the central image. The king as representative of Western culture's ruling principles consciously faces the queen, who represents the cultural feminine, which had been subordinate since the times of Classical Greece. From the queen's calm attitude and her newly elevated position, we anticipate a shift in consciousness.

The presence of human figures indicates a progression from the previous image, with its statues of naked children. There is also a movement from the imperfect symbol of the *solutio* as urine to the *solutio* as the milk of the virgin, *lac virginis*.[66] Instead of raw mercury and sulfur, the opposites are represented by the king and queen as Sol and Luna, sun and moon. As Jung pointed out,

> The elevation of the human figure to a king or a divinity, and on the other hand its representation in subhuman ... form, are indications of the *transconscious character* of the pairs of opposites. They do not belong to the ego-personality but are supraordinate to it.[67]

Within the main image, the king and queen are standing on bases suggesting their elemental nature. Wherever you see the elements represented as pure – as Earth, Air, Fire, or Water – it refers to the archetypal level of the unconscious, which lies unseen beneath everyday conscious life.

Jung referred to this plate in his essay entitled, 'Individual Dream Symbolism in Relation to Alchemy.'[68] The patient under consideration had a visual image in which, 'The veiled woman uncovers her face. It shines like the sun.'[69] Jung characterized this image as analogous to the alchemical stage of *solificatio*, as a 'lighting up' of the unconscious, which he contrasted to rational enlightenment.[70]

Later in the same series of visions, the patient had the impression of, 'A globe. The unknown woman is standing on it and worshipping the sun.'[71] (We can see the parallel between the dream and the queen in Plate I–4, except that here the queen does not appear to be worshipping the sun. Rather, she looks expectantly toward what the king may offer.) What Jung says about the image in his patient's vision helps us understand its psychological context:

> the globe is rather an image of the earth, upon which the anima stands worshipping the sun. . . . Anima and sun are thus distinct, which points to the fact that the sun represents a different principle from that of the anima. The latter is a personification of the unconscious, while the sun is a symbol of the source of life and the ultimate wholeness of man (as indicated in the *solificatio*). Now, the sun is an antique symbol that is still very close to us. We know also that the early Christians had some difficulty in distinguishing ἡλιοω ανατολη̣ω (the rising sun) from Christ. The dreamer's anima still seems to be a sun-worshipper, that is to say, she belongs to the ancient world, and for the following reason: the conscious mind with its rationalistic attitude has taken little or no interest in her and therefore made it impossible for the anima to become modernized (or better, Christianized). It almost seems as if the differentiation of the intellect that began in the Christian Middle Ages, as a result of scholastic training, had driven the anima to regress to the ancient world.[72]

Jung's commentary exposes a problem of cultural development in the Christian world and exemplifies the importance of reading archetypal images in their cultural context.

Jung goes on to say,

> It may not be superfluous to point out here with due emphasis that consciously the dreamer had no inkling of all this but in his unconscious he is immersed in this sea of historical associations so that he behaves in his dreams as if he were fully cognizant of this curious phenomenon in the history of the human mind. He is in

fact an unconscious exponent of the autonomous psyche and its development, just like the Medieval alchemist or the classical neoplatonist. Hence one could say, with a grain of salt, that history could be constructed just as easily from one's own unconscious as from the actual texts.[73]

This shows us why we talk about a cultural unconscious, which is an awareness of our cultural background that comes to light in dreams and is quite distinct from both the personal life and the archetypal level of the unconscious. And Jung's statement, quoted above, seems to verify that distinction.

The motto at the top of this picture says, 'Particularia,' and at the bottom it says, 'Via Universalis Particularibus Inclusis,' which means, 'the universal way including the particular.' In the light of our work in analytical psychology we could easily say that *Particularia* represents the ego with its personal connections, as well as influences from specific aspects of the culture. And the *Via Universalis*, the Universal Way, represents the way of the Self. This might serve as a good motto for analytical psychology, since we consider the larger personality of the Self in relationship to the particulars of the individual's personality and experiences.

At first we might confuse the Self with personal identity, the *Particularia*. This happens inevitably, in the early part of treatment, when the patient has established a transference to the analyst – and the analyst has a countertransference to the patient. The danger at this point is to take it too personally. For instance, one may think, 'Aha, I've met my soul mate, and we belong together, forever and ever, or at least for the duration of this journey.' Even though the analyst's and the patient's conduct is restrained, the fantasy about what is going on can be very personal, very specific. But, like the alchemist, the analyst, if he knows his craft as he should, realizes that this is an illusion and that underneath there is an archetypal basis for the feeling of deep connection. The elemental level, if it is allowed to speak, says, 'No, this is a universal experience. It is much bigger than anything that could possibly be understood in a personal context.'[74]

The inner emotional states or attitudes of the analyst can be seen in the expressions on the faces of the king and the queen: the king especially looks upset, quite possibly anxious about the whole situation, whereas she is serene and self-assured. She holds her hand out to him with great confidence. In this period of analysis, the analyst feels very competent to take whatever projections may come and deal with them, like the receptive, feminine queen. But there is another side expressing doubt: 'How are we going to do this?' The king, charged with the duty to maintain order, is standing on a blazing fire, which poses the question, 'Will the emotional intensity of this relationship become so overheated that we won't be able to contain it?' In fact, both attitudes are necessary at this stage, for no-one knows how to direct the process, which can't be assumed to be only benign. This intensely human encounter – bringing to bear the personal, cultural, and archetypal dimensions of the psyche – is not the *coniunctio* (the ultimate union of opposites) but does anticipate it.

Plate I-5 Digging for Gold

This painting shows two small, hooded men (dwarves or *cabiri*) quarrying at a steep, rocky up-cropping. The man on the left wears a dark costume but has golden shoes,

PLATE I–5[75]

whereas the one on the right has a golden costume and dark shoes. Just above the bottom of the circular frame, in the center foreground, a bronzed crescent moon with a human face is reflected in the water, creating the illusion of a floating moon-boat. The sun shines through an opening in storm clouds, while in the distance dark streams of rain pour down. A path winds along a ridge in the left foreground. Within the scene itself, the plants and trees have golden highlights. To the right, young plants can be seen growing out of the thick tree stumps.

In contrast to the rustic scene of the central image, the golden frame and pedestal are elaborately crafted. To either side, at the base of the golden columns of the pedestal, are naked women: those on the left have arms curved into spirals, whereas those on the right have legs in spiral form. Cameos of a man and a woman face each other from columns at either side, just above the pedestal. In the triangle between these columns and the frame, naked children sit on fire-breathing dragons. To the outside of the columns sit figures that are half woman, half beast. Dynamic, free-standing figures are seen above the frame. In the center is a child's head with wings on either side. Wingless dragons with spiraled tails and extended tongues in the form of vines (rather than the usual flames) face outward, beginning to entwine two nude figures of children, a boy and a girl. On the left, the boy holds a fruit, upon which a red and black bird alights; on the right, the girl reaches out and offers a flower to another bird.

The pedestal of the frame depicts a crucial scene from the biblical story of King Ahasueros and Queen Esther, representing a new kind of relationship between a pair of opposites. Just below the word 'Esther,' the pedestal opens to reveal the interior of the palace of King Ahasueros, who is seated on a throne and handing his scepter to Queen Esther. This gesture seems to say that the masculine, which has heretofore ruled, is now willingly sharing its authority with the feminine. Although the feminine stands in contrast to the power of the masculine, it also is to become one with it. According to the story, King Ahasueros, 'who reigned from India to Ethiopia over one hundred and twenty-seven provinces,'[76] had renounced Vashti, his Queen, after she disdainfully refused to come into his presence with her royal crown 'in order to show the peoples and the princes her beauty.'[77] He 'proclaimed throughout all his kingdom, vast as it is, [that] all women will give honor to their husbands,'[78] making it law in Persia and Medea. King Ahasueros then made the beautiful Jewish maiden, Esther, his Queen. She later risked her own life by requesting that the King overturn an order (promoted by his chief counselor Haman) condemning to death all the Jews in his kingdom. In response, King Ahasueros handed her his scepter, the emblem of his power and authority. Accepting the power to rule, she not only prevailed, but her foster father and protector, the wise Mordecai, became the most influential man in the court, to the great benefit of the Jewish population. These events were the origin of the ancient Jewish Festival of Purim, which is still celebrated every spring. The freeing of the Jews from persecution can serve as a metaphor for the recognition of the real worth of something or someone that has been devalued, even scapegoated. The theme of Purim might very well be appreciated more widely today as an historical precedent for the wish that men and women become partners in meeting the difficulties posed by their relationships and also a sign that trust in mutuality will be rewarded with a favorable outcome.

The analytical interpretation of the central image is clear from the picture itself. The digging, which requires a conscious effort, is analogous to the beginning of the analytic process of 'working through.' Digging also symbolizes what we mean by the term, 'Depth Psychology.' In order to go deeper, we must dig. The patient, with the help of the therapist, repeatedly has to bring material from the unconscious. This digging, to some extent, is what Jung would have called the reductive phase of analysis, an unearthing of the origins of what has gone wrong in the patient's life and sent it in a neurotic direction, as well as instinctual strivings which can be processed differently by the more mature ego. During this stage, the unconscious material, like valuable ore, is sought out by the ego, with a new attitude of respect and interest. This is in contrast to the attitude toward the unconscious expressed in the first Plate (I–1), where the ego had been so on guard against the unconscious that the conscious attitude is symbolized by a coat-of-arms.

The gold or treasure of this regressive stage may well be found in the subtleties of behaviors rather than in the form of images or words. Analytic work requires patience and endurance, as well as attention to the detail and nuance of nonverbal experience and communication – including attitudes about time and money, the tone of voice, eye contact, postures, body sensations, and so on. In this regard, the analyst must attend carefully to the process and, when appropriate, comment on it in a sensitive way. This calls to mind the archaeologist, who uses tiny brushes to gently uncover ancient relics and bones.

The image of digging also suggests that there is a possibility of finding a buried treasure, a deeper meaning or value in the unconscious. It is not just digging back for the sake of tidying things up and saying that, if you had had a better mother or father, all would have been well. The work has a deeper purpose than that: it is regression in the service of the Self, not just in the service of the ego. In this sense, the serious regressions that the analytic work triggers, though painful, can offer a reward that is greater even than relief from neurosis.

If we imagine the scene of Queen Esther and King Ahasueros as representing the activity in the unconscious, its color and three dimensions suggest that the unconscious is now experienced as very active and real – possibly as a result of the charged encounter between the king and the queen in the previous painting (Plate I–4). We might even think of this scene labeled 'Esther' as representing the attitude that needs to be adopted by the ego toward what might be found by the men who are digging. Jung pointed out that,

> we are confronted, at every new stage in the differentiation of consciousness . . . with the task of finding a new *interpretation* appropriate to this stage, in order to connect the life of the past that still exists in us with the life of the present, which threatens to slip away from it. If this link-up does not take place, a kind of rootless consciousness comes into being . . . With the loss of the past, now become 'insignificant,' devalued, and incapable of revaluation, the saviour is lost too, for the saviour is either the insignificant thing itself or else arises out of it [symbolized as the archetypal lost child, *puer aeternus*, or child-god]. . . . In folklore the child motif appears in the guise of the dwarf or the elf as personifications of the hidden forces of nature. To this sphere also belongs the little metal man of late antiquity, . . . who, till far into the Middle Ages on the one hand inhabited the mine-shafts, and on the other hand represented the alchemical metals . . . [79]

The painting's elaborate golden frame, with its dragons, children, women, and theriomorphic figures, hints once again at the value of instinct, of childlike playfulness, and of the feminine. At the top of the frame, birds, perhaps representing spirit, come down toward the naked children, who are offering them a fruit and a flower.

The moon-boat floating on the water in the foreground seems to be watching the dwarves at work. This suggests a certain fascination with the opus on the part of nature, and also reminds us that consciousness itself is a natural activity. Here the moon is a purely receptive feminine presence, both above and below, observing the toil of the two dwarves but not interfering. Jung makes the following relevant observation:

> It seems that nature is out to prod man's consciousness towards greater expansion and greater clarity, and for this reason continually exploits his greed for metals, especially the precious ones, and makes him seek them out and investigate their properties. While so engaged it may perhaps dawn on him that not only veins of ore are to be found in the mines, but also kobolds [gnomes that haunt underground places] and little metal men, and that there may be hidden in lead either a deadly demon or the dove of the Holy Ghost.[80]

Images of digging appear frequently during active imagination[81] but infrequently in dreams. Perhaps this is because the digging symbolizes a conscious engagement of the ego required to bring previously unconscious material into awareness. During my own analysis with Jung, I (J. H.) imagined that I literally bought a pick and shovel, and a ladder to lift me out of the cavity I intended to dig. I never got to the bottom of this, but the image did me good. It made the value of the unconscious more real.

An example of digging as metaphor can also be seen in the treatment of a woman in her fifties, who came into therapy during a severe depression. The process of her therapy revealed a tendency to be either overly optimistic or pessimistic. She focused on the wishes of others and found it very difficult to attend to her own experience unless its content was extreme or dramatic. It was as if she had an unusually elevated attentional threshold (in part, the defense of denial) that allowed her to maintain her optimistic or pessimistic state in spite of accumulating proof that her situation was not so black or white as she supposed. Whenever she was forced to see the other side of any situation, her emotional state and attitude reversed. Her life was dominated by her idealization of her father, and she lived in fear of his disapproval. He had never been able to express ordinary feelings, and when he did express emotion, it was with a critical and demeaning outburst that left her feeling unworthy of his approval or love.

After she and her analyst had spent considerable time exploring her difficulty tolerating ambivalence, especially in the transference, she recalled accompanying her father while he used a pick and shovel to terrace a barren, rocky hillside next to their home. She spent many quiet and happy hours helping him to carry away small rocks and playing in the dirt while he worked. She treasured this time, because it was the only time in her childhood when she had felt truly safe and calm in his presence.

At her analyst's suggestion, she called up this memory, when she became anxious; she was then able to move into a calmer state. With her anxiety lowered, she could tolerate more ambiguity of feeling and began to appreciate the value of her capacity to observe. Digging became a living metaphor for her, and she spoke of digging from within her body her own buried, unacknowledged feelings, which she experienced as tight lumps or rocks in her throat, chest, solar plexus, and stomach. This digging felt connected to her father in an additional way because she was able to use the determination and work ethic she had learned from him to support the therapeutic process. In this way she could both identify with positive aspects of his personality and extend his model of diligence to a kind of work, psychological digging, that he apparently had been unable to do. The patient learned to recognize her own feelings before they overwhelmed her, and she stopped vacillating between extremes of emotion. In the transference, she was better able to state her own opinions without anticipating the therapist's attitude, and she could appreciate that gains were based upon her own hard and careful work.

Although we seldom see images of digging in dreams, we do find images of caves. This often represents the discovery of a hidden and mysterious state of being and comes after there has been an intense period of working through personal material. It is like a mysterious opening to the transpersonal psyche. For example, a woman in analysis, whose mother was deeply critical of her, was in turn critical of her own children. After a long period of unearthing her self-directed demands for achievement and perfection, she dreamt that she was in a mysterious underground cave where tiny spots of light shone like stars. She felt a new peace in this place and freedom from constant anxiety about her limitations. Although she had yet to realize this state of being in ordinary life, she was given a felt experience of the possibility, as well as the realization that there was a deeper meaning to life than worldly achievement.

Plate I–6 The Philosophical Tree

Here the emphasis is upon growth[82] as the central symbol, represented by a tree with golden roots and gold-highlighted branches and leaves. Its fruit have a silvery tinge. From a psychological point of view, this plate refers to the growth that has come from the labor of working-through, preparing the way for an encounter with the unconscious which goes deeper than the personal complexes and issues derived from childhood. The tree has a golden crown around the base of its trunk, rather than at the part of the tree we call its crown, signifying that this is the tree of the philosophers. This placement of the crown naturally draws one's attention to the base of the tree and its golden roots. As Jung pointed out in his essay, 'The Philosophical Tree,'

> The secret is hidden not in the top but in the roots of the tree. . . . The roots extend into the inorganic realm, into the mineral kingdom. In psychological terms, this would mean that the self has its roots in the body, indeed in the body's chemical elements.[83]

A young man has climbed to the seventh rung of a ladder. The number seven reiterates the theme of initiation, seen in Plate I–3, where seven stars were around the head of the knight. Now initiation is more than an idea or ideal: it has become an effective way of reaching higher consciousness. The young man on the ladder, dressed in black with gold leggings and boots, reaches down and hands golden branches to two priestly figures. One of these figures has red outer garments and white inner garments, while the other has white outer garments and red inner garments. Once again we see the play of the opposites, here between the alchemical stages of *albedo* and *rubedo*.

The man on the left gazes at the leafless golden bough in his left hand, while the

PLATE I–6

man on the right reaches with his left hand to receive a bough from the young man on the ladder. The two men are conversing – so here again is the idea of a conversation and of a relationship between two people, which we saw in the very first plate.

The young man – perhaps representing the ego – performs the physical work in the service of the priestly figures, who may represent the observing and reflecting aspects of the personality, as well as the search for deeper meaning. The figure on the ladder is bringing new growth down to earth. This attitude is echoed in the humble cottage that is seen in the background. According to the text of the *Splendor Solis*:

> Hermes,[84] the First Master of this Art, says as follows: 'the Water of the Air, which is between Heaven and Earth is the Life of everything; for by means of its Moisture and Warmth, it is the medium between the two opposites, as Fire and Water, and therefore it rains water on earth, Heaven has opened itself, and set its Dew on earth, making it as sweet as honey, and moist. Therefore the Earth flowers and bears manifold coloured blooms and fruits, and in her interior has grown a large Tree with a silver stem, stretching itself out of the earth's surface. On its branches have been sitting many kinds of birds, all departing at Daybreak, when the Ravenhead became white. . . .'[85]

In the painting, a raven with a white head pecks at the golden fruit. When the bough is taken, the thirteen black and white birds fly away from the tree, setting in motion the movement from the *nigredo* to the *albedo*. Two of the birds are green-tinged, a suggestion of plant-like growth. The upward flight of the birds represents a movement that is quite different from a practical adaptation to life. Here begins the search for a higher level of meaning.

In another passage of the text that accompanies this image, there is a reference to an episode in Book 6 of Virgil's *Aeneid*. According to Virgil, Aeneas and Silvius were led by two doves to a tree with golden boughs, boughs which always regrew where they were broken off. Aeneas took a golden bough, which secured his passage into the underworld and allowed him to return across the River Cocytus (one of the five rivers of Hades) unscathed. So we might at first say that taking the golden bough robs nature, but according to the myth, the bough can only be obtained if it allows itself to be taken. The hero, Aeneas, does not overcome nature or Fate; in other words, man cannot act unless the nature principle agrees. The Sibyl, an oracle of Apollo, told Aeneas:

> Anchises' son, the downward path to death
> Is easy; all the livelong night and day
> Dark Pluto's door stands open for a guest.
> But O! remounting to the world of light,
> This is a task indeed, a strife supreme.
> Few, very few, whom righteous Jove did bless,
> Or quenchless virtue carried to the stars,
> Children of gods, have such a victory won.
> Grim forests stop the way, and, gliding slow,
> Cocytus circles through the sightless gloom.
> But if it be thy dream and fond desire
> Twice o'er the Stygian gulf to travel, twice

On glooms of Tartarus to set thine eyes,
If such mad quest be now thy pleasure – hear
What must be first fulfilled. A certain tree
Hides in obscurest shade a golden bough,
Of pliant stems and many a leaf of gold,
Sacred to Proserpine,[86] infernal Queen.
Far in the grove it hides; in sunless vale
Deep shadows keep it in captivity.
No pilgrim to that underworld can pass
But he who plucks this burgeoned, leafy gold;
For this hath beauteous Proserpine ordained
Her chosen gift to be. Whene'er it is culled,
A branch out-leafing in like golden gleam,
A second wonder-stem, fails not to spring.
Therefore go seek it with uplifted eyes!
And when by will of Heaven thou findest it,
Reach forth and pluck; for at a touch it yields,
A free and willing gift, if Fate ordain;
But otherwise no mortal strength avails,
Nor strong, sharp steel, to rend it from the tree.[87]

The notion that man's use of nature requires a willing sacrifice on nature's part is unfamiliar to the modern Western psyche, with its focus on developing better and better tools in order to overcome and control nature. However, we do recognize it from the study of totem magic and the belief that the animal who is killed by a hunter is in an intimate relationship to him and must be willing to be killed. In recognition of the animal's sacrifice, the animal becomes sacred. Hence we see in hunter-gatherer cultures that the animals which provide sustenance were considered to be sacred and their spirits were honored.[88]

Just as Aeneas went up into the tree to take a golden bough, prior to his descent into the Underworld, in the *Splendor Solis* a descent will follow the ascent up the ladder, recalling Eliade's descriptions of the shaman's initiatory journey either up into the sky or down to the underworld, or both.[89] According to Jung, ascent and insight are not enough for psychological development: one must also take the light of consciousness down into the world of the unconscious.

But even more is happening in this picture. If we look next to the base of the tree, we can see a stream flowing, presumably from an underground spring near its golden roots. Apparently, the stream flows out of the space of the central image and into a bath that is within the structure of the frame below. In the bath is a fountain with a naked child riding a horse and blowing a horn or trumpet. Water flows from the horse's mouth and from the mouths of decorative faces on the pedestal of the fountain. In Plate I–3, the silvery-golden fluid from the fountains flowed out into nature. Now we see water contained in the bath, within a highly cultured setting, yet flowing from a subterranean source in nature.

This image symbolizes the healing of a split in the European psyche, its separation of spirit from its natural source. Jung commented:

The early Christians repudiated nature worship of every description – nature was not to be looked at nor admired – while the antique religions consisted of an intense nature worship, particularly Mithraism. Therefore the mithraeums are always found in lovely places, near a spring in the woods perhaps, or in natural grottoes and caves. There is such a place in Provence ... where a beautiful clear spring comes out of the green under a wall of rock, ... [The] Romans ... erected the temple right beside the spring. The spring was always outside for the sacred ablutions, and there the mystery rebirth was performed ... It was a beautiful form of worship, and there Christianity met its most formidable enemy; the natural joy one feels in nature had to be combatted by the Christian spirit. They said the devil was tempting them, luring them away to natural beauty, to the beauties of the flesh, and making them dull in spirit.[90]

The women in the bath, which is fed from an underground spring, represent receptivity to what flows from below, permitting the contents of the unconscious to be transferred to consciousness effectively. It is like the transcendent function – 'the cooperation of conscious reasoning with the data of the unconscious ... progressively unit[ing] the opposites'[91] – that allows nature to change human life. In contrast, the intellectual recognition of a union of opposites doesn't reconcile them, but it can be a transition of an unconscious idea into consciousness. A symbol, on the other hand, can emerge as a meaningful image and pattern of behavior that *does* reconcile what was experienced previously as irreconcilable from either a rational or from an emotional point of view.

The golden frame has taken the form of a palatial building, shown in cross-section like the stage of a theater. As spectators watch from what looks like boxes at the opera, four naked women are bathing on stage. The women, elegant in their nakedness, wear red and gold jewelry. One woman hands a flask or alembic to another woman. The four bathing women are served by two female attendants, dressed in yellow and red. Here again we see colors that represent alchemical stages: yellow, or *citrinatis*, which is transitional to the final stage, represented by red or *rubedo*.

Behind the women is a frieze (Figure 16) that depicts men on horseback and on foot, rushing as if to battle toward a central disk inscribed with '1582' (thus the date of the illuminated paintings for this manuscript of the *Splendor Solis*). The rush to battle reminds us of the tendency to act destructively when threatened by something that challenges our interests or beliefs. In contrast, the men within the scene are hiding in the boxes or standing in the balconies, looking down at the women. A king wears a red robe with a fur collar and holds a lyre. The men watch the women but do not interfere; they

FIGURE 16 Frieze of Men Rushing to Battle. Located behind bathing women, left side, Plate I–6. (Harley 3469, by permission of the British Library)

observe but do not act. And the women allow themselves to be seen. The lyre suggests a potential for harmony: what might happen if the king were to play a musical instrument to the women, rather than try to rule them?

We might imagine that the men who view the women are eager to look but are trying to stay out of the women's view because they are embarrassed. In analysis, as in life, it is possible to experience forms of curiosity that are embarrassing. For example, a patient may be reluctant to reveal curiosity or fantasies about the analyst's private life, as well as fantasies or behaviors of an aggressive or sexual nature. Similarly, patients may feel reluctant to recount a dream because it shows them at a painful disadvantage from a conventional point of view. But it is usually quite releasing when they do open up and the therapist responds with tact and interest. This is particularly true when the patient has had a transference dream of a sexual nature. The analyst's tact and related-ness are especially important at these times. For example, the psychoanalyst, Ralph Greenson, described his work with 'Mrs. K,'[92] a woman who needed badly to be loved, which he attributed to her mother's irresponsibility and her father's abandonment. She came to her initial analytic session (following preliminary interviews), where she used the couch for the first time, and reported a dream:

> 'I come to my first analytic hour, but you seem different, you look like Dr. M. [the referring physician]. You lead me into a small room and tell me to undress. I am surprised and ask you whether you're supposed to do that as a classical Freudian. You assure me it is alright. I get undressed and you begin to kiss me all over. Then you finally "went down" on me. I was pleased, but I kept wondering if it was right.'[93]

Her associations were related to feeling unworthy; she also revealed that she could only have an orgasm when a man performed cunnilingus, which she thought must be disgusting for a man to do. Dr. Greenson was faced with the question of how to respond to the overt sexual content in the dream in the very first analytic hour. Failure to respond could be interpreted by the patient as an indication that she should not have told him about it or that he was uncomfortable with it. He decided to make a 'reconstruction upward,' and said, 'You must have been very worried after the last hour when I seemed brusque and you wondered if I would really take you as a patient. Then you dream that I use my mouth on you sexually as proof that I really do accept you.' Dr. Greenson interpreted the sexual content as *symbolic* of Mrs. K's psychic needs and her anxious feelings with regard to passivity and vulnerability, perhaps stirred by her first session on the couch. His interpretation was also a communication to her about the work of analysis: there is a deeper, or higher, meaning, beyond the manifest content. Making this kind of interpretation, rather than urging her to associate more fully to her sexual experiences, fantasies, or wishes, actually brought them into relationship with each other and began the work of building a therapeutic alliance.

The scene in the painting, however, suggests a later stage of analytic work: the transference and countertransference are now familiar and perhaps can be acknow-ledged more directly. The analyst and the patient have grown more comfortable with the situation, as though analysis were something that could even be enjoyed instead of endured. Often, at this point in the work, there comes a period of interchange, where the material brought up by the unconscious[94] becomes an opportunity for a shared experience of learning and for relating in a more intimate way than we are usually able to do in everyday life. In certain instances, both the analyst and the analysand may feel they are sharing in a soulful way that is not possible even in their most intimate personal relationships. The libido activated at these times may tempt them to cross the analytic boundaries of physical and social contact. (On the analyst's part, intrusive erotic and/or aggressive fantasies about the analysand, along with the temptation to reveal them during the work, are warning signs that require immediate and careful professional consultation.) There must be a mutual understanding that fantasies and wishes will not be acted out. The process can then go forward with more freedom of expression than before. Indeed the openness is possible because the purpose is greater consciousness and healing.

The painting of the women bathing suggests that the principle of masculinity and kingship is in abeyance. The Feminine, now on center stage, is no longer symbolized by an archetypal figure but by real women, open to full view and at ease with their nakedness. We might ask, 'How can these women be so comfortable with their nakedness in this open place?' The theater's elegance suggests a cultural value to their activity – but as *theater*, an imaginal reality, not everyday life. The women's elegant public bath is not a formula to emulate concretely. However, through the use of the creative arts, there are, in fact, ways to express feelings and ideas that one might feel conventionally inhibited to express.

The allegory of the golden bough suggests what the patient may be learning: that the initially disconcerting failure of certain ego-adaptations can result in new growth, that the personality has its roots in the center of the earth or the Self, like the tree with the golden boughs. There is even the anticipation of an unseen source of vitality – like the spring providing water for the women's bath – which can flow into a fresh experience of life and culture. This image, then, beautifully elaborates the relationship between primal source and ultimate goal.

Plate I–7 The Drowning King

The seventh picture shows an androgynous masculine figure, a young prince or king, draped in a loose and flowing gold-embroidered robe trimmed with silvery white fur. The landscape around this beautiful youth is also very beautiful, with slender trees and gold-tipped flowers and leaves. In the middle distance, in a flooded valley, an aged king, with a long white beard, struggles, half-submerged in water, reaching his arms out and calling for help to save his life.

According to the text of the *Splendor Solis*:

They further saw the King of the Earth sink, and heard him cry out with eager voice: 'Whoever saves me shall live and reign with me for ever in my brightness on my royal throne,' and night enveloped all things. The day after they saw over the king an apparent Morning Star, and the light of day cleared up the darkness, the bright sunlight pierced through the cloud with manifold colored rays of brilliant brightness, and a sweet perfume rose from the earth, and the sun shone clear . . . the King of the Earth was released and renewed, well appareled, and quite handsome, surprising Sun and Moon with his beauty. He was crowned with three costly crowns, one of iron, another of silver, and the third of pure gold. They saw in his

PLATE I–7

FIGURE 17 The Morning Sun and Star. Detail from Plate I–7. (Harley 3469, by permission of the British Library)

right hand a scepter with seven stars, all of which gave a golden splendor, and in his left hand a golden apple, and seated upon it a white dove, with wings partly silvered and partly of a golden hue, . . . [95]

The golden sun, with a serene human face, throws its straight rays behind the youth (Figure 17). To the left of the sun, the luminous morning star also directs its rays downward. A rocky up-cropping just behind the youth may allude to the digging or mining shown in Plate I–5. In stark contrast to the golden rays of light emanating from the star and the sun, dark rays descend beneath large gray clouds in the sky above the drowning king.

This picture represents the death of the Old King and the birth of a youthful king[96] with a kingly nature rather than the established authority derived from a worldly position. From a psychological viewpoint, this plate represents the capacity of the Self – like the tree with the golden bough – to regenerate, to grow a new way of being.[97] The text of the *Splendor Solis* puts it simply, 'The destruction of one thing is the birth of another.'[98] The Old King represents the outworn aspects of the personality, the eternal *senex* that we tend to forget about until we run up against it: our conventional attitudes, our habits, even our loyalties that have hardened into rigid postures.

Another alchemical image depicting the theme of death and rebirth in Nature – this time through destruction by fire rather than water – is a tree with flames at the base (Figure 18).[99] The leafy, beautifully formed, mature tree is dropping its branches into the flames below.

Often, the symptoms felt by the patient in analysis are signs of an unconscious rebellion against the dominant and rigid postures of consciousness. People may begin to have uncomfortable dreams about floods, tidal waves, rain coming down, or the roof

FIGURE 18 Tree with Flames at Its Base. From the title page of *Le Tableau des Riches Inventions*, 1600, Paris, Guillemot, based upon a 1546 edition. (Beinecke Rare Book and Manuscript Library, Yale University)

leaking. They experience pressure from the unconscious and don't know what to do. The analyst can become worried too, wondering how to keep the process afloat.

In contrast to the king in his *senex* aspect, the androgynous king seems very young. His robe is too big, suggesting that he is not ready to take on the full responsibilities of kingship. Psychologically, we often encounter awkward, untried, or unseasoned new attitudes, rather like the young king who would trip over the hem of his garment should he try to walk. A new attitude or way of being functions naively or awkwardly when a person begins to apply it in real life. The therapist may need to help the patient to understand that the new attitude will need to learn from contact with reality. If the patient does not grasp that she must learn anew how to operate in the world, the new attitude may be discarded on the basis of a misstep before it has a chance to develop. For example, when a person has learned not to express negative personal reactions and then tries to, they may at first be poorly expressed. Such an attempt may backfire, with others reacting badly or with the person's feeling embarrassed by the display of emotion. This is one reason that 'practicing' in the therapeutic relationship can be very helpful, since the therapist can presumably not overreact in a personal way but rather help the patient learn to express these feelings more comfortably and effectively. In this sense, the analysis is a laboratory or theater for improvisation.

However, the death of the old king and the appearance of the young king have a more profound psychological meaning than a simple change of attitude. They represent the transformation of the person's very way of being in the world, a revolution of the personality. At such a time, a person often experiences premonitions of death and/or anxiety about whether it will be possible to function in everyday life. The dominant organization cries out in terror to be saved, like the old king sinking into the waters of the unconscious.

At this point the patient is not fully aware of the Self, hidden like the roots of the tree, whose existence in a paradoxical way can only be known by enduring the inner experience of death and rebirth. The new way of being, represented here by the young king, may have appeared to the patient as symbols and figures in dreams or have been glimpsed insightfully. But the ego may not trust that something new can really be embodied and may fear that it is not possible to survive the internal change, much less weather the inevitable changes in relationships. The patient may prefer to rescue the drowning king, for example to flee from treatment – a flight into 'health.' Hopefully, by this point in the treatment, there have already been many therapeutic experiences of tolerating anxiety rather than automatically defending against it, so that the patient has trust in a process. The analyst's role in helping the patient to embody the new developments can be crucial at this time and may come in part from the quality of the analyst's presence, which is itself a way of *being* different from the patient's.

The young king's crown has three tiers: iron, silver, and gold. The dual principle of male and female, as represented in Plate I–4 by the king and queen, has now become a trinitarian symbol. In 'The Philosophical Tree,' Jung refers to the number three and the *coniunctio triplativa*, which is a combination of earth, moon, and sun.[100] Jung also quotes from the 'Scala Philosophorum':[101] 'The threefold coniunctio: that is the union of the Trinity is composed of body, spirit, and soul. . . . thus the Trinity is in its essence a unity for they are coeternal and coequal.' The spirit, the soul, and the body also appear in alchemy, as symbolized by a forest (body) in which live both a stag (soul) and a unicorn (spirit) (Figure 19). The unicorn may also be viewed as a symbol of the creative animus.

Deinceps fine cura fcitote
In fylva cervum & unicornu latere.

TERTIA FIGVRA.

In Corpore eft Anima & Spiritus.

FIGURE 19 The Stag and the Unicorn in the Forest: Symbols of Body, Soul, and Spirit. Lambspringk, 'Figurae et emblemata,' in *Musaeum hermeticum*, 1625 edition. (By permission of the New York Public Library)

According to myth, the unicorn sought refuge with the Virgin Mary when pursued by hunters, which tells us that a woman must protect her inner spirit from men who want to possess it and use it for themselves. Jung's concept of the Self would be the whole image: spirit, soul, and body – separate and inseparable.

The lowest tier of the young king's crown is composed of iron. Like lead,[102] iron stands for the *prima materia* to be transformed. Iron was particularly associated with the Earth and connected with the Greco-Roman Ares/Mars, with blood, passion, and man's violent instinctual nature. This aspect of human life was represented in the bas-reliefs on the frames of the previous plates by the images of Achilles and Hector (Figure 12), Alexander (Figure 13), and the men rushing as to battle (Figure 16). Jung quoted a contemporary of Paracelsus:

> 'This man [Mars] is a man whose complexion is choleric. . . . This hot and bilious man is iron . . . it is called a man because it has soul, body, and spirit. . . . That metal, although begotten in the earth by virtue of the most high and mighty Pole Star called the Great Bear. . . . he walks in the midmost bowels of the earth, and is there hidden . . . not begotten of any.'[103]

We see from the symbolism of the three-tiered crown that the passions are not to be banished (or repressed) but rather transformed. Without them, there is no passion for life, no life force, no *basis* on which other developments may rest.

The next tier is silver, associated with the Moon and the Feminine, whereas the gold of the upper tier is associated with the Sun and the Masculine Principle. This symbolism contrasts to the more specific color symbolism of the knight's crest in Plate I–3, which refers back to changes in color observed during actual chemical processes in the experiments of the alchemists. The metals refer to the instinctual *prima materia* and to the Feminine and Masculine Principles, Luna and Sol, which emerge as the *prima materia* is refined to reveal its spirit and its soul. Here we see that what begins as an attempt to transform matter begins to be taken inside, as a process of interior transformation.

The three-tiered crown suggests an evolution of consciousness from iron to silver and finally gold. This transformation is symbolized here by the crown because at this stage there is only an insight or intuition about the nature of transformation and its value. The process to come is anticipated, and one feels an overall potential for development; a true change in consciousness is yet to be achieved. Like the alchemist dressed in red in the first plate, who may glimpse the goal of his journey far in the distance, but cannot know what the journey may bring. In the crown, the iron, silver, and gold are united and separate, and so this intimates that the final result will not be gold alone.[104]

The young king is holding a golden apple, perhaps a reference to the Greek myth of the golden apples of the Hesperides, which has survived from pre-patriarchal times (Figure 20). Joseph Campbell described the garden in which the tree grew:

> An immense horned snake coils up around the tree, and from a cave in the earth at its root water wells from a spring with a double mouth, while the lovely Hesperides themselves – a family of nymphs known to antiquity as daughters born without father to the cosmic goddess Night – are in attendance round about . . .

and commented:

FIGURE 20 Hercules confronts the Snake Ladon, who guards the Golden Apples of the Hesperides. (From a Greek vase, 340 BCE, red figure calyx crater; Louvre N3157. By permission of Réunion des Musées Nationaux, France/Art Resource, NY)

For it is now perfectly clear that before the violent entry of the late Bronze and early Iron Age nomadic Aryan cattle-herders from the north and Semitic sheep-and-goat herders from the south into the old cult sites of the ancient world, there had prevailed in that world an essentially organic, vegetal, non-heroic view of the nature and necessities of life that was completely repugnant to those lion hearts for whom not the patient toil of earth but the battle spear and its plunder were the source of both wealth and joy. In the older mother myths and rites the light and darker aspects of the mixed thing that is life had been honored equally and together, whereas in the later, male-oriented, patriarchal myths, all that is good and noble was attributed to the new, heroic master gods, leaving to the native nature powers the character only of darkness – to which, also, a negative moral judgement now was added.[105]

Indeed, in later versions of the myth, Hercules, with his great masculine strength, perseverance, and cunning, obtains the apples of thc Hesperides. In some accounts, he gives the snake a sleeping potion, while in others he slays it.[106]

The garden of the Hesperides was at the western end of the earth:

The sky is green, yellow, and red, as if it were an apple-tree in full bearing; and the Sun, cut by the horizon like a crimson half-apple, meets his death dramatically in the western waves. When the Sun is gone, Hesperus appears. This star was sacred to the Love-goddess Aphrodite, and the apple was the gift by which her priestess decoyed the king, the Sun's representative, to his death with love-songs; if an apple is cut in two transversely, her five-pointed star appears in the centre of each half.[107]

Thus the golden apples could not be possessed by a mortal and therefore were a symbol of immortality. A white bird is alighting upon from the golden apple, symbolizing a renewal of spirit as well as body.

A different mythological association to the apple introduces a developmental point of view. Joan Chodorow has pointed out that the apple and ball are the ancient toys associated with the Divine Child and that they were used during initiation into the Dionysian mysteries: 'Ball games, rolling balls, tossing a ball in the air, catching it . . . modulate the experience of loss. Every time a beautiful round object leaves the hands, there is a momentary image of loss. But the game is joyful, completely voluntary – and the ball is likely to return. . . .'[108]

The golden frame, depicted once again as two-dimensional (as in the first three plates), is wider on the left than on the right. It contains beautiful butterflies, strawberries, birds, and flowers. The lower portion of the frame contains a pinkish rectangle, only slightly darker than the frieze behind the bathing women in the previous image. A small, square, bluish-gray intaglio is on each side (Figure 21). The one to the left depicts a naked woman sitting on the ground with a satyr,[109] who leans against a tree; they hold up their arms to ward off an imminent blow from a bludgeon held by a naked man. The intaglio to the right is similar – except for a fourth figure, a man who tries to prevent the man with the bludgeon from striking the other two.

The shift in attitude, shown by the right intaglio as compared to the left, represents the removal of both masculine hostility toward the feminine and of a man's guilt about his own instinctual desires, as represented by the satyr. The redemption of the feminine in this context is also redemption of the body and its affects from the shame that attends them in the attitudes of European culture and religions. The debate between the body and soul was a popular topic in medieval texts. In one well-known example, 'Soul described herself as a noble creature blackened by Flesh, which must be overcome by hunger, thirst and beatings.'[110]

FIGURE 21 Images of Men Attacking Women. From the base of the frame, Plate I–7. (Harley 3469, by permission of the British Library)

The symbolism of this plate helps us to understand the dream of a professional woman in her thirties:

> I am alone in a large shopping mall, wishing for a purpose and looking at all the colors. Suddenly I am in a huge public building with glass and marble, very imposing, a bastion of male authority. There has been a terrible catastrophe, and people are running everywhere. I have gone down some stairs and then ascend in an elevator, which I would not normally do in a catastrophe. I think of looking for my mother, and even though my rational mind tells me that I will not find her in such a place, my mother appears at my left. She is young, fit, and confident – not as I think of her in real life – and she takes charge in a natural way, leading me to a set of elevators. I look into one, and a man is drowning. Water is rising from the depths, so that is not the way to go.

This was a woman whose keen intelligence and determination had earned her success in academic and professional realms. However, she often experienced depersonalized states and had difficulty discerning her own priorities and values (introverted feeling). When feeling did begin to assert itself and she questioned the true value of her 'success,' she experienced a new kind of crisis. The very aspects of herself that had given her a sense of agency felt threatened. The elevator in the dream might represent hierarchical organization, which allows her to ascend easily, as she had in her professional life. The cultural transmission of tools, including machinery that seems to allow us to defy gravity, has inflated our confidence in the power of masculine values over natural law. For the patient, the facility with which her animus adopted patriarchal attitudes had led her to overestimate the ability of reason and ego mastery to control nature, including her own human nature. Water rising in the elevator shows that the unconscious is going to assert itself; reliance upon a hierarchy, with rationality at the top, has now become dangerous.

Her awareness of many colors, which preceded the change of scene early in the dream, represents a potential for a variety of emotions and for a relational (as opposed to structured, hierarchical, logos-oriented) experience. The colors also symbolize the goddess in her many forms. The appearance in the dream of her mother as a young and vital woman, at her left, is like the living personification of a saving grace. (An image of redemption by the Feminine will be seen in the next plate in this series.) However, the way out of her dilemma (out of the building in the dream) is not apparent at the dream's end.

Plate I–8 The Ethiopian

The next picture is often called, 'The Regeneration of the Ethiopian.' It depicts a naked man emerging from a muddy stream to face a beautiful, pale queen with wings of white peacock feathers. She wears a crown and neck ornaments, all made of gold and inlaid with rubies. Above her head floats a silver, six-pointed star. Her dress is golden across the breast, with a pale bodice and long yellow sleeves. Her long white skirt is decorated with green foliage and red and blue flowers, whereas her cape is blue with golden edges. The queen's too-long skirt alludes to the young king's robe of the previous plate, while her peacock-like wings predict the dawning of a new day.[111] This is but one example of imagery that looks both backward and forward at the same time, which is found throughout the *Splendor Solis*. It reminds us that each development is rooted in what came before and contains the possibility of what is to come.

The queen offers a robe edged with gold to the naked man, who is standing up to his knees in black mud. A transparent red helmet covers his head, all but the profile. His right arm, neck, and head are blood red, while his left arm and hand are white. His entire body is tinged with gold, showing us the potential value of the transformation now taking place. He holds his right hand over his right thigh, as if to cover his genital nakedness. He holds his left hand, palm up, toward the queen, ready to accept her help. The queen seems to be encouraging him to accept her gift of renewal or regeneration.

The sky is calm, with layers of small clouds. No sun is visible in the sky; light reflected from the man's helmet suggests that its source is from above and to the left. A horse-drawn wagon and people on foot approach a town, and in the distance a ship sails on a broad river toward the sea.

The arched golden frame surrounding the picture is filled with beautiful flowers and birds. Below, there are no human scenes, as in Plates I–4 to I–7; deer, seen previously in Plate I–2, have reappeared. This time, however, both are stags. One stag appears to be listening to a monkey, whose teeth are bared, while the other walks toward the right, with its head beyond the edge of the frame, as if leaving the picture to lead us on to the next stage.

This painting is a good example of the process by which the concrete operations of alchemy took on symbolic, sometimes personified forms. The male figure is the personified representation of a substance that the alchemists called 'Ethiops,' or 'Moor,' a black substance obtained by mixing mercury with melted sulfur. When the Ethiops was baked, it gave off a vapor (mercuric sulfide) that condensed into a brilliant red pigment known as vermilion, or cinnabar.[112] Cinnabar was highly valued for painting, and its deep red was associated with blood. Unless the alchemist knew how to capture the vapor, he would be left with only a clotted black residue. Therefore, the red helmet may refer to the man's having captured the sublimated vapor (or spirit) from the

PLATE I–8

blackness below. In alchemical terms, the *nigredo*[113] has yielded up the *rubedo*, one of many names for the goal of the process.

Another example of this symbolism can be seen in an image from a fourteenth-century manuscript of *Aurora Consurgens* (Figure 22). In this case, the symbolism of the Ethiops and the redeeming feminine are combined in one figure, that of Sophia, who stands on the moon[114] in a simple white dress. Her green, outstretched wings link the growth of spirit to the growth of green plants, and she radiates a mandorla of red light. She opens the front of her dress to reveal a sword or staff with intertwined snakes, like the caduceus of Hermes (Mercurius).

From a psychological point of view, the images of the Ethiopian and Sophia refer to the spirit or consciousness that can emerge from rejected or undervalued aspects of the personality. From these examples, we can see how concrete chemical operations took on a life of their own in the imagination of the alchemist. They are like visions or dreams, rife with symbolism and unconscious projections of the psyche's archetypal process.

The image of the man emerging from the mire also brings to mind Dante's description of a muddy swamp in the underworld, where those guilty of the sin of *acedia*, or spiritual indifference, live for eternity. These are the people who met life's challenges

FIGURE 22 Sophia Reveals her Mercurial Nature. From a late fourteenth-century manuscript of *Aurora Consurgens*. (Zentralbibliotech Zürich, MS. Rh. 172, f. 29v)

with anger or sullen apathy: we might say that they failed to capture the precious sublimate and ended as clotted masses of *prima materia*. Dante described their torment:

> Within that bog, all naked and muddy – with looks
> Of fury, striking each other: with a hand
> But also with their heads, chests, feet, and backs,
>
> Teeth tearing piecemeal.
> . . . These are the souls whom anger overcame,
> . . . under the water are found
>
> Others, whose sighing makes the bubbles come
> That pock the surface everywhere you look.
> Lodged in the slime they say: 'Once we were grim
>
> And sullen in the sweet air above, that took
> A further gladness from the play of the sun;
> Inside us, we bore acedia's dismal smoke.
>
> We have this black mire now to be sullen in.'[115]

Psychologically, the appearance of the Ethiopian also represents an encounter with the dark side of human life. This is a period in analysis that we all recognize, when people begin to have dreams or symptoms indicating deeper levels yet to be explored. We saw in the previous plate that the young king was wearing over-sized kingly robes, suggesting that he was not at the end of the work. Actually, he was split off from the shadow.

Genuine transformation must always include what Jung referred to as 'shadow,'[116] 'the "negative" side of the personality, the sum of all those unpleasant qualities we like to hide, together with the insufficiently developed functions and the contents of the personal unconscious.'[117] (The word 'functions' in this context has a specific meaning. In Jung's terminology, it denotes two pairs of complementary ego functions: thinking/feeling and sensation/intuition.[118] For each person, one of these four functions is superior, i.e., is naturally the most 'capable.' The other member of its pair is the inferior function, i.e., the one that functions most poorly unless developed. For example, a person who processes experience most naturally by thinking will find 'feeling,' or knowing what to value, to be most difficult.) The shadow side of life is often discovered in what is missed by the inferior function.

In this context, the man coming up out of the mud represents the appearance of that which has never been cultivated and presents the greatest potential for growth, something that has to be redeemed from the unconscious. This development is more profound than the *weakening* of the formerly dominant principles and functions (represented by the old king in the previous painting). This can be seen in the dream of a man in analysis:

> I was staying in a small town next to a river, where dead bodies formed a barrier or dam, blocking some boats. I realized that everyone in the town knew about the dead bodies, but they were pretending they didn't know. I said, 'We all swim in

this river, and we know there's death out there. You may deny it but it's creating a neurosis for me.' I went out and began moving dead bodies. I took pieces of the dead bodies and tried to place them in a toilet, but they wouldn't fit. A male figure, my 'father' in the dream, was young and strong. I wanted to show him the bodies. He didn't believe me, but he went with me. The bodies weren't where I had found them, but we came upon a burial place: he was shocked that it had actually occurred.

The patient's dream-ego is recognizing a horrifying problem – although there is still much resistance, represented by the denial of the townspeople. The horrifying problem is the reality of death, the putrefaction of the body. This man, who was very intelligent, sensitive, and creative, had been terribly neglected and abused as a child. In order to survive, he had retreated to a world of fantasy and spent a great deal of time in lethargic, dreamy states, seeking 'bliss' and 'enlightenment.' He put off really living his life, but near the time of his fortieth birthday he had this dream.

We see in the dream that at first he tries a regressive solution, 'flushing it down the toilet.' A helpful male figure appears, who is at first skeptical but allows himself to be led by the patient. This 'father' was entirely unlike his real father and represents a new and potentially redeeming part of the patient's personality, one that possesses a new strength and vigor and also respects his feelings. Something has happened to the bodies; they are no longer blocking the river but are buried in the earth, where their decomposition might provide food for new growth rather than contamination.

A new attitude toward life, represented by the 'father,' could help the patient leave his fantasy world (of denial) so that the river of life might flow. After the analytic session in which he talked about the dream, this man felt the need to take some action that would give him direct and immediate experience of this new part of himself. He went on a long hike and found a small stream, following it to a blockage. He dug out sand and rocks until the water flowed freely, and this activity made him feel alive and powerful. This helped him fix in his mind and body the living symbolism of his dream.

If you think again of the previous image of the beautiful and innocent-looking young king in Plate I–7 – seen at the moment when the white bird of revelation has landed on the golden apple in his hand – he is too good to be true: it is more like wish-fulfillment or an idealized possibility. This picture (Plate I–8) shows that real change comes from below, where life is imperfect. The psychological stages of development, like the alchemical stages, black, white, yellow, and red, shine through the muck.

The Ethiopian is a figure that appears often in alchemy, reminding us of the essential nature of the problem of the shadow, which is not just a single stage. As Jung pointed out in 'Psychology of the Transference': 'It must be emphasized that in alchemy the dark initial state of *nigredo* is often regarded as the product of a previous operation, and that it therefore does not represent the absolute beginning.'[119] Nor is it the end – for this is a process that repeats itself throughout life, as long as individuation continues.

The alchemical colors are represented on the Ethiopian's body, signifying an embodied transformation, not just a change in mental attitude. At this stage, the conscious personality, with its red and white symbolism (on the head and arms), now confronts the shadow, which naturally arises following the death of the old king, or the old way of functioning. It is important to understand that this old way of functioning, including unconscious defenses, may have been very necessary at a particular point in development and in a particular context. However, the person may no longer be served by this way of functioning, which limits or cuts off aspects of the personality that could potentially be integrated to allow a fuller experience of life. Often, defenses may be rigid and automatic, interfering with the person's ability to make discerning or flexible choices.

The task of acknowledging shadow is unbearably painful and usually surrounded by shame. It is not a task that can be accomplished by the ego alone. Integrating shadow aspects of the personality requires help from a 'guardian spirit,' in the form of a living symbol that comes from the generative depths of the unconscious. Sometimes the analyst carries this projection for the patient; at other times, the guardian spirit may take the form of a beneficent deity, such as Kwan Yin, Tara, Avalokitesvara, or the Virgin Mary. Baudelaire expressed the need for strength that transcends the ego, when, in *Les Fleurs du Mal*, he cried out, 'Oh God, give me the courage to face my own true image without disgust!'

In Plate I–8 the Feminine Principle is fully manifest as a saving grace, a guardian spirit represented as a woman, a queen who is also an angel, i.e., transcendent. She has the power to rescue the alchemical/analytic process from the folly of mere insight by recasting it as a relational process rather than one of mastery. The wings suggest that the white bird in the previous picture has now taken shape and form, to be *experienced in an embodied way*. In Jung's terms, she represents the Feminine Self for women or the anima for men.

Over the queen's head is a six-pointed star, formed by two triangles, one pointing up, the other down. The six-pointed star is a good example of a symbol that expresses some fundamental but ineffable quality of inner experience, transcending personal and specific contents; it is found in many cultures and eras. In ancient Indian Tantrism, it symbolized the union of Shiva and Shakti and was also associated with the heart chakra in Kundalini yoga. In Jewish iconography (as the Star of David or Solomon's Seal), it denoted wisdom. As a Christian symbol, it represented the union of the upper and lower trinities (Father–Son–Holy Ghost and Animal–Vegetable–Mineral). In alchemy, the triangles were the symbols for fire (pointing up) and water (pointing down), so the six-pointed star could symbolize fiery-water.[120] In other contexts, it symbolized the mercurial union of spirit and matter, Sol and Luna, heaven and earth.[121] *The Chinese Book of Changes*, or *I Ching*, consists of interpretations of hexagrams that are formed by two trigrams. Each of the six lines can be either a *yin* or a *yang* line, either feminine/receptive or masculine/creative.

This plate is a useful reminder of the attitude necessary to establish a healing relationship with the emerging shadow, as opposed to shaming or denial and projection. Initially, the patient's shadow may be acted out in the analytic relationship and also projected onto the analyst before it can be faced consciously by the patient. The analyst's task is to see the shadow and then relate to it incisively through the Masculine Principle and also compassionately, through the Feminine Principle. The analyst may struggle internally with negative reactions – hatred, disgust, rage, contempt, lust, or greed – in response to the patient's shadowy transference behavior. Unless the analyst can pass the patient's half-consciously created tests, the shadow will not emerge and the therapy will become stymied. The patient will be exquisitely sensitive to the analyst's tolerance or lack of tolerance (as shown, for example, in moralizing judgment), as well as to the analyst's strength to confront, as well as contain, the powerful energies constellated by the shadow. In meeting these challenges, the analyst will no doubt learn more about her own shadow during the course of each therapy.

PLATE I–9

Plate I-9 The Hermaphrodite

Standing in the foreground of a magnificent landscape is an exquisite hermaphroditic human figure dressed formally in a black tunic, with a gold-tinged orange collar and belt and clasps of red and gold down the front, as well as black tights and shoes. The hermaphrodite stands on a high grassy mound strewn with lovely plants bearing golden flowers and gold-tinged leaves. Trees, a river flowing to the sea, and towns can be seen below. Above, the blue sky is turbulent with white cumulus clouds. The arched golden frame surrounding the scene is decorated with beautiful birds, flowers, and fruit.

The figure has two heads and necks: one is a clean-shaven man with sandy hair and blue eyes; the other is a woman, also with blue eyes and fair, reddish hair.[122] A golden halo radiates from the male head, while a silvery radiation emanates from the female head. The male face is to the left of the picture, his profile overlapping the back part of the female head. The black of the Ethiopian is still manifest, but in a new light as the impressive clothing. This symbolizes the value of the transformed shadow. The red wing on the man's side and the white, purple-tinged wing on the side of the woman refer to a common alchemical expression for the meeting of the opposites as *coniunctio*, known as 'the red man and his white wife.'

In its left hand, the hermaphrodite holds an egg, upon which both heads look intently. According to alchemical tradition, the Four Elements are contained in the symbolic egg. The outer shell represents Earth; the membrane between the shell and the white, Air; the white itself, Water; and the yoke, Fire. Thus the egg is a symbol of totality, of the Four Elements distinct yet combined in a harmonious relationship: 'all the elements combined with matter to form a source of perfect nature, just so as it is necessary in this noble art.'[123] The text of the *Splendor Solis* contains some additional symbolism of the egg: the membrane around the yoke represents 'subtle air, which is more warm and subtle, as it is nearer to the Fire, and separates the Fire from the Water.'[124] The center of the yolk is a Fifth or Quintessential Element out of which the chick grows. The egg represents the potential for further growth, even wholeness, as an egg contains everything needed to develop into a living being. As with the egg, inner development may remain unseen during a period of gestation.

A circular shield, with an outer band of gold-tinged orange, is held in the hermaphrodite's right hand. A grayish, marbled band is within the orange band, within which lies a third band, dark with indistinct edges. These bands encircle an image of the surrounding landscape, as it would be seen in a convex mirror. The symbolism of the hermaphrodite's mirror suggests a stage of development in which both the inner and the outer can be imagined as coming together. The mirror is an accurate reflection, but of a reduced size, symbolizing that the microcosm reflects the macrocosm. If the egg is the microcosm experienced inwardly, the inner man, then the landscape would represent the macrocosm, which is the outer world. The egg is the Four Elements in harmony, together with the embryo, the quintessential and mysterious capacity of life to develop, diversify, and reproduce. The adept may now consciously ponder this mysterious and wonderful truth.

Although a new synthesis has appeared, we must note that the union is really awkward and artificial: one body split into complementary halves, with two heads. The result, therefore, is an idealistic model of union. Nevertheless, the hermaphrodite is a provisional attempt to unite what seemed irreconcilable. In fact, the picture suggests that at this stage a person may feel both ecstatic and humbled by the realization that one is truly a part of nature, a part of something that transcends an individual identity and lifetime.

This kind of symbolism in the context of analysis may coincide with a man's first conscious inner (not projected) experience of his feminine side – of his anima or soul. It may also represent a conscious recognition of *participation mystique*, the realization that one is part of the entire world rather than separate from it. There is finally the *feeling* that some kind of resolution of the original problem is possible, that there is some possibility of unification. According to this view, the hermaphrodite symbolizes the prospective Self,[125] in which the opposites (which were separated in the earlier stage, shown in Plate I–2) may come together. However, the lack of integration of masculine and feminine in the hermaphrodite's appearance shows us that the opposites have not been fundamentally transformed. We then might ask whether the hermaphrodite represents a prospect of the Self or whether it represents the conscious ego's acceptance of the problem of the opposites and the possibility of an attitude that is neither one-sided nor conventional.

To Marie-Louise von Franz,[126] the image of the hermaphrodite illustrated the in-between, or 'stuck,' nature of a complex. She gave the example of a peasant girl who practiced black magic: the girl dreamt that her grandfather, who had held seances, appeared to her in the form of a hermaphroditic 'monster.' Von Franz interpreted this image as showing both the girl's undeveloped mind and her repressed, feminine passions: a combination that drew the girl into the empty pining of black magic. During analysis, the girl dreamed of her grandfather's death and the miraculous birth of a child, deep in a cave. After that, the girl's energy was more available for pursuits that could really meet her needs in life.

Von Franz's interpretation emphasizes the negative, regressive aspects of the hermaphrodite, which were represented in medieval alchemy as a hermaphrodite associated with the devil rather than with the divine. Alexander Roob[127] has reprinted striking images of the 'holy' hermaphrodite and of the 'evil' hermaphrodite from the fifteenth-century *Buch der heiligen Dreifaltigkeit*.

What the image of the hermaphrodite means in specific terms in the therapeutic relationship between the patient and the doctor is unique in every clinical situation. Generally, one can say that there is always a danger at the point when a symbolic resolution has presented itself through dreams or active imagination. When such a solution presents itself after the intense efforts of working through regressive material and confrontation with the shadow, the analyst and patient may both feel relieved that the end of treatment appears to be in sight. Even if they both realize consciously that there is even more to face before the 'resolution' is integrated into inner and outer life. It is tempting at this juncture to think, 'This is the end of the process, what more? The analysis is a success and all we have to do is just tidy things up a bit and we can both be on our way.'

Likewise, when a solution has presented itself in both a microcosmic and macro-cosmic way, the patient and analyst may both believe that the fundamental conflict has been resolved and that the patient is now contained within an ongoing and well-established individuation process. After all, the patient has already confronted neuroses or complexes, has had an experience of the deep unconscious, has confronted the shadow, and has now begun to integrate the anima or animus.

Nevertheless, this is not the end. In fact, if the process should end here, the patient will very likely be left with an inflated sense of the power of insight. The patient may then continue to act out the unsolved problem because he is unable to *really live* the life that had been intimated by the insight.

I [J. H.] have previously reported a dream of my own that I think addresses the problem of unifying the macrocosm and the microcosm:

> The mountain ranges in [this] dream were not at all like those real mountains [near my childhood home in Nevada], nor like any other mountains I have ever seen, but they were similar in some way. Moreover, there was a remarkable symbolic element that emerged from the far side of each of these ranges: a round object surmounted by a vertical eagle's feather. Altogether, there were four ranges and four eagle's feathers. The whole scene, with its symmetrical arrangement of symbols, did not seem strange or in any way frightening. The image gave me the impression that the outer world of nature, the macrocosm, is not alien but akin to our own unique inner vision. The symbol bridges the inner and the outer.[128]

This dream was not an end in itself but a potential, an anticipation, of something that would manifest later in life:

> I later understood the round object to symbolize an earthbound sense of whole-ness and unity, whereas the eagle feather represented a magic flight into regions of higher consciousness. Together they generated a promise that these need not be polar but [were in fact] complementary opposites, unified through symbolism.[129]

This dream, like the reconciling symbols representing the microcosm and macrocosm in the painting, does not make a final statement denoting the wholeness of comple-mentarity. That statement of wholeness can only be made by life itself and must wait for events in real life to realize its meaning. In other words, after I had my dream of the four feathers, I did not know how to bring its symbols into reality, but in fact they did become a reality in my life. In another place, I [J. H.] have also recounted that Jung told me, when I visited him in the 1950s, about a similar anticipatory dream which he understood only years later.[130]

Plate I–10 The Golden Head

This painting shows for the first time a scene that takes place entirely inside the walls of a city. Yet here we are confronted with a shocking beheading and dismemberment. A ferocious man with a dark face and wild, disheveled black hair holds an enormous sword in his right hand. Although his head is turned toward his left, he appears to gaze out at the viewer. In his left hand, he grasps a golden human head, with closed lids and an almost peaceful countenance. The wild man with the sword wears an orange shirt and tights. His white tunic is transparent, revealing the contours of his torso. At his feet lies the decapitated, naked corpse, with all four limbs freshly severed. Its white torso is strangely similar to that of the man standing above it, and the cross-sections of the severed limbs reveal the red of the flesh and white of the bone within.

The assassin is standing on green ground, with grass and golden-tipped foliage, next to a large courtyard and palace. Just to the swordsman's right is a column whose base is decorated with a frieze of knights riding to battle (Figure 23). Toward his

PLATE I–10

FIGURE 23 Knights Riding to Battle. Portion of a frieze from Plate I–10. (Harley 3469, by permission of the British Library)

left, beyond the courtyard and palace, gondolas ply on a waterway. Castles and fine mansions are seen in the distance, like Venice in her glory. Several people are strolling and lingering on the grounds, within view yet oblivious to the scene here depicted.

In the background, near the center of the picture, a man steps onto a porch, toward an open doorway in which stands a woman. This doorway is on the ground level of a three-storied, domed building with the statue of a knight on its roof. The first domed building in Western Europe was the Pantheon, completed in Rome 27 BCE. The essential meaning of the domed space is inner life. Thus, the man going in the door could represent the Renaissance man entering the inner sanctum in contrast to the activity outside.[131]

Beneath the main picture there are two small golden bas-reliefs (Figure 24). The one on the left shows a clothed female figure in an ordinary boat, calmly holding reins

FIGURE 24 Mythological Scenes of Water-chariots. Base of frame, Plate I–10. (Harley 3469, by permission of the British Library)

attached to a swimming horse. She encounters the naked Poseidon, whose billowing robes and three prancing horses evoke the energy of the wind and sea. In the relief to the right, a woman holds a trident in her right hand and with her left guides three energetic horses. In classical Greek mythology, the trident was associated with Poseidon, the brother of Zeus and god of waters, earthquakes, and horses, but Robert Graves has speculated that it was a symbol of the tripartite mother goddess prior to the advent of the patriarchy.[132] A man or merman[133] accompanies two women, whereas on the right one woman stands while another reclines upon a man with a serpent's tail and lower limbs like the roots of a tree.

It would appear that the union of opposites that took place in the last picture was not final. The hermaphrodite, though easy to imagine and idealize, is always troubling in the sense that it is very hard for us to think how it would really be possible to exist as both a man and a woman in the same body at the same time. In fact, the hermaphrodite represents a stage of the work at which the opposites have come too close together for comfort. One might say that the image of the hermaphrodite as a resolution of the problem of the opposites is contrived, facile, or too intellectual. So we see that as we move along from one plate to the next, there is an anticipation of a solution to the problem of the opposites, followed by a more integrated, embodied, and lived solution, only to be followed by destruction and then a new anticipation.

Once again we must be reminded that fresh insight into the problem of the opposites involving an artificial union can easily be overvalued. There is always the danger of getting fixated upon the insight without the embodiment of the trans-formation. This frequently occurs in analysis, especially of intuitive individuals, who respond enthusiastically to the idea of achieving the goal as soon as it comes to mind. Nevertheless, some statement of the possibility of union is necessary to prevent the individual from getting stuck in confusion, fear, or dissociation. The hermaphrodite, then, is an imperfect, or premature, image of the Self, but not a final image. First, there must be another separation (recall the knight with his sword in Plate I–2). Hence the ruthless *separatio* of the present picture.

At this stage, separation involves a sacrifice. We are reminded of the theme of sacrifice and decapitation in the vision of Zosimos,[134] discussed in the Introduction, and of the theme of decapitation found in East Indian Tantrism.[135] Psychologically the rendering of false integrity is often experienced inwardly as a bodily dissociation or dis-memberment. The patient may suffer with physical pain, numbing, intense sensations of heat or cold, or hypersensitivity to sensory stimulation. The analyst, who may experience some of the same symptoms while with the patient, must work with the bodily symptoms and note any changes that occur while they are processing psychological material. This destructive energy of the shadow is essential: the inner experience of the body and all it symbolizes must be taken apart so it can come together in a new way.

The text of the *Splendor Solis* reads,

> In [the murderer's] left hand was a paper on which the following was written, 'I have killed thee, that thou mayest receive a superabundant life, but thy head I will care-fully hide, that the worldly wantons may not find thee, and destroy the earth, and the body I will bury, that it may putrefy, and grow and bear innumerable fruit.'[136]

The shadow figure, in other words, has rescued the essential value, as represented by the golden head, which signifies the coming into consciousness of the Self, beyond the opposites. The golden head also represents the lasting and unique value of the process up to this point, which needs to be rescued from the danger of slipping back into a conventional or an infantile form of adaptation (i.e., the solution sought by the 'worldly wantons' in the quote). Understanding and insight must not be discarded, even though they are helpless to prevent the suffering of this stage.

A clinical example of this symbolism and its healing power can be seen in the case of a woman in her early fifties, who returned to analysis because of marital discord. Her creative development, which had blossomed during her analysis, had begun to clash with expectations that her husband and his extended family should be her first priority. After she re-entered treatment, her husband began to pressure her about the money she was spending: he could not acknowledge the value of her analytic work, just as he could not understand her inability to set aside her painting. He disparaged her need for an inner life as a luxury the couple could not afford. His skepticism reinforced her own doubts, and she felt ashamed every time she came to a session. However, she could objectively see that her earlier work had brought her out of a profound and long-lasting depression and had changed the quality of her life. She dreamed that,

> I had taken photographs of landscapes, and for the first time I noticed that in each picture someone had died. Then I was observing a movie scene being filmed. As a heavy-set, dark-haired woman was saying her lines, someone (perhaps myself) handed her the head of a dark-haired man, with blood running from it. She grabbed the head, jumped in her car, drove over the curb to make a U-turn, and sped away. As she sped away, she became thinner.

This dream addressed her difficulty holding onto the value of her own psychological growth in the face of the authority she gave to her husband's opinion. When she acknowledges her loss of libido (the dead bodies), she becomes energized. The large woman reflects her use of food to substitute for emotional nourishment while she devoted herself to the care of others. Her mobilization into action suggests assumption of responsibility for her situation and reversal of direction. She has come into touch with her masculine side in a positive, active sense, rather than favoring an all-giving maternal ideal. The potential suggested by this dream emerged later, and she dreamt that she was joining a group of women who wore colorful costumes and performed acrobatics without anxiety. She expressed this in life by building a studio and setting aside time for her painting.

Plate I-11 The Alchemist in the Bath

In the eleventh and final picture of this series, we see the courtyard of a magnificent palace. The naked alchemist sits chest-deep in a cylindrical bath, which rests upon a circular furnace. The furrows between his eyes and his flushed complexion show his distress, yet he remains. The alchemist has chosen to suffer in the bath of personal transformation.

A workman kneels and very intently uses a pair of bellows to blow air at the roaring fire beneath the furnace. His blouse is a reddish gold, and his vest is black, edged with white; his leggings are blue and his apron white. His hair is long and careless.

PLATE I–11

Next to the stove is a pair of tongs as well as coal to fuel the fire. On a piece of masonry next to the stove, sits an alembic containing a gaseous yellow substance, suggesting a *sublimatio*. In the background, two figures stand on a raised corridor: a woman, in red garments and a golden cap, carries a flask in her hand, and a bearded man, dressed in pale purple, gazes down upon the alchemist. In two niches below them are figures of Mercury and Jupiter (Figure 25).

On the pedestal of a column on the right is an *intaglio* of Vulcan working as a blacksmith, while a woman, naked but for a diaphanous drape, stands and looks on (Figure 26). Vulcan, or *Hephaistos* the blacksmith, is the great shaman of Greek

FIGURE 25 Jupiter and Mercury. Framing a column in Plate I–11. (Harley 3469, by permission of the British Library)

FIGURE 26 Hephaistos. At the base of a column in Plate I–11. (Harley 3469, by permission of the British Library)

mythology. According to Homer, Hephaistos came to Hera's aid when Zeus threatened her. Zeus hurled Hephaistos off of Mount Olympus, and he was crippled by the fall. He had to fend for himself apart from the rest of the gods, but he learned how to transform base metals into valuable things, including beautiful jewelry. He stands for that ability to create order and beauty out of what would otherwise be chaos.

A reflection by Erich Neumann in another context provides an apt commentary for this image:

> The symbolism of the vessel appears even at the highest level as the vessel of spiritual transformation. Although Christianity did its best to suppress it, this matriarchal symbolism has survived. . . . The pre-Christian plunge bath signifies return to the mysterious uterus of the Great Mother and its water of life. The plunge bath . . . became in Christianity the baptismal bath of transformation that . . . is a return to the primordial egg of the beginning.[137]

The Christian ritual of baptism as an alchemical *solutio* can be seen in Figure 27, which is a mosaic of Christ being baptized by John the Baptist, who was Christ's cousin and lived in the wilderness, preaching to pagans. As Christ is plunged into the swirling

FIGURE 27 The Baptism of Christ. Mosaic from the Cathedral of San Marco, Venice, thirteenth century. (By permission of the Procuratoria di San Marco, Venezia)

water, he blesses the fishes,[138] a suggestion that animals as well as humans have souls. In the water at the lower right, we see a boy, perhaps representing the soul of Christ, looking up at three angels. The baptism takes place beneath a seven-pointed star, symbolic of initiation. A white dove, here representing spirit or the Holy Ghost, faces downward.

The image of the alchemist in the bath takes the integration a step further: the objective psyche is fully manifest and aware of itself. It is nothing less than transformation of the whole person. The white bird that we saw perched on the golden fruit of the youthful king (Plate I–7) now appears upon the head of an ordinary human being. What was formerly the wish of the adept to transcend the limitations of material reality has resulted paradoxically in a humble and embodied spiritual attitude. The man is not flying; rather, he remains sitting in the great iron cauldron, still suffering and being transformed. This alchemical symbol conveys that the work done on the chthonic, or earthly, level has released the white bird, which ascends – the reverse of the Christian dogma that spiritual enlightenment comes only from above through divine revelation, as symbolized by the white dove descending in Figure 27. In alchemy, salvation comes not only from above: it comes also from below.

The dream of a Catholic woman in analysis illustrates this discovery:

> I am in my yoga class. I am not paying much attention to the postures; rather I am reading a book. During a break in the class, the teacher says, 'I want you to grab the book, hit it on the edge of the table, and say "Ptah!"' I do this, and then I see a table at the far end of the room, on which stands a wooden box that looks like a tabernacle, the house of the deity. Someone puts a dove inside and closes the door.

The dreamer commented, 'Ptah is the Egyptian god of creation. He created beings from mud by saying a word.' This woman was a talented writer who had not developed her potential. Her dream demonstrates the value of the word that comes through bodily experience. She has been captivated by the intellect, but her teacher intervenes, giving her some very specific and puzzling instructions. She nevertheless follows, without asking first to understand. The dove, the Christian symbol of the Spirit or Holy Ghost, appears only after the patient has used the book in its concrete physical form to make a sound and has spoken the name of an ancient god who created life from mud, i.e., from the *prima materia*. This gave her the key to her creative potential as a writer.

Edward Edinger has recounted the dream of a young woman in relation to this image. In the dream, she is in a dark place and is feeling an exterior pressure to give birth. In active imagination, she continued the dream and saw a girl screaming, as in Munch's lithograph. White doves fly out of the circular mouth. Edinger interpreted this dream as informing the patient that the anxiety she was suffering was part of a larger process of transformation, but it could also be seen as a transference dream about the pressure the patient was feeling about the expectations of the analyst or the analytic situation.

Edinger speaks of the released bird as the white soul,[139] the *anima candida*, and cites an alchemical text quoted by Jung in *Psychology and Alchemy*:

> At the end of the sublimation there germinates through the mediation of the spirit, a shining white soul which flies to heaven with the spirit. This is clearly and manifestly the stone.[140]

Edinger continues, referring specifically to the image in Plate I–11:

> This 'white soul' is often represented by a white bird being released from the material being heated. One picture shows a man being cooked in the water bath with a white bird emerging from his head.[141]

There are many parallels to this picture, which show spirit arising from the chaotic material of the unconscious.[142] They refer to an *increatum*, something that was not created by God but created by the human being from the depth of suffering, the white soul brought forth to enrich higher consciousness and the whole of his life.

This image of the alchemist's personal transformation through the opus completes this series.

THE SECOND SERIES

Introduction

THE SECOND SERIES REPRESENTS a seven-stage alchemical process[1] that builds upon the transformations shown in the First Series. The Second Series simultaneously conveys a broad, objective perspective and an intensely felt but contained internal experience. Each painting in this series has the same basic structure: a large central niche containing an alembic, surrounded by scenes of people engaged in the affairs of everyday life; in the sky above, a Greco-Roman god or goddess rides in an ornamented chariot with astrological signs of the Zodiac on its wheel(s), each chariot drawn by a pair of animal or human figures.

In medieval astrology, each known planet had a 'ruler,' personified as a god or goddess, and in medieval alchemy, each of the seven planets was associated with a stage of the alchemical opus in the following order: Saturn, Jupiter, Mars, Sol (Sun), Venus, Mercury, and Luna. This order begins with what was believed to be the most distant planet from earth and progresses to the nearest.

The scenes in the paintings draw upon medieval woodblock and miniature illustrations known as 'The Planets and their Children.'[2] The term 'children' referred to the people born under the astrological signs governed by the planet; they were believed to share traits and occupations consistent with the character of the ruling god. More technically sophisticated prints depicting the planets as the patrons of certain occupations were produced into the Renaissance (Figure 28), so we may infer that this theme was a popular one in Europe for at least several hundred years. These paintings of the Greco-Roman gods/planets and their human 'children' find a parallel in Jung's psychology with his thesis that each archetype contains both the archetypal image (symbolized here by the Greco-Roman deities) and the corresponding pattern of behavior (the activities of the deity's 'children').

The depiction of a god in the sky above with typical human activities below also reminds us of the saying in the Emerald Tablet of Hermes: 'What is below is like that which is above, and what is above is like that which is below . . .'.[3] In Figure 29, we see an illustration from an early fifteenth-century edition of *Mandeville's Travels*, showing astronomers making observations, while their colleagues are using divining rods on the ground, suggesting the link between the earthly and heavenly spheres. As the author of the *Splendor Solis* wrote, 'All corporeal things originate in and are

FIGURE 28 Saturn, or Cronos and His 'Children.' Woodblock, Hans Beham, 1530–1540. A similar imagery is found in Plate II–1, but with the addition of an alembic in the center of the picture. (From *Astrology: The Celestial Mirror*, by Warren Kenton, published by Thames & Hudson Ltd., London and New York, 1989)

FIGURE 29 Astronomers and Geomancers (*John Mandeville's Travels*, Bohemia, 1410–1420). This scene takes place on Mt. Athos in central Macedonia, known for its beauty and ancient monasteries. (Addison 24189, f. 15, by permission of the British Library)

maintained and exist of the Earth, according to Time and Influence of the Stars and Planets.'[4]

Another example of the alchemists' worldview relating the opus to the Zodiac is shown in Figure 30. In this late fourteenth-century illustration for the *Aurora*

FIGURE 30 The Signs of the Zodiac in Relation to the Alchemical *Opus*. (From a fourteenth-century *Aurora Consurgens* (Zentralbibliotech Zürich, MS. Rh. 172, f. 11r)

Consurgens, a woman appears ready to give birth. According to the author of the *Aurora Consurgens*, the ripening of the philosopher's stone requires nine months, the same time as the gestation of a human fetus. The woman holds a simple astronomical instrument for viewing the stars and looks toward the moon (originally silver but now oxidized), which radiates its own light (as we saw earlier in Plate I–4). The moon was associated with the tides and water, and the breaking of the water prior to birth was associated in alchemy with the *albedo*. The apparent ease with which she awaits the birth in this case may indicate that the timing is in harmony with the positions of the planets and so is not painful.

Recall that in medieval and early Renaissance times, the earth was believed to lie at the center of the universe with other heavenly bodies moving around it (Figure 31). The telescope had not yet been invented, so the only known heavenly bodies were those visible to the naked eye. The seven 'planets' of the astrologers of those times were in fact the five planets visible with the naked eye (Venus, Mercury, Mars, Saturn, and Jupiter), plus the Sun and Moon. Each of the five actual planets 'ruled' over two signs of the Zodiac – here depicted on the wheels of the chariots – whereas the Sun and the Moon each ruled over one sign. In this way, all twelve signs of the Zodiac are represented in the series.

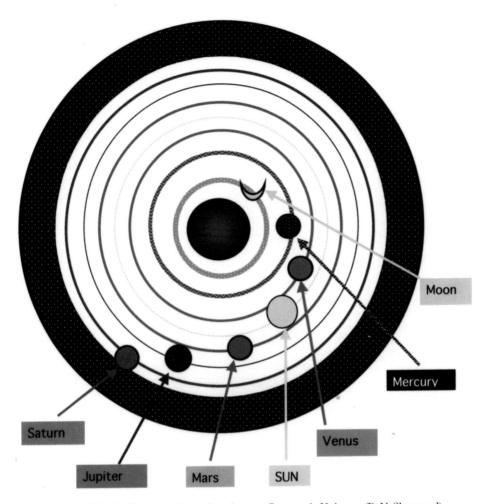

FIGURE 31 The Medieval and Early Renaissance Geocentric Universe (D. N. Sherwood)

Astrology had developed even more complex symbols and attributions to explain human destiny. For example, each sign of the Zodiac is identified with one pole of various pairs of opposite qualities (antinomies). The result is that the two astrological signs 'ruled' by each planet form a pair with opposing qualities – such as, masculine/feminine and fixed/mutable – that may be viewed either as in conflict or as complementary (Table 1). We might recall how in the First Series we saw such pairs of opposites symbolized by human figures. For example, in Plate I–4, the king was associated with both masculine qualities and the sun (fixed), whereas the queen was associated with feminine qualities and the moon (mutable).

Each sign of the Zodiac was also associated with one of the four elements (the basic constituents of all matter according to the belief at that time): Earth, Water, Fire, and Air. Earth and Water were considered to be 'passive,' while Fire and Air were

Table 1 Signs of the Zodiac

DATES	SIGN	PLANET RULER	ELEMENT	HUMOUR	CROSS
12/22–1/20	CAPRICORN	Saturn (p)[1]	Earth	phlegmatic	cardinal
1/21–2/19	AQUARIUS	Saturn (a)	Air	sanguine	fixed
2/20–3/20	PISCES	Jupiter (p)	Water	melancholy	mutable
3/21–4/20	ARIES	Mars (a)	Fire	choleric	cardinal
4/21–5/21	TAURUS	Venus (p)	Earth	phlegmatic	fixed
5/22–6/21	GEMINI	Mercury (a)	Air	sanguine	mutable
6/22–7/22	CANCER	Moon	Water	melancholy	cardinal
7/23–8/23	LEO	Sun	Fire	choleric	fixed
8/24–9/23	VIRGO	Mercury (p)	Earth	phlegmatic	mutable
9/24–10/23	LIBRA	Venus (a)	Air	sanguine	cardinal
10/24–11/22	SCORPIO	Mars (p)	Water	melancholy	fixed
11/23–12/21	SAGITTARIUS	Jupiter (a)	Fire	choleric	mutable

[1] a: active; p: passive

Source: Adapted from Kenton, *Astrology*, p. 126.

deemed 'active.' In the astrological schema, the two signs 'ruled' by a planet are always associated with different elements, one active and one passive. Astrology was also used in the diagnosis and treatment of diseases, a practice that dated back at least to Hippocrates. Contemporaneous with the paintings of the *Splendor Solis*, the physician would classify a patient according to 'humour' or temperament based on the sun sign at birth. Fire signs were choleric (associated with yellow bile, irritability, bad temper), air signs, sanguine (associated with blood, ruddy complexion, passion, optimism), water signs, melancholic (associated with black bile, gloom, sudden anger), and earth signs phlegmatic (associated with mucous or phlegm, sluggishness, evenness of temper).[5] Parts of the body (as microcosm) were associated with signs of the Zodiac (as macrocosm) (Figure 32), and every disease was associated with a sign and a planet.

Jung pointed out that we have a tendency to experience and conceptualize the opposites as 'either confronting one another in enmity or attracting one another in love.'[6] This series contains depictions of many such relations between pairs of opposites, including above/below, inner/outer, image/behavior, masculine/feminine, nature/artifice, active/passive and eternal/changing. In the series of images we are about to examine, the astrological signs of the Zodiac – characterized by various pairs of opposites – appear on the wheels of the chariot of the planetary ruler or god. We know that in order for the chariot to move forward, the wheels must turn in concert, a beautiful image suggesting to us that at the archetypal level, where the gods rule, opposing qualities can somehow work together. The progression of the seven planetary rulers in their chariots across the sky suggests that life is not just cyclical, not limited to an eternal return as represented by the yearly cycle of the constellations of the Zodiac. Rather, the planetary rulers and

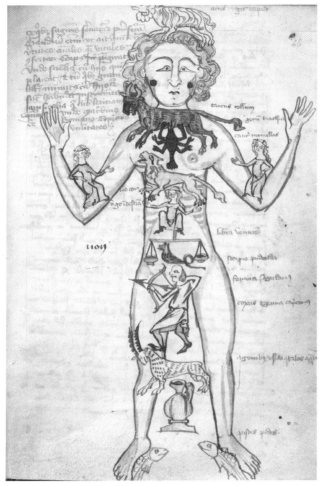

FIGURE 32 Zodiac Man. From a fifteenth-century German manuscript. Particular parts of the body were associated with signs of the Zodiac, and astrological information was important in reaching a diagnosis and choosing a treatment. This view linked the human microcosm with the macrocosm, with the constellations of the Zodiac also giving human meaning and form to the sky at night. (Arundel MS 251, f. 46, by permission of the British Library)

their astrological signs present us with an archetypal[7] depiction of the dynamic tensions involved in a forward movement of transformation.

In this view, each return is not to the original beginning. It begins with the *prima materia* left over from the last cycle. This is represented in various psycho-spiritual systems as a spiral.[8] Jung wrote in 1935:

> The way to the goal seems chaotic and interminable at first, and only gradually do the signs increase that it is leading anywhere. The way is not straight but appears to go round in circles. More accurate knowledge has proved it to go in

spirals: . . . which may in certain circumstances appear even in the initial dreams. As manifestations of unconscious processes the dreams rotate or circumambulate round the centre, drawing closer to it as the amplifications increase in distinctness and in scope. Owing to the diversity of the symbolical material it is difficult at first to perceive any kind of order at all. Nor should it be taken for granted that dream sequences are subject to any governing principle. But, as I say, the process of development proves on closer inspection to be cyclic or spiral. We might draw a parallel between such spiral courses and the processes of growth in plants; in fact the plant motif (tree, flower, etc.) frequently recurs in these dreams and fantasies and is also spontaneously drawn or painted.[9]

The images of the *Splendor Solis* go beyond astrology to represent the awareness of an interior dimension of human experience, depicted symbolically by the alembic[10] and its contents. This was anticipated by the last plate we viewed (I–11), which showed the alchemist in the bath, implying that he was the *prima materia*. This new capacity for containment, achieved through the transformations in the First Series, is symbolized by the alembic (melted shut at its neck[11]).

From a psychological standpoint, the alembic represents a conscious, purposeful, contained activity. As Jung noted, 'The bottle is an artificial human product and thus signifies the intellectual purposefulness . . . of the procedure . . .'[12] Therefore, we can imagine the symbols in the alembics as representing a consciously undertaken internal process of change. Analysis is an activity that, like alchemy, requires containment rather than acting out. In analysis, we also engage in conscious reflection upon the archetypal images and their corresponding patterns of behavior.

A golden king's crown encircles the neck of the alembic, denoting alchemy as a 'Kingly Art.' From a psychological point of view, the crown here is a symbol of totality and unity[13] and therefore an indication that the transformation is taking place under the auspices of the Self. The three-dimensionality of the alembic and its niche suggests that the process, while interior and symbolic, is substantial and real, bringing to mind Jung's term, the 'reality of the psyche.' The significance of the alembic is the recognition of, and reflection upon, man's capacity to transcend a life-as-fate through psychological and spiritual transformation.

We observe a progression in the colors of the alembics: the first three are black, the fourth is white, the fifth is black with stripes of bright white light, the sixth is black with an inner oval of muted golden light, and the seventh is black with stripes of white light and contains an oval of radiant golden light. This reminds us of the color sequences from black to white (to yellow) to red that became familiar in the first series. If we reflect on how the container itself changes through the series, we may wonder what this symbolism is meant to convey.

To the rational mind, the symbols within the alembics may at first make no sense either in themselves or in relation to the surrounding scene. However, the medieval mind was fascinated with images of the monstrous, just as nowadays are seen in many science fiction and horror films. Imaginary creatures not found in the natural world challenge our capacities for conceptual or ontological closure.[14] They can be frightening or disturbing yet exciting and stimulating at the same time. Irreconcilable to the rational mind, their contemplation moves one out of ordinary experience and into the larger world of poetry, allegory, image, paradox – and inner turmoil. These comments apply to this series as a whole: it is nearly impossible to present clinical material or process in words that can convey the quality of transformation that is going on. This difficulty brings to mind the belief of Albertus Magnus that chemical *analysis* had a physical basis but that *synthesis* required the influence of the soul.[15]

The relationship between the contents of the alembic and surrounding scene is not a direct correspondence but a dynamic interplay. The *contents* of the alembic sometimes complement but more often compensate the behavior patterns, in a way similar to Jung's view of dreams as compensatory to the dreamer's conscious attitude.[16] The dynamic moving us from one image to the next suggests how the unconscious often anticipates developments that cannot be foreseen through introspection or rational analysis. As Jung put it,

> the unconscious is not just a 'subconscious' appendage or the dustbin of consciousness, but is a largely autonomous psychic system for compensating the biases and aberrations of the conscious attitude. . . . it also extends beyond consciousness and, with its symbols, anticipates future conscious processes. It is therefore quite as much a 'supraconsciousness.'[17]

The commentary to follow is meant as an introduction to the imagery and symbolism of inner transformation, as expressed by the painter of the *Splendor Solis*, and the relevance of the play of opposites to the process of analysis. It is also an invitation to the viewer to discover fresh connections and meanings within this rich symbolism of the *mundus imaginalis*. The images, with their brilliant colors, evoke responses in the viewer's conscious and unconscious psyche that amplify their richness in new ways, each time they are encountered.

Plate II–1 The Heart of the Dragon

At the top of the picture, Saturn, or Hermes, rides in a chariot pulled by two prancing, fire-breathing dragons. He holds a sickle in his right hand and a caduceus in his left hand. The sickle refers to Hermes' Saturnine aspect as the Great Reaper, the representation of Death or Limitation. In life, Hermes' Saturnine aspect is associated with resignation and with futile, useless repetition and suffering.

At an archetypal level, death is always associated with rebirth,[18] and so we see a baby or small child[19] sitting in front of Saturn and surveying the scene below. This aspect of Hermes, the youthful Mercurius, represents the promise of renewal. Jung pointed out that 'Saturn is the father and origin of Mercurius, therefore the latter is called "Saturn's child".'[20]

It might at first seem puzzling that Saturn, associated with suffering and repetition, could be viewed as the origin of Mercurius, the youthful god, full of child-like imagination and possibilities, but psychologically what is most leaden and fixed is the most valuable source for the work. For example, a competent and productive woman came into analysis after a shocking dream just after her sixtieth birthday that she had committed a heinous crime and could no longer face living. In telling her story, she admitted to a dreadful boredom: 'I do what I do extremely well, but there is no life in it for me.' Upon starting analysis, she began to dream prodigiously, and in one dream she saw a woman lecturing from a podium, and to her surprise, babies in swaddling clothes flew out of her

PLATE II–1

mouth. The dream prompted her to drop her professionally correct style and to write with the feeling quality she can bring to her subject. New life had begun to flow.

Hermes' staff, the caduceus, with its male and female snakes, suggests a union of the opposites. According to myth, the caduceus gave Hermes the power to change into any form he desired or to touch others and put them into a dream state. (The tails of the dragons pulling the chariot are also intertwined like the two snakes of the caduceus.) The origins of this symbolism probably predate Greek culture, since they are identical to the more ancient Tantric symbolism found in Kundalini yoga: the central rod represents a subtle channel, *susumn*, which ascends along the spine to the brain and through the top of the skull; the left snake represents *ida*, the lunar channel, while the snake on the right represents *pingala*, the solar channel.[21] As Kundalini yoga was a method for embodied spiritual transformation,[22] the symbolism remained remarkably constant even though its origins were obscured. We can now see Figure 22, in which Sophia opens her body to reveal a caduceus, as a reference to the secret of transformation through the body. Jung used the symbolism of the caduceus to speak about psychotherapeutic process: 'But the right way to wholeness is made up, unfortunately, of fateful detours and wrong turnings. It is a *longissima via*, not straight but snakelike, a path that unites the opposites in the manner of the guiding caduceus, a path whose labyrinthine twists and turns are not lacking in terrors.'[23]

The dragons pulling the chariot represent the energies associated with Saturn. The symbolism of animals associated with gods goes back to ancient times. For example, in the picture-writing of the ancient Near East (by 1500 BCE in Mesopotamia), an animal 'determinant' specifying the character of a god or goddess was added beneath the anthropomorphic figure.[24] Psychologically, the animal-vehicles are the instinctual energies that are contained and transcended by the god or goddess, who in effect has put them under conscious control.[25] (A shamanic interpretation offers a different perspective: the animal-vehicle willingly carries the shaman to non-ordinary states of experience.) It is fitting that the Great Reaper is carried along by the primal energy of terrifying creatures not to be seen in this world.

The symbols on the chariot's wheels are the signs of Capricorn and Aquarius. Capricorn, the tenth sign of the Zodiac, is represented by a mountain goat with a fishtail, signifying the opposing human tendencies to fall into the waters of the unconscious or scale the heights of spiritual development. These alternatives present the possibility of returning to the Wheel of Existence (related to the wheel of the Zodiac), the endless round of birth and death, or departing from the cycle of suffering.[26] Aquarius, the eleventh sign, the Water Bearer, finds its duality in the life-giving and life-destroying potential of water.

As the most distant and dark planet, Saturn, the shadow of the Sun or *Sol niger*,[27] was associated with the cold, dark, wet winter months on earth, with the struggle for survival but also with the kind of wisdom that comes from endurance. Yet Capricorn begins at the Winter Solstice when the daylight hours begin to lengthen. Negative aspects of both Capricorn and Aquarius are related to impulsive actions and stubborn beliefs, also associated with the negative sides of the Trickster and the *senex*. In the words of a medieval verse in doggerel, the 'children' of Saturn were

. . . vicious, dry and old,
Envious, weary, wretched, cold

Deep eyes, hard skin, their beards are small.
They're lame, misshapen, depraved withal
Traitorous, brooding, greedy, pale,
They often find themselves in jail.
They grub the dirt, dig graves, plow land,
In foul and stinking clothes they stand.
Condemned to die or live in sorrow,
Swear and strain, or trouble borrow,
Always needy, never free,
It's Saturn's children there you see.[28]

The scenes around the alembic show us the Saturnine aspects of life. In the scene just beneath the alembic, an old man is drawing water from a well and pouring it into a barrel, from which the water flows out of a hole and onto the ground. This is a *senex* or old man, representing an attitude that simply repeats itself, an outworn pattern that has become counterproductive. To the left, we see two men bargaining. Beyond them a woman in blue, rosary in hand, supports herself with a stick. The river appears to end, rather than to flow on, at a point beyond the woman where a man gives alms to crippled beggars. In the upper left, a funeral procession approaches a gate next to a cathedral, beyond which graves are being dug, and to the right, a crowd watches a man being hanged on a hilltop gallows. A prisoner is beaten with a stick as he walks toward the hill, while below a man beats a plough horse. A woman feeds a pig, while a man catches another pig by the ear and rear leg, in order to butcher it. A dead pig lies in a trough behind the man. In the lower right, a man is tanning an animal hide.

As we saw earlier in Plate I–7 of the old king drowning, the idea of death is paramount. Men mourn death, yet they can also make a spectacle of it. Other scenes indicate that we make do with what we have and can't expect true happiness, that life is simply suffering with some kind of survival. So this series begins by bringing to conscious attention the shadow aspect of life itself – and the kind of deadly or deadened psychological state that can drive one to analysis.

The gray alembic, sealed at the top, rests on a green wreath, within a mottled red and golden niche with a red rectangle on its base. As we examine the contents of the alembic, we enter the paradoxical world of alchemy. The symbol in the alembic is a little monster, or dragon, with scales, wings, and large paws. It appears to be submitting to a naked boy, meaning that the spirit of youth is working on it. With one hand, he is pouring a dark substance with gold highlights into the mouth of the dragon. This is the *prima materia*, the raw ingredient necessary to begin the alchemical opus. Joseph Cambray[29] has suggested that this *prima materia* is the residue or sludge, the inert substance, left behind after the *sublimatio* in the final 'alembic' of the previous plate (I–11). In this context, the containment of the dark substance within the alembic (of the current plate) can be seen as representing a *conscious* awareness of the Saturnine aspect of life.

With his other hand the infant Mercurius holds a bellows to fan an invisible fire within the dragon. The green wreath at the base of the alembic emphasizes that the fire is within and not applied from without. In fact, the English word 'wreath' comes from the Indo-European root *wer*, which also is the root for *wind, winding*, and [turning] *inward*.[30] In his essay on 'The Spirit Mercurius,' Jung wrote that, 'The mercurial fire is found in the "center of the earth," or dragon's belly, in fluid form.'[31]

David Williams, in his study of the symbolic functions of the monster in medieval European thought and literature, has aptly summarized the dragon's essential symbolism:

> Its form combines all that nature has kept separate, and upon this separation humans have constructed their cognitive systems. This monster is simultaneously a being of water, earth, air, and fire, and thus the sign of the potency and plenitude of being itself. At the same time, the dragon is a powerfully negating sign, since by combining the four realms constituting the phenomenal universe, it denies the distinctions between them. Transgressing the borders between the fundamental principles of the world, the dragon erases their identity and destroys the efficacy of our cognitive schemes.[32]

Williams also reminds us that in Greek and Roman mythology the dragon was often associated with cities, enclosures, and boundaries (for examples, Cadmus and the founding of Thebes and the dragon Ladon who guarded the golden apples in the garden of Hesperides). In the medieval legend of St. George and the Dragon, a dragon has laid siege to a city and, full of rage and hunger, demands a daily human sacrifice. Thus the inhabitants of the city are protected by the city walls from the dragon (who wants to come inside), but they are unable to go safely out. Each day someone must pass across the wall of the city and be consumed by the dragon. Saint George arrives as the dragon is about to eat the king's daughter, and he subdues the dragon. The princess then leads the dragon into the city with her girdle.[33] In Figure 33, we see the episode (possibly a Christian addition to an originally pagan myth), in which St. George slays the dragon, as painted by Carpaccio in Venice between 1502 and 1507.

In many tales, the dragon, with its embittered attitude toward life and its unquenchable greed, has hoarded a great treasure in its cave or lair. In other tales, the dragon has abducted a fair maiden and imprisoned her in his cave. However, in Plate II–1, the dragon's large paws and head are suggestive of a young dragon, symbolizing a return to the beginning, to a natural, not-yet-developed or differentiated instinctual potential.

This return corresponds to a different quality of regressive work, when the container provided by the analytic situation permits the experience of less differentiated

FIGURE 33   St. George Slays the Dragon. 1502–1507, Carpaccio. (Studio Böhm, Venice)

states that are not to be confused with a return to a developmental experience of infancy. Furthermore, this 'regression' must be contained and attended by the patient's ego, which has been tempered by the analytic work up to this point (symbolized by the alembic). The challenge for the patient and the analyst will be to contain but not mortally wound the young dragon, with its threat of madness and its essential but unchanneled vitality.

Within the alembic, the naked boy subjects the *prima materia* to the two processes known as the *solutio* and the *calcinatio*, which are often said to be the beginning of the alchemical work. Since the mercurial fire is in fluid form, the young Mercurius is both dissolving the *prima materia* and heating it up at the same time. This is a psychological state that is almost impossible to describe in words, but we do often see the enlivening combination of healing water and divine fire depicted in dreams and in fantasies that invigorate and enliven us.

The configuration also suggests an initiation by fire and water, an archetypal state that frequently appears at points in analytical work, when a deeper level of the entire psyche is engaged. This may occur after a long period of therapy in which the patient has struggled with issues of adaptation and problem-solving. This may also happen at any point in the treatment when a return to something fundamental is required by the psyche.

The primal experience symbolized by fire and water appears in many cultures and eras. In Mozart's opera, *The Magic Flute*, Pamina and Tamino – a couple kept separate while longing to be united – must pass first through a cave containing fire and then through another cave containing a torrent of water. In this story, the hero and heroine undergo the ordeal together, with the help of the magic flute. In ancient China, fire and water were observed to be powerful natural forces, which could be destructive if uncontained but could support civilization if channeled properly. The Confucian scholar, Xunzi (310–219 BCE) wrote that both fire and water have vitality (*qi*). *Qi* was also closely associated with breath, clouds, and vapor. A later Chinese text (second century BCE) referred to lightning as the meeting of fire (*yang*) and water (*yin*).[34] It is this meeting of the opposites that releases tremendous and unpredictable energy. A more contemporaneous example of this energetic moment is Wassily Kandinsky's 1913 *Composition VI*,[35] originally entitled *Deluge*. Painted at a time of intense creativity, when Kandinsky was exploring the boundary between representational and 'abstract' art, i.e., art expressing something spiritual and ineffable,[36] the painting suggests a violent storm with flashes of lightning. One of the studies for *Composition VI*, shown in Figure 34, is less suggestive of the primordial darkness but also represents a chaotic and dynamic inner state.

The meeting of fire and water as lightning also appeared in a painting by one of Jung's patients,[37] and he commented that, 'Lightning signifies a sudden, unexpected, and overpowering change of psychic condition.'[38] In his essay 'The Visions of Zosimos,' Jung pointed out that,

> [B]eginning with the treatises of Democritus and Komarios, which are assigned to the first century A.D., alchemy, until well into the eighteenth century, was very largely concerned with the miraculous water, the *aqua divina* or *permanens*, which was extracted from the lapis, or prima materia, through the torment of the fire. The water was the *humidum radicale* (radical moisture), which stood for the *anima*

FIGURE 34 'Improvisation Sinflut.' Wassily Kandinsky. (Auch genannt 'Grosse Studie zu Komposition 6' (Sinflut), 1913, Inv. Nr. GMS 76, by permission of Stadtische Galerie im Lenbachhaus, Münich)

media natura or *anima mundi* imprisoned in matter, the soul of the stone or metal, also called the *anima aquina*. This anima was set free not only by means of the 'cooking,' [cf. Plate I–11] but also by the sword dividing the 'egg,' or by the *separatio*, or by dissolution into the four 'roots' or elements. The *separatio* was often represented as the dismemberment of a human body [cf. Plate I–10].[39]

Edward Edinger refers to Plate II–1 of the *Splendor Solis* in connection with the inflammation of desire. He points out that the opening to the unconscious in analysis exposes the ego to long-dormant desires, including the erotic.[40] He compares it to another alchemical image, 'The King in the Sweatbox.'[41] This is a graphic illustration of the autonomic response of breaking into a sweat while in a state of contained arousal, desire, or anxiety. The central image in the alembic symbolizes a resurgence of primitive libido – but libido that is contained and endured, not acted out. This can signal the beginning of a process that has the power to break through long-established, but meaningless and repetitive, patterns of behavior.

Patients who suffer from compulsion often feel burdened by apparently meaningless but seemingly necessary tasks that prevent the enjoyment of natural impulsiveness or play. Other people are bound unconsciously to a dutiful persona, but they obtain only the sterile reward of conventional approval. Frequently dreams show how these habitual patterns fail to serve the individual or cause needless suffering. By way of compensation, a dream may occasionally reveal a glimpse of the healing water or fire of new life, helping the individual to bear the pain and fear that accompany the breaking down of what is known and comfortingly familiar, if no longer helpful. For example, a woman in analysis dreamed that a star entered her room and then transformed into a grandmother figure. She offered the dreamer a shaman's drum with a pair of drumsticks from a child's drum, festooned by cloth streamers that were red and kinetic, like fire. The grandmother said to the dreamer, 'Do not be afraid. The fire is your fire.' This dream reassured the woman that several recent and startling inner experiences, accompanied by intense affects, had some meaning and were not simply the signs of a breakdown. It also illustrates the way in which the psyche reaches back to release libido in order to move toward a fuller expression of the personality.

The recognition of the Saturnine aspects of life – that creation and destruction are inseparably linked in Nature, that one's death must certainly follow one's birth[42] – can jar a person out of the complacency of conventional attitudes. This may create tremendous anxiety but also has the potential to awaken something within that searches for a deeper meaning and purpose in life. For example, a woman in her thirties, who had been quite deprived both materially and emotionally as a child, had built for herself a comfortable and cultured adult life. Then the following words came to her in a dream: 'You have a lifestyle but not a life.' She was so shocked by this statement, which she painfully recognized to be all too true, that she began to spend more time alone and to meditate. During her early morning meditation practice, she became so hot that she perspired even though the room was unheated. In her analytic work, the focus moved from the recitation of relationship difficulties and her wish to have a child to the meaning of her own life. With a feeling of necessity, she began to paint and to make clay images. The experience of matter being formed in ways that arose spontaneously during a creative process became a crucial aspect of her psychological transformation. The results, she knew, were not intended as works of art but rather were deeply meaningful expressions of her own being.

Jung himself worked with sand and stone, and he painted images that emerged from his dreams and from inner dialogues, which he called 'active imagination.'[43] In his essay, 'On the Nature of the Psyche,'[44] Jung recounts how he developed this method. He had the impression that patients in their waking state had access to the unconscious that they could not quite put into words. Beginning with an association or a dream image, he asked the patient to allow this image to develop by having a dialogue with a dream figure or using one of the expressive arts. He found that this often helped to reduce the pressure arising from the unconscious. Jung was careful not to prematurely interpret the productions:

> I had to try to give provisional interpretations, at least, so far as I was able, interspersing them with innumerable 'perhapses' and 'ifs' and 'buts' and never stepping beyond the bounds of the picture lying before me. I always took good care to let the interpretation of each image tail off into a question whose answer was left to the free fantasy-activity [imagination[45]] of the patient.[46]

Over time Jung was able to identify some basic themes that emerged: 'chaotic multiplicity and order; duality; the opposition of light and dark, upper and lower, right and left; the union of opposites in a third; the quaternity (square, cross); rotation (circle, sphere); and finally the centring process and a radial arrangement that usually followed some quaternary system.'[47] He found that these expressions of the inner world of the patient led to improved therapeutic results. We might add that there is something mysterious that happens in such a process: the qualities of the material world – the clay,

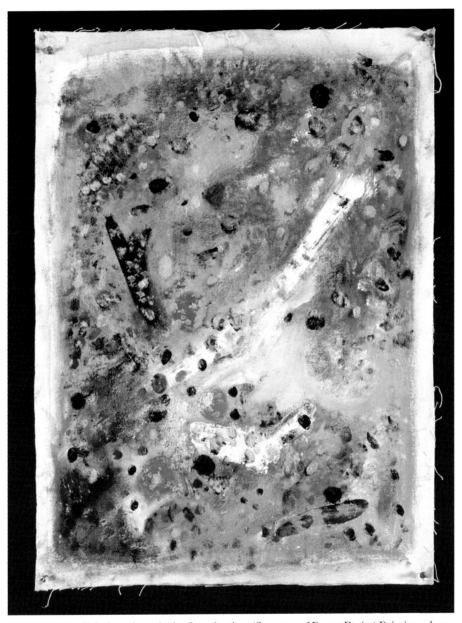

FIGURE 35 Paintings from Active Imagination. (Courtesy of Penny Etnier) Paintings done as active imagination may begin with an image, but the image may also emerge as directed by an inner, non-cognitive process while making the painting. The first painting suggests a shock or revelation that is full of energy, while in the second, some form and order are emerging. A. 'Big Bang.'

B. 'Dark Matter.'

stone, body movement, musical sounds – seem to stimulate and guide the inner world, so that there is a creative process that is bi-directional.

For Jung, soul and psyche were not abstractions but embodied realities. Like the alchemists, Jung saw the material world not only as something into which we project soul but also as a source of soul. Patients in Jungian analysis today may engage in 'active imagination,' in the form of dance or movement,[48] drama,[49] painting,[50] sculpture, music,[51] or writing. Analytic patients may work with a body-therapist or study yoga and meditative practices. Many participate in a 'sandplay'[52] process, either with their own analyst or as an adjunct. These approaches allow the developing psyche to express its depth and complexity in differentiated ways. Meanwhile, the analyst of course attends to the possibilities of a pathological or defensive use of working with other modalities, but often the other modalities act synergistically with the analytic work. An example of painting used as a form of active imagination can be seen in Figure 35. The first painting, entitled 'Big Bang,' shows the release of powerful but unformed energies, such as we might expect from the young dragon in Plate II–1. In the next painting, made several years later and entitled 'Dark Matter' forms appear but not yet in a way that is easy to conceptualize or digest, as we shall see in the next painting from the *Splendor Solis*.

Plate II–2 Three Birds

The symbolism here is very different from the previous plate. Instead of limitation and suffering, the value of conventional life has asserted itself. Human activities are under the sign of Jupiter, the king of the gods, whose chariot is drawn by a pair of peacocks.[53] Jupiter holds two arrows, while a soldier or knight kneels before him, making an offering. The symbols on the wheels are the two signs ruled by Jupiter, and they come just before and after the signs ruled by Saturn. Sagittarius, which precedes Capricorn, is the active side of Jupiter, whereas Pisces, which follows Aquarius, is the passive side.

Sagittarius is symbolized by the Centaur (often with a bow-and-arrow), a mythological creature half-horse, half-man, whose unrestrained passions but skill in hunting evoke the potential of mankind's animal nature. The positive potential of this combination was found in the centaur Chiron, the great healer of Greek myth, who was struck by a poison arrow and could neither die nor heal himself. He was at home in the darkness of suffering, and unlike other centaurs, Chiron was kind. He was an excellent hunter and tracker, and he used his connection with nature together with the skills he had learned from Apollo (including playing the lyre) to care for and teach young men. One of his pupils was Achilles. Another was the famous healer of Greek myth, Asklepios, to whom Chiron taught incantations and the healing powers of plants and snakes. Asklepios, whose staff had a snake twisted round it, slept in a sanctuary and attended to dreams as part of his healing ritual.

Pisces, represented by two fish swimming in opposite directions, is the last sign of the Zodiac and holds within it the potential to swim backwards into the cycle of life or forward to something new. Pisces is associated with intuition, sensitivity, insecurity, and adaptability. We can see the interplay of these characteristics in the scenes depicted in the lower part of the painting.

The scenes around the central alembic are very different from those in Plate II–1, which suggested poverty and deprivation. The human activities in this plate echo the theme that those with greater power are in a benevolent relationship to those who are beneath them, and that those who are below show proper deference to those in power. Everything appears to be orderly and harmonious and to assure that there is continuity to life. In the scene at the lower left, the pope crowns a king. In the center, there is a wide landing, where a man seated at a table is looking over a large book. There are two black trunks at his feet and on the table is a pair of scales, in perfect balance, along with two heaps of gold, some paper, and an ink-pot and quills. A paper at the end of the table may be a sample of calligraphy, suggesting that this man is a scribe. The heaps of gold represent the importance of the state or empire and the worldly power of the church during the Middle Ages. A man holding an illuminated manuscript (a self-portrait of the artist?) converses with another man. Behind them, a man or woman with a fur-lined black hat and fur-lined violet coat points toward a black bird, perhaps representing the *prima materia*, on the sleeve of a man's yellow robe. A man in blue looks on, while a man in white has removed his hat and is kneeling.

Beyond them, in a courtyard, we see two alchemists at work (Figure 36): a man in a gold robe and blue cap holds an alembic, while a workman dressed in blue fills a vessel with the distillate from a large retort or still, contained within a square oven. Here

PLATE II–2

FIGURE 36 The Alchemist and the 'Puffer.'
From Plate II–2. (Harley 3469, by permission
of the British Library)

again we see harmony, this time between the philosophical alchemist and the 'puffer,' the alchemist's assistant, whose frequent task was to use the bellows to raise the temperature of the fire, in the belief that transmutation would proceed more easily at higher temperatures. (We saw this in Plate I–11. The term also was used disparagingly to refer to naive alchemists who believed they could learn to make ordinary gold.[54])

In the courtyard with the alchemists are two hounds, one in an alert posture of open curiosity and anticipation, the other carefully sniffing the ground. The social historian Carlo Ginsburg has explored the metaphor of hunting and the reading of animal tracks:

> Man has been a hunter for thousands of years. In the course of countless chases he learned to reconstruct the shapes and movements of his invisible prey from tracks on the ground, broken branches, excrement, tufts of hair, entangled feathers, stagnating odors. He learned to sniff out, record, interpret, and classify such infinitesimal traces as trails of spittle. He learned how to execute complex mental operations with lightning speed, in the depth of a forest or in a prairie with its hidden dangers.[55]

Ginsburg relates the hunter's reconstruction from particular, apparently insignificant details to the methodology of human disciplines (medical diagnosis, paleontology, history). He has also shown that Sigmund Freud was influenced in his method of psychoanalysis by the writings of the nineteenth-century Italian physician, Giovanni Morelli, who propounded a method of examining the apparently insignificant details of a painting in order to detect forgeries.[56] This reminds us of the clinical significance of what may be a momentary affective reaction, an 'incidental' remark or gesture, or an odd detail in a dream, behind which may lie repressed emotions or dissociations between affect and content.

Beyond the alchemists, another man rides away on a horse. In the distance, in a verdant countryside, we see a horseman riding with his hounds, and still further, at the horizon, a castle surrounded by trees. The cooperation and liveliness between man and animal in the hunt contrasts with the adversarial relationships shown in the previous scene, where a man hit a plough horse with a stick and another man was subduing a pig.

The central alembic is very dark, nearly black. The rectangle on the base of the golden niche repeats the same blue-gray of the alembic of the preceding plate. At the upper corners of the niche, two naked people look across at one another. In the rear of the niche, behind the sealed neck of the flask, a naked child tries to lead a reluctant young horse.

In contrast to the harmony of the outer scenes, the compelling symbol within the alembic is three birds of different colors – black, white, and red. The black bird is on its back, its claws up to defend itself. The white and red birds are overpowering it. They are not only working together: they appear to be passing through one another, something not possible in the ordinary physical world. Now that the youthful Mercurius has used a bellows to heat the mercurial fire at the heart of the dragon, the interior process has become much more active and mysterious. The red and the white have become active against the black, which is, of course, the way the alchemical process of transformation moves, from black to white to red. The number three is a dynamic number, upsetting the balance of two-in-opposition, as shown by comparing the three birds in the alembic to a painting by Hilma af Klint, where two swans are in a moment of great dynamic, yet balanced, tension (Figure 37).

Psychologically, outer harmony may allow for a clearer experience of inner factors and conflicts, as well as a search for new information, as represented graphically by

FIGURE 37 Two Swans. Hilma af Klint (1915). (Series SUW group 9/Swan number 24, oil on canvas, by permission of the Hilma af Klint Foundation, Stockholm)

the explorations of the alchemists and the hounds. This is a phenomenon well-known to analysts: when the analysand has achieved a reasonable stability in outer life, the inner life is free to stir.

The differentiation of the initial chaos into distinct colors immediately produces inner conflict. The process is represented by birds, suggesting spiritual potential now that the *separatio* has begun. The transformation is active, but still in the unconscious, well-contained and not having any immediate effect on the outer scene. For the patient in analysis, an agitation may be felt bodily or appear in dreams in fragmentary form. It is not yet something that can be consciously understood or fully symbolized. However, it may easily lead to outer discord, given the propensity of the human psyche to translate inner conflict into action rather than to tolerate the inner tension.

The wish for worldly power and the fulfillment of desire is frequently seen at times when the patient's inner life begins to differentiate, as it is freed in part from its ingrained habits and awakens to new possibilities. This resonates with Freud's theory that dreams reflect the fulfillment of desires incompatible with outer harmony or convention. At such a time, the analyst has to work hard to shepherd the impulse to act, returning the energy back into analysis, sometimes with 'reductive' interpretations hopefully showing the patient the potential destructiveness of the wish to translate affect immediately into behavior, without the benefit of reflection. The analyst does this while also supporting the *creative* expression of the patient's inner conflict and the imaginal exploration of new possibilities. This is where the creative 'third,' as opposed to the duality of black and white, inner or outer, comes into play.

The analyst's constant task is to enable the insight that inner experience neither requires nor demands immediate action. In this regard, we might think back to Plate I–6, where the theater is the imaginal space, combining inspiration and expression. The intense creativity arising from inwardly channeled energies can be seen in letters written by Hermann Hesse in 1921 during his analysis with Jung (quoted in a recent biography of Jung):

> 'My psychoanalysis is causing me a lot of trouble, and Klingsor [the main character of a novella he was working on at the time] often feels old and incorrigible. The summer no longer belongs to him. I shall stay on here. I have bitten into fruit that must be finished . . . Analysis . . . has become for me a fire I must pass through but which hurts very much . . . Already duties and dangers have emerged which I can scarcely yet confront.' . . . [I]n another letter he [Hesse] compared the methods and techniques of the early monks with those of analysis, which 'can fundamentally have hardly any other objective than to create an internal space in which God's voice can be heard.'[57]

The role of contemplation is suggested by the left-hand side of this plate (shown in detail in Figure 38). There, above the ecclesiastical dignitaries crowded behind the king, rise two loggias in a palatial blue tower. In one is a woman, solitary and pensive; in the other, two men engage in conversation. We might speculate that the figures in the loggias represent the idea that both contemplation and dialogue can transcend the worldly and religious pomp shown in the scene below.

Plate II–3 A Three-Headed Bird

In contrast to the previous scene of ebullient wealth and power, both religious and worldly, we have here a battle scene under the sign of Mars. The god of war, with his shield and spear, rides in a chariot drawn by two galloping wolves. At the front of the chariot is a coiled serpent, representing a readiness to strike but also 'emotionality and the possession of a soul.'[58]

The wolf, a predator and scavenger, was recognized for its energy, ferocity, and capacity for survival. Yet wolves show qualities of loyalty and devotion to their young that

FIGURE 38 Loggias above the King's Coronation. From Plate II–2. (Harley 3469, by permission of the British Library)

PLATE II–3

are also valued by humans: the Roman myth of Romulus and Remus, who were suckled by a she-wolf, was well-known in medieval times. In alchemy, the wolf was particularly connected with Mars,[59] as the personification of the passions that both animate and consume. The wolf can also be an initiatory animal.[60] In Freud's case of the 'Wolf-man,' his patient's earliest childhood dream was of seven white wolves sitting in a tree outside of his bedroom window and staring at him. Carlo Ginsburg recently suggested that this was an initiatory dream, based on associations to Russian folk tales told to the 'Wolf-man' by his nurse.[61] We also find a wolf In Canto I of Dante's *Inferno*: when the poet tries to make a hasty retreat from his approach to the underworld, he encounters a wolf:

> Then, a grim she-wolf – whose leanness seemed to compress
>   All the world's cravings, that had made miserable
>
> Such multitudes; she put such heaviness
>   Into my spirit, I lost hope of the crest.
>   Like someone eager to win, who tested by loss
>
> Surrenders to gloom and weeps, so did that beast
>   Make me feel, as harrying toward me at a lope
>   She forced me back toward where the sun is lost.[62]

On the wheels of the chariot, we see the signs of the Zodiac ruled by Mars. Aries, or the Ram, the first sign of the Zodiac, symbolizes the original cause or thunderbolt rising from the primordial waters of Pisces, which ended the previous cycle. It is associated with thunder and spring, with the potential becoming actual.[63] In contrast, the eighth sign, Scorpio is associated with the fall season, death, and the hangman. In the Middle Ages it symbolized treachery and was used to refer to Jews,[64] who were made scapegoats because of their refusal to desert their faith for Christianity. The signs of Aries and Scorpio pair impulsiveness, energy, and passion with strong will, emotional control, and decisiveness. As a medieval verse puts it, the human 'children' of Mars are, 'All those who deal in fire and blood.'[65]

Within the foreground of the painting, knights are confronting peasants, who have only sticks to defend themselves. On the left, brigands are robbing peasants. In the distance, to the left, buildings are burning, and only beyond them do we see a river flowing off toward the horizon. On the right, knights lead away sheep and cattle stolen from the peasants. Still further in the distance, we see a forest and steep rocks that look almost like those seen in a Chinese landscape.

This scene shows that those with superior arms can brutalize and ruthlessly plunder the fruits of those who labor. In the foreground, on the right, a large group of armed peasants faces the knights on horses, so some of the people who are subjugated are no longer content to be victims but are rising up against their oppressors.

Clearly, these scenes show that in the movement from the second to the third plates the outer harmony has been lost. This development may at first appear to be solely regressive. However, analysis is a process that moves forward and backward and then forward again. In Jung's dream seminar in Zürich in 1930,[66] he asked his students to draw diagrams of the movement of the dream images of the patient whose dreams he was studying. Some students drew graphs of a linear type, but others drew circular or spiral forms to illustrate this movement. No one was able to make a definitive final assessment as to the pattern of movement of the unconscious, but the students learned that there was a psychic response to therapy that moves according to a principle of progression alternating with regression. This is why in subsequent years this type of therapy came to be called a 'process.'

Why, we may ask, is this movement of progression and regression not simply a repetitive, and frequently compulsive, activity, like the activities depicted in Plate II–1? Why should it not be controlled and eventually stopped by the intervention of consciousness? The answer is that the movement of progression and regression does not just repeat. When the movement of progression reaches its apex, it does not return to a baseline of regressive movement but only goes back far enough to recover its momentum for moving forward again (*reculer pour mieux sauter*). There is a design in Greek art (shown in Figure 39) which expresses this pattern of progression and regression. After each regression, the new forward movement emerges from a transforming center at the heart of the spiral.[67]

What makes this clinically important is that this process of returning each time to the unconscious center is a healthy reaction to analytic insight, and if this is not present, or if it is interrupted sporadically, we must look for some pathology to account for it. On the other hand, therapists must learn to separate themselves from the many urgent and repetitive demands of patients who would unconsciously try to drag the process down into a pathological dependency. If this aspect of the transference is not managed very carefully, both the patient and the analyst will become mired in the *prima materia*.

The alchemical illustrations of the *Splendor Solis* show both the danger of a movement which is apparently only forward and the danger of a complete regression. In this way, the study of alchemy may provide a new appreciation of the tensions and apparent contradictions in the analytic process, a process that of course fully includes the therapist as well as the patient. We see dramatic examples of the tension of forward movement in the psychosomatic ailments that may appear during treatment. Paracelsus reflected an ancient therapeutic wisdom when he said, 'The body is the dwelling place of the soul, and the one must open "access" to the other.'[68]

The niche containing the alembic is decorated with painted flowers and squares of green, red, black, and lapis-blue. The rectangle on the base is red. Within the blue-black alembic, a three-headed white bird, wings outstretched, its feet far apart, is apparently unable to move. This is a startling contrast to the three birds in the previous alembic. The colors black and red are no longer within the alembic; however, the alembic itself is now black, and the large rectangle at the base of the painting is red.

In the last image, the conflict was internal, the result of the patient's seeing the shadow side of life and facing the reality of death. The patient turns inward and asks

FIGURE 39 Wave Design in Greek Ornamental Art. (D. N. Sherwood, based on Fig. 1, J. L. Henderson, *Shadow and Self*, Wilmette, IL, Chiron, 1990)

from a mature perspective about the meaning of his or her life. While outwardly there may be harmony, inwardly there is confusion and turmoil when the primal chaos in the unconscious undergoes a new *separatio* or differentiation that produces an intense life-or-death *inner* conflict. How, we wonder, did the three birds transform into the white bird that now occupies the alembic? The differentiation shown by the three birds can only come into mental awareness when it has been synthesized into a form that can be consciously apprehended, and this new consciousness is represented by the three-headed white bird. The dilemma it symbolizes feels both painful and insoluble. Moreover, the person is probably emotionally and physically depleted from the inner struggle. The patient may ask, 'I haven't been *doing* anything. Why am I so exhausted?'

Each of the heads is turning in a different direction. The imbalance symbolized by three may be considered here in relation to the number four, symbolizing wholeness. According to Jung,

> In psychological language we should say that when the unconscious wholeness becomes manifest, i.e., leaves the unconscious and crosses over into the sphere of consciousness, one of the four remains behind, held fast by the *horror vacui* of the unconscious. There thus arises a triad. . . [and] a conflict ensues. . . . [The fourth] has remained in the realm of the dark mother, caught by the wolfish greed of the unconscious, which is unwilling to let anything escape from its magic circle save at the cost of a sacrifice.[69]

So the single body suggests both the possibility of wholeness, as a fourth, and the fourth that has remained in the body, i.e., remained in the unconscious.

Psychologically, the three-headed bird could represent a situation where the intellect feels ungrounded, dissociated, and thrown into an immobilizing state of confusion. Things that used to make sense just don't. However, a golden crown on each of the bird's heads shows that it is still very much the Kingly Art, in other words, in the service of the Self, straining toward wholeness.

We might guess that it would be a mistake to try to get the three heads to agree on one point of view. The temptation to find an intellectualized solution carries with it the danger of using clever ideas derived from insight to create a debate that obscures, rather than acknowledges, certain manifestations of the unconscious. We are not dealing with ideas alone but with their growth from the fertile earth of natural philosophy. The imagery of alchemy shows us a wholesome shift, where concepts – instead of controlling psychic activity – are themselves fed from that visionary source.

A more detailed examination of the white bird in the alembic reveals its long necks and long, curved bills. This bird is most likely an ibis,[70] a water bird associated with the moon in Egyptian mythology. When it sleeps, the ibis tucks its head under its wing, which Egyptians saw as the shape of a heart (also suggested by the body-shape of the three-headed bird), symbolizing wisdom. The ibis was associated with temple building because its long stride measured a cubit, and it was valued near humans because it eats harmful insects.[71] Thoth, the Egyptian god of wisdom, the originator of writing and measurement, was represented as an ibis (or a man with the head of an ibis). He carried other gods and goddesses on his wings to the underworld and fulfilled the role of messenger to the gods, represented in Greek mythology by Hermes. His cult center became known as Hermopolis during Classical times.[72]

The white bird's heads seem to be looking through the dark glass of the alembic into the surrounding scene with agitation or alarm. Yet the bird is confined in the alembic, straining at its inner surface, unable to fly up to escape or to enter the scene. Might this represent the unbearable inner state of witnessing the suffering that man inflicts on man, the way of the world, to feel one's own humanity profoundly and to know that one is powerless to change the needless suffering once and for all? This scene is also played out in the memory of the harm one has caused in life and the knowledge that, being human, one will harm others in the future. In James Joyce's *Portrait of the Artist as a Young Man*, Stephen Daedalus refers to Aristotle's statement in the *Poetics* that 'tragedy represents incidents that cause pity and terror,' and comments, 'Aristotle has not defined pity and terror. I have. I say ... Pity is the feeling which arrests the mind in the presence of whatsoever is grave and constant in human suffering and unites it with the human sufferer. Terror is the feeling which arrests the mind in the presence of whatsoever is grave and constant in human suffering and unites it with the secret cause.'[73]

It can feel impossible to go on living in such a brutal, unjust world: to quote T. S. Eliot:[74] 'Humankind cannot bear very much reality.' At this point, a person may fall into utter despair, regress back to intellectualization or frantic activity, decide to join in the spoils ('Living well is the best revenge'), or try to renounce the world and lead an ascetic life. Now, rather than death being the problem, life is. The body may feel dead inside – there is no red, no blood, no chthonic source of energy in this white bird. It is stuck, not in the *prima materia*, but in the terrible knowledge of clear sight. There is no turning away from the surrounding scene, and there is no way forward or backward. The analyst, as well as the patient, must bear this new darkness and not try to move out of it with suggestions for solutions or impatient withdrawal of interest.

What might it take to move ahead? A series of four paintings by a woman in analysis[75] show such a process (Figure 40), which arose only after many years of intense analytic work. At that time, she endured a long and agonizing period of facing the utter darkness and evil she had experienced in her life, as shown in the first two paintings (Figures 40 A and B), and mourning her lost innocence, expressed in the third painting (Figure 40 C). While only she alone could undergo this ordeal, apparently compelled by her psyche, she did it with the support of her spiritual practice, her creative expression in painting, her husband, and her analyst. She came to see herself more clearly, as if cleansed of poisons she had been forced to swallow at an early age, and she also saw with compassion the tragic limitations and misery of the people who had repeatedly brutalized her as a child. Just before she made the fourth painting (Figure 40 D), which she entitled 'Facing It,' she had a dream about a woman in red and also formed a significant friendship with a woman who shared both her integrity and her dedication to the work of transformation. We see that the painting alternates red and white, and the profile is facing toward the right. With the introduction of the red, the transformation included her body, and in fact, she began to care for her body in a more loving way. This image of 'Facing It' leads us to the next painting of the *Splendor Solis*.

Plate II–4 A Three-Headed Dragon

In contrast to the last picture, we have here a peaceful scene of cooperation in the diplomatic meeting of a beneficent king with his courtiers. Instead of actual fighting, we

FIGURE 40 'Facing It.' (Courtesy of the works of Jean Schellenberg, Ph.D.) A. 'Torture.' B. 'Freed.' C. 'Baby Girl.' D. 'Facing It.'

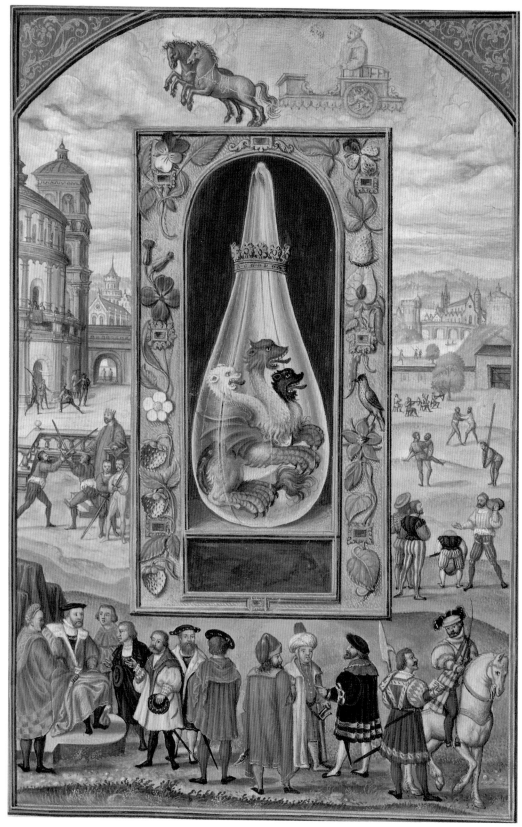

PLATE II–4

have sporting scenes. In the background to the right, we see a large, arched bridge spanning a river, perhaps symbolic of a new connection between two sides.

In the pale green and gold chariot at the top of the painting, we see Sol, or the personified solar deity, who rules this scene. He is dressed in golden garments and is carrying a text or tablet. The Sun was believed to govern the 'growth' of sulfur in the earth, and in the medieval mind it connected with the sulfurous fire blazing within the earth. The golden sun is just in front of Sol's face, which also appears to radiate light. He holds two prancing, silver-gray horses with golden reins and harnesses. The Zodiac symbol on the wheel is Leo, the lion, associated with expressiveness, nobility of character, and creativity.

If we think of Sol as a symbol of the Self, we might speculate that just when strife and confusion seemed to be about to overwhelm the psyche, the brightest light of consciousness has appeared. This may at first seem magical, but we might remind ourselves that the three-headed bird, for all its problems, did remain in the alembic. In other words, the process continued, was contained, and was not disrupted.

Applied to clinical work, this image would correspond to the situation where there was enough containment in the analytic process to make the pain and confusion bearable. We might think of this as analogous to the traveler who, having thoroughly lost his bearings in a blinding storm, reorients himself to the sun as the weather clears. At such times, mandala symbols may arise from dreams or active imagination, sometimes through painting or sculpture.[76] In Figure 41, we see such a painting, produced by a woman in analysis. The form of the painting emerged as she worked to express her inner circumstance. In it we see that four snake-like forms seem to orient toward the red central disk. Powerful libidinal forces, which had the potential to careen off in all directions, creating chaos, now orient to a newly emerging center. We might also think of this process as analogous to subduing the dragon rather than slaying it.

Returning to the plate, we see that this alembic, too, is contained within a niche framed with gold, but now the interior is a deep crimson. The frame is decorated with flowers, birds, berries, and seed pods. The rectangle on the base of the niche is darker, brownish crimson with flecks of blue. Within the alembic, rears a three-headed dragon, glaring with teeth bared and lashing tongues. The body of the dragon is yellow with blue-green spots, while its large brown feet, claws, tail, and wings give it the appearance of a young animal.

The three heads of this dragon are the colors of the alchemical process, but the central head is red, meaning that the final stage of the work, the *rubedo*, is about to come into view. Both the white and the black heads take slightly lower positions, with the black head at the rear looking almost like a shadow. Unlike the white bird in the previous alembic, all three heads of the dragon are now pointed in the same direction, towards the right, so the process is once again moving forward.

Why is the figure in the alembic a dragon? That miserable little dragon in the first picture, far from being bad, *is* the life process, and having been stirred up, thrown into conflict, then arrested, it is now afire to move ahead. This dragon is positive, like the Chinese dragon, in contrast to the Western view of dragons as so negative that heroes (like St. George) have to overcome them. Chinese dragons, like this dragon, represent the embodiment of the life force in Nature, which creates from the ground up and not from above by the bidding of celestial gods. If you compare this dragon with the three-headed bird, you can see how very much more grounded, flexible, and energetic this

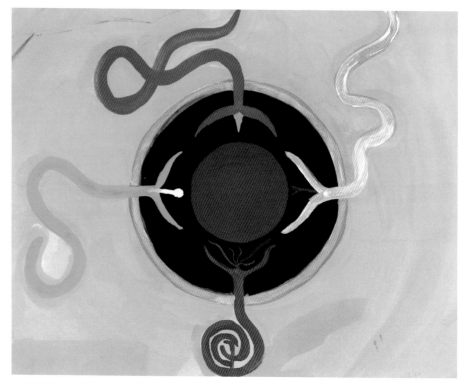

FIGURE 41 Mandala with Snakes. (Painting by a woman in analysis)

dragon is. Each of the dragon's heads is extremely alert, as if something of the chthonic, instinctual psyche has moved up and into the head. It also has wings, meaning that there is a spiritual potential in the libido coming from below. So, looking at the previous picture, we can now say that white bird was ethereal, perhaps an abstract notion of spiritual perfection horrified by the rapacious energies of the body.

Jung suggested that the triadic aspect of Mercurius, who was often represented as a three-headed snake, is the chthonic counterpart to the Christian Trinity.[77] In *Aurora Consurgens*, the lower Trinity is described as earth, which von Franz interprets as

> a psychic reality which has to do with the nature of matter. Matter thus acquires an importance of its own and is even raised to divine rank – in complete reversal of the medieval scholastic view, according to which matter, unless it is given form, has only potential reality. The text is, in effect, proclaiming a glorification of the feminine principle, of the body and matter. From this we can see what a shattering breakthrough of unconscious contents was needed before a man of the Middle Ages could hazard such a statement, . . . for these are the compensatory statements of the unconscious and not the conscious views of a man of that age.[78]

Jung also referred to the pre-Christian origins of this symbolism, pointing out that a three-headed Hermes (Mercury) was worshipped in Arcadia. In Plate I–4, we encountered the basilisk, which in some versions has three heads.

Hermes also had a quaternary nature, as three-in-one. An example of this symbolism that combines features of the three-headed bird of the previous plate with the dragon seen in this plate is found in the frontispiece for volume 13 of Jung's *Collected Works* (Figure 42). It comes from an illuminated alchemical manuscript (*c*.1600) and shows a dragon with three bird-like heads, labeled with the signs for the Moon, the Sun, and Mercury. Its serpent's tail winds up and around the three long necks. It has the wings of a peacock, the head of *mercurius senex* on its breast, and human legs with red, winged boots.

The Sun in Leo at the top of Plate II–4 represents the fullness of the *rubedo* as spiritual strength. In an analytical context, this plate might represent a stage where conflict and shadow no longer threaten to destroy the process itself. Still, the breadth of view required for the work at this time is well represented by the panorama afforded by the Sun in a clear sky. The analyst must maintain a broad view, supporting but not directing the particular course of the patient's newly emerging energies and developing talents.

For comment on the process in the alembic up to this point, we turn to Jung:

> Right at the beginning you meet the 'dragon' the chthonic spirit, the 'devil' or, as the alchemists called it, the 'blackness' the *nigredo*, and this encounter produces suffering. . . . until the *nigredo* disappears, when the 'dawn' (aurora) will be announced by the 'peacock's tail' (*cauda pavonis*) and a new day will break, the *leukosis* or *albedo*. But in this state of 'whiteness' one does not live in the true sense of the word, it is a sort of abstract ideal state. In order to make it come alive it must have 'blood,' it must have what the alchemists call the *rubedo*, the 'redness' of life. Only the total experience of being can transform this ideal state of the *albedo* into a fully human mode of existence.[79]

Plate II–5 The Peacock

At the top of the painting, a contented-looking Venus dressed in gold rides upon fluffy blue clouds in a golden chariot drawn by two birds. Cupid rides at the front of the chariot, poised to shoot an arrow toward what lies ahead. Venus holds a second arrow in her left hand, and in the right she holds a golden thread which loops around Cupid's waist. A heart, pierced by an arrow, appears in a wreath on the sun. The astrological signs ruled by Venus, shown on the red wheels, are Taurus, the Bull, associated with fecundity, and Libra, the Scales, symbolizing equilibrium. As the seventh sign, Libra is associated with initiation and the attainment of spiritual harmony. These signs of the Zodiac are associated with partnership, reliability, productivity, tactfulness, creativity, and aesthetic satisfactions. Venus and Amor (or Cupid), the goddess of love and her son, represent what we know from allegory as the Greek idea of love. Translated into Jung's psychological terminology, it is the Eros Principle, which is not just love or sexual attraction but true *relatedness*, the human capacity for communication of discriminated feeling. This is the essence of relationship, the opposite of narcissistic self-love.

The central alembic rests in a larger golden niche supported by ornate columns and with an interior of deep reddish-gold. The rectangle on the base of the niche is pink, representing the mixture of red and white that occurred symbolically in the last painting. The ceiling of the niche has a circular opening, as if to allow the pointed top of

FIGURE 42 Mercurius as a Three-Headed Dragon. Illuminated drawing from a German alchemical MS., *c.*1600. (Beinecke Rare Book and Manuscript Library, Yale University)

PLATE II-5

the glass alembic to rise through it, were it not for a pair of golden chains, fastened to the columns at each side and meeting above in the center of the dark opening. We can't know what this means, but it reminds us that 'spirit' refers to something lighter than air, so perhaps the previous reaction in the alembic has produced a volatile substance that could lift the alembic and its contents.

The iridescence seen in the *nigredo* at the moment in the process just before it changes into the *albedo* was likened to a peacock's tail. This stage represents the beginning of any real process of redemption of the shadow in a psychological sense. When people have fully accepted the shadow side of life, then they know that it enriches their experience of life and they feel ready to affirm a new and healthier attitude toward what was formerly *only* painful and problematic. This change may be seen in a painting by a woman in analysis. She named it 'Honey Girl,' suggesting an inner source of nourishment that could flow out into the world. The color red is in the flowered crown adorning her head, and her body is full of the possibilities in her unique life (as shown by the fan of paint samples); she is serene and joyous.

The people in the scene ruled over by Venus are in a pastoral setting, eating and drinking, reading poetry, playing music, making love, dancing, riding, swimming, and simply conversing with each other.[80] The symbols in the alembic and the surrounding scene are no longer in opposition. This really is a turning point, truly the dawn of a new day in the psyche, where outer activity and the inner state are in harmony, neither opposing nor compensating one another. As a result of the process, a partnership has been forged between an open relationship to contents emerging from the unconscious and a more conscious living of life. This is reflected in the harmonious interactions between men and women in the scenes surrounding the central alembic and may be contrasted with the charged meeting of the king and queen in Plate I–4, where each has yet to know the other, either in relationship or within.

The combination of trust and tactfulness are qualities in the therapist that are essential for the process, crucial prerequisites for the development of a working relationship and for carrying the transference. This is particularly important to patients whose capacity for warm and open relationship has been wounded early in development.

However, true relatedness is not reached in every analysis. A successful businessman entered analysis in midlife because he could not find a woman to marry, even though this is what he thought he most wanted. He had developed a good social persona and was eagerly sought by hostesses as the extra man for parties. He met many eligible women but no spark ignited. In one of his dreams, he saw a dinner table at which everyone was paired, but he sat alone at a single small table appended to the large one. When he talked about this with his analyst, he understood only intellectually his peculiar isolation in the midst of social opportunity. His lack of capacity for rapport also manifested in his relation to his analyst. At one point he said, 'I think I should find an analyst that would teach you how to help me.' Perhaps he was right. Although the analyst invited him to talk about his discomfort with the analyst and his ideas about how the analyst might do a better job, the patient was unwilling or unable to express his own feeling reactions.

So although many plausible causes for this stalemate came to light in his analysis, such as early childhood fixations of various kinds, the ice in his heart never melted. The impasse persisted, and the patient left analysis, disappointed in the pairing of analytic work, and still ruminating on what was unsatisfactory about others.

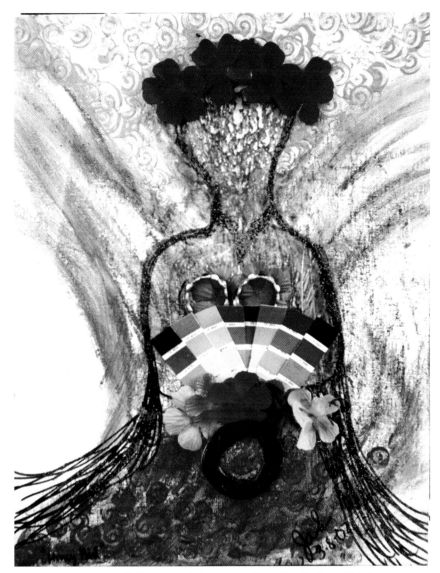

FIGURE 43 'Honey Girl.' (Courtesy of the works of Jean Schellenberg, Ph.D.)

Many other patients, fortunately, do find the ability to develop the eros function rising as a product of the analytical situation itself, overcoming either shyness or a tendency to dominate in social situations. This is not simply a matter of developing better social skills: as the obstacles and projections caused by personal complexes and cultural attitudes are diminished, *genuine relating* becomes possible. The Buddha's teachings are exemplary in this regard: he answered questions through stories that were skillfully *related* to the individual person and situation at hand.[81]

The need for eros may also arise in situations that are not obviously relationship problems. For example, one sees many people who suffer from performance anxiety, and their dreams may be very instructive about how to overcome this. In one case, a woman was a gifted pianist but was too frightened to perform very often. After a period of suicidal depression, she dreamed that she was part of a traveling circus where she found comfort and security from her fellow performers. Her situation emphasized the need for establishing a warm family feeling even among strangers. This can be a kind of cure for fear, mediated by Venus as she appears in this picture.

The peacock, with its unfurled tail, is a state often accompanied by joy and enthusiasm for the possibilities in life and relationship. However, it can be an inflating image, because it does not represent the new day itself: it only represents the *dawn* of the new day. Once again we have both the transformation and the anticipation of what is still to come.

Plate II–6 The Muse

The scene in this picture shows the arts, sciences, and crafts in many forms: in an urban setting we see musicians and singers who read from a score, scribes, scholars, masons, astronomers, vendors, merchants, and shoppers. At the base of the stone wall beneath the niche, a large rectangular stone bears the inscription 1582, the presumed date of these paintings.

This scene of city life and industry is a fitting representation of what we mean by the activities animated by the Logos Principle. These activities involve tangible creativity: philosophy, the arts, and the sciences all governed by rational planning and discrimination. Here the focus is not on interpersonal relating but upon an inner capacity for work, the performance of skilled tasks with joy and inspiration in a context ruled by a *principle* of discipline (often thought of as patriarchal in Western culture). Here, the fair exchange of goods and services is assured and anxiety about survival is not paramount. Now it is possible for devotion to work that is genuinely fulfilling.

In the sky above, two cocks pull the pale blue chariot of Hermes/Mercurius, who wears a blue robe tinged with gold and a golden *petasos*, his broad-rimmed traveler's cap. He holds a sickle in his left hand, and in his right, a shining golden caduceus. The brilliant caduceus contrasts with its backdrop of dark rays, presumably sunlight darkened as it is filtered through the clouds. This evokes the symbolism of fire and water from the beginning of the series, but in a less violent form. Here we are reminded of the natural sublimation of water into clouds through the heat of the sun and of the natural darkening of the sun's rays when the sky is cloudy. Thus light and dark are seen here as inextricably part of the natural order, not culturally imposed, black-and-white cognitive distinctions.

The signs of the Zodiac on the wheels of the chariot are those ruled by the planet Mercury: Gemini, the Twins, and Virgo, the late summer sign, represented by a virgin holding a shaft of wheat, or sometimes by a six-pointed star.[82] These signs combine the qualities of curiosity, change, practicality, and attention to quality – especially in relation to communication and vocation. In the sign of Gemini, the twins symbolize the pairs of opposites: here, one is black, the other is white; one is immortal, the other mortal. Psychologically, we might think of Gemini as a conscious acknowledgement that two opposing tendencies or attitudes are always co-existent in every situation. This contrasts with the tendency to identify with one side, and to consign the other tendency or attitude

PLATE II–6

to the unconscious, to be projected onto the other. If we think of the psyche as having lived through the events in this series up to this point, then we can see that it has already experienced the to-and-fro of the opposites, what Heraclitus called *enantiodromia*. After this, a person can no longer maintain the hope for one-sidedness as a stable reality.

We see in this plate that Hermes – the messenger of the gods who could travel down into the underworld, over the earth, and up into the heavens – is now above as the 'ruler' or archetypal representation of the human activity below. Hermes is certainly appropriate for the activities in the painting in the sense that he can represent the creative intuition necessary to inaugurate something new, as well as the ability to bring it to some kind of fulfillment. This idea is central to the concept of a hermeneutic.

At the beginning of this series (Plate II–1), Hermes appeared in his most undeveloped form as the infant Mercurius, as *prima materia*, paired with his fixed, Saturnine form. Now we see the caduceus of Hermes, with its pair of intertwined snakes, representing the unification of the opposites, but lifted from a chthonic level. The two snakes are less tightly wound together as they ascend the caduceus. Their heads are held away from the caduceus and face one another. Hermes, in turn, seems to contemplate the two snakes and their awareness of one another.

The infant Hermes in the initial plate reminds us of Michael Fordham's concept of the primal self, or the undifferentiated self *in potentia*:

> Jung's material shows many features of infantile states . . . and his interpretation of the *quaternio* as representing the *prima materia* in which the elements of the self are not integrated is one of them: it represents deintegration of the self resulting in identity of subject and object such as we find in infancy as well as in alchemy. . . It is the splitting processes on which Jung lays emphasis and he shows that they lead on to states of integration . . . My own experience of full analysis . . . depends upon reaching, through representations, the initial state of wholeness – the primary self – from which maturation can proceed.[83]

In contrast, the Hermes in this plate reminds us of the ultimate self[84] that arises later in the development that Jung called individuation. This ultimate self is conscious of the opposites.

Returning to the image, we see that the dark gray alembic is contained in a golden niche, but it casts a reddish brown shadow on the interior, as if there is for the first time something truly substantial in the alchemical vessel. The sides of the niche are painted with large flowers and leaves, and the rectangle at the base is again pink.

Within the alembic is a beautiful queen, who wears a diaphanous, pale blue robe fastened on her right shoulder, exposing her firm, round breasts framed between three golden necklaces and a gold belt. In her right hand, she carries a golden ball or fruit and in her left a scepter. These symbols appeared in the First Series: in Plate I–5, in which King Ahasueros hands Esther his scepter, and in Plate I–7, where the youthful king holds a scepter and a golden fruit or orb.

The queen stands upon a yellow substance or light, on which there appears the profile of a man's head. It might remind us of Plate I–10, where the golden head has been severed from the torso. The profile in the alembic, however, refers to an individual man whose mental faculties and skills are now at the service of the Feminine Principle of relatedness rather than an end-in-themselves or a source of power or dominance.

The yellow may also refer to a transitional stage of the alchemical process, the *citrinatis* or yellowing, found between the *albedo* and the *rubedo*. (This stage was not emphasized by alchemists in the fifteenth and sixteenth centuries.[85]) The author of *Aurora Consurgens* (thirteenth century) made an association between this yellow–red

FIGURE 44 Projection Of The Tincture From The Heart Of The King Onto The Base Metals. (MS Ferguson 208, f. 73ʳ. By permission of the Department of Special Collections, Glasgow University Library)

145

transition and the dawn: 'The dawn [aurora] is midway between night and day, shining with twofold hues, namely, red and yellow . . .'[86] Marie-Louise von Franz commented:

> Psychologically this 'aurora' symbol denotes a state in which there is a growing awareness of the luminosity of the unconscious. It is not a concentrated light like the sun, but rather a diffused glow on the horizon, i.e., on the threshold of consciousness. The anima is this 'feminine' light of the unconscious bringing illumination, gnosis, or the realization of the self, whose emissary she is.[87]

The queen in the alembic is surrounded by an aura composed of an inner yellow band and an outer blue band. The color blue was sometimes used to represent the quintessence, a fifth stage that followed the *rubedo*. Paracelsus introduced the symbolism of a sapphire from the Cabala in connection with the blue quintessence. The process at this stage, called 'projection,' used the tincture or philosopher's stone to convert the spirits of ordinary metals into sophic gold.[88] In Figure 44, we see a seventeenth-century image of the tincture at the heart of the king projecting into the metals and transforming them. Psychologically, we may think of this as the beneficial effect that someone who is truly developed and compassionate may have on others.

The beautiful queen in the alembic corresponds psychologically to the Creative Feminine. In particular, she may personify the 'muse' in creative men, which can feel to them like a very personal relationship. She can also serve as a symbol for anyone who is in the process of creating something of lasting value; the work itself is felt to come from a feminine source infused with eros. The life force is manifest within the individual, who lives in a loving relationship to feminine qualities of grace, patience, wisdom, and creativity.

When these themes emerge in analysis, the patient may search for a more suitable vocation or feel the need of a change from one form of creative activity to another. The scene in this plate shows people in an urban setting, performing practical and aesthetically expressive tasks, interdependent upon one another in their daily lives, reminding us that a person's choice of profession may appear to be an individual choice but it is also culturally conditioned. It might be said that culture consists of the historical union of many such forms of Logos which express the Eros of the age, thus whole periods are characterized by a certain spirit or Zeitgeist.

Plate II–7 The New Sun as Inner Light

The figure in the alembic of the seventh and final symbolic painting of the Second Series is a youthful king in gold and red, symbolizing the end of the process that has passed through the stages of black to white to yellow to red. The young king's muscular torso is apparent through his thin garment, and his strong arms and legs are bare. In his right hand, he holds a golden scepter, perhaps with a five-pointed star at its top. In his left hand he holds a golden orb. He is surrounded by a golden aura, radiating light.

The rectangular niche behind the alembic is deep red-brown speckled with gold, flanked by golden columns decorated with red and blue flowers balanced with regard to upper/lower and left/right. In the center of each column, there is a decorative mandala formed by a rectangular blue or red jewel, with a half-circle along each edge and contained within a larger circle with pearls at the cardinal points. A bird stands on the

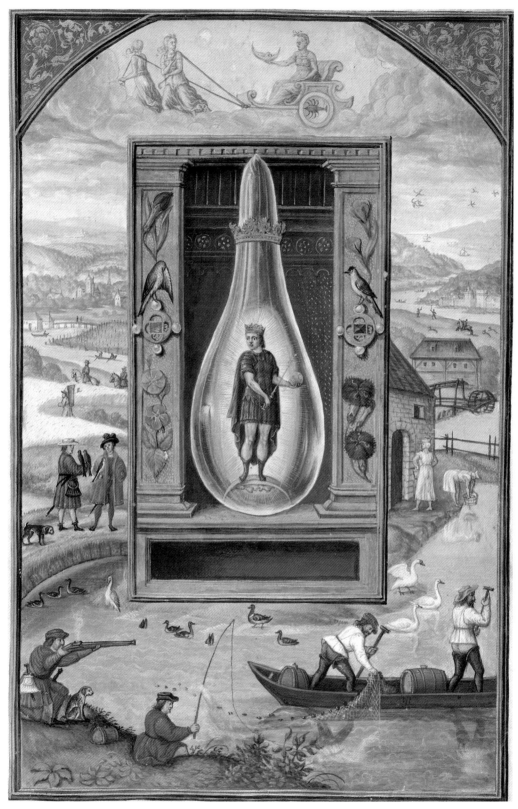

PLATE II–7

upper pearl on each mandala: on the right, a bird looks toward the bird on the opposite side, which is hiding its eyes behind an upraised wing. The large rectangle on the base of the niche is red.

We might be tempted to say that at last the Masculine Principle is triumphant, as expressed by the wonderful sun-like radiance. But the picture tells us something different. There is no sun in evidence; the planetary ruler is the moon. This young king is under the sign of the moon, and he is standing on the convex surface of a golden crescent moon. So he is not a symbol of the Masculine only but rather a symbol of the Masculine tempered by the Feminine.

While the planet ruler above is clearly Luna, the moon, the interpenetration of opposites is at work here, too: both she and her chariot are a radiant gold (the sun's color), not the silver usually associated with the moon. Behind her are pale violet and gold-tinged clouds. Her chariot is drawn by two maidens, dressed in flowing, pale orange robes. The maidens suggest that, at the culmination of the process, the instincts (represented by the animals pulling the chariots in the previous images) have become humanized.[89] The maidens look to the left and right, while Luna's gaze is focused on a golden upturned crescent moon, which she holds in her right hand.

The moon rules over the astrological sign of Cancer, or the crab, seen in a contrasting silvery-gray color on the golden wheel of the chariot. Cancer is associated with the Home, with nurturing and support; according to Orphic belief, it represents the threshold for incarnation of the soul.[90] The culmination of the work contains the two poles of the opposites, sun and moon, Sol and Luna. The kingly presence in the alembic, represented in human form, expresses the fullness of the *rubedo*, the red color that represents the end of the process. In order to appreciate the significance of what has been accomplished, the reader might want to think back once again to Plate I–4 and the initial meeting of the King and the Queen, to compare those figures with the youthful King and youthful Queen in the final two alembics of this series.

The symbols in this plate may be viewed as an attempt to solve a paradox posed at the beginning of the First Treatise:

> The Philosopher's Stone is produced by means of the Greening and Growing Nature . . . our Art but adapts and prepares the Matter as becomes Nature . . . and provides also, with premeditated Wisdom, a suitable vessel. . . .
>
> For Art does not undertake to produce Gold and Silver anew, as it cannot endow matter with its first origin . . . Art goes quite another way to work and with different intention from Nature . . .
>
> For that reason can Art produce extraordinary things out of the aforesaid natural beginnings such as Nature of herself would never be able to create . . .
>
> Here Nature serves Art with Matter, and Art serves Nature with suitable Instruments . . . and although the before mentioned Stone can only be brought to its proper form by Art, yet the form is from Nature. For the form of every thing be it living, growing, or metallic, comes into existence by virtue of the interior force in matter – except the human soul.[91]

In other words, higher consciousness is from Nature and yet is something which Nature alone could not create. Edward Edinger refers to this passage from the *Splendor Solis* and comments,

This is a profound idea. In one sense the opus is against Nature, but in another sense the alchemist is helping her to do what she cannot do for herself. This surely refers to the evolution of consciousness. Although the urge to consciousness exists with nature – within the unconscious psyche – an ego is needed to realize fully that natural urge. It is required that the individual cooperate deliberately in the task of creating consciousness.[92]

A passage from the work of Erich Neumann could apply to the stage of the work symbolized in this final plate of the series: 'What in the primitive stage was realized as an unconscious bond, now returns on a higher level as the possibility of a symbolic realization of life's meaning when lived out to its fullest extent.' He adds this interesting comment, 'Now neither the extravert's outward vision of the world nor the introvert's inner vision remains in force but a third type of vision remains . . .'[93]

This is true on an empirical level. The initiatory events seen in the normal psychological development of young people move from a primal source through experiences associated with the Great Mother, the Great Father, and the Group as the young person arrives at a first awareness of his or her own unique identity. This discovery may become manifest with the appearance of a Guardian Spirit,[94] for example during what the American Indians call a 'vision quest.' In this ceremony, the young person must stay alone in nature without food or water for several days, praying for the strength to endure the suffering of body and psyche. Such an initiation serves to reorganize the youth's patterns of dependency on parents and relatives and to temper youthful inflation. The youth may have a vision, which is told following the vision quest in the sacred space of the sweatlodge.[95] This introduces that third type of vision, of which Neumann speaks, but on the humble level of youthful self-discovery.

The symbolism of a full experience of life can also be found in the imagery of Kundalini Yoga (Figure 45).[95] A vertical movement of the Kundalini serpent, arising from its root chakra, passes through seven areas of psychophysical energy from the perineum up to the crown of the head, and then winds down again to its source. The seven-fold scheme reveals a similarity between the visualizations of Kundalini Yoga and the developmental sequences of the alchemical opus that we have just observed, which also moves up and down a psycho-spiritual ladder. For people who are not ready, alchemy or yoga may be pure poison, a sort of *ignis fatuus*, or illusion. They are not in themselves psychological methods, and their images should not be used uncritically as *techniques* or offered as premature amplifications in analytical psychology. However, for people already engaged in deep psychological work, there is much to learn from such imagery.

Returning to the images in Plate II–7, we might ask about the pattern of behavior associated with the symbolic expression of the Masculine tempered by the Feminine. We are shown images of hunting, shooting, fishing, and falconry, and of women washing.[97] A boat moves down a river toward the sea, using the energy of the wind in its sails. And the wheel of the mill turns, harnessing the energy of the flowing river. We see many birds in the sky, as well as ducks and swans below. If we look again at the first picture of this series, we might now think of it as 'Nature Exploited.' This final picture is about mankind using Nature while also honoring Nature, so that none of the human activities are really against Nature. Humans recognize themselves as part of nature and try to live in balance with it. This is perhaps what the Chinese call living in the *tao*, suggesting the

FIGURE 45 Chakras. A. The Psychic (Kundalini) Centers. Copper with gold wash, South India, *c.* eighteenth century (Private Collection. From A. Mookerjee, *Kundalini: The Arousal of the Inner Energy*, Thames & Hudson Ltd., London, 1982)

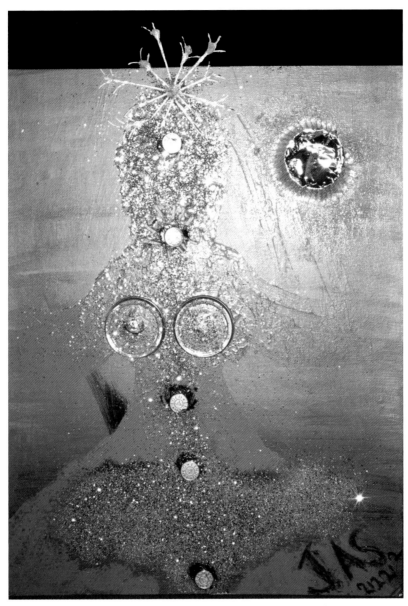

B. 'Opening the Chakras.' (Courtesy of the works of Jean Schellenberg, Ph.D.)

possibility of living more harmoniously with nature and human nature. The dreams of modern people in analysis today often address the dilemma of how to honor nature and protect the environment from the brutal exploitation in a technological age.[98] This is an example of a growing movement, coming from the unconscious, to reverse or moderate a cultural trend.

The process in the Second Series

Any attempt at summary must be made with the proviso that we are talking about a process that by its very nature cannot be conveyed through words but only through experience.

We began with an undeveloped psychological state characterized by lack of awareness and repetitive but futile patterns of perception and behavior, a state consistent with unconscious complexes or ego adaptations that have become counter-productive.

In order to break out of a pattern of compulsive repetition, the shadow aspects of these behaviors and mental tendencies must be experienced consciously. This stimulates a resurgence of previously dormant or repressed instinctual energies, represented by the dragon (Plate II–1). The dream of a woman in analysis vividly represents this stage:

> I enter a cave near the ocean and see my mother, who is sitting on a sofa covered with gelatin. Marine micro-organisms have multiplied in the gel, and I start to remove it from her. Suddenly I am standing by a tide pool that has no water. I can see what it is – that it sucks people up. There is a creature consisting of many moving internal organs, a brain, and big sharp teeth (incisors here and there). It is in constant motion. I say, 'It's like the Charybdis.'

The mother sitting on the sofa is an image of the feminine persona that the dreamer developed through identification with her mother. The gelatin on the mother's skin suggests that the persona is being eroded. The marine organisms evoke the capacity of living cells to organize themselves in relationship to the environment and often to one another, as seen in single-celled animals that aggregate into colonies that act as a single large organism. As the dreamer is beginning to remove the gel from her mother, she realizes that she is next to a tide pool with a strange creature inside: the transformation cannot be accomplished like a spa treatment, only skin deep. In the tide pool is a *teratoma*, the monster that represents the undeveloped aspects of the dreamer, namely her aggression and incisiveness, as represented by the teeth, and her intellectual capacities, as represented by the brain. Of course, her fear is that she could become this primitive creature, sucked into the unconscious and into madness.

Emergence of the shadow into consciousness eventually produces a rebellion against the well-ordered, hierarchical, or one-sided psychological adaptation (cf. activities shown in Plate II–2). The same woman had a dream showing that the shadow had broken through her persona, as predicted by the earlier dream:

> I am in bed, at night or before dawn. There is no sunlight. The shades are down. I get up and go to the bathroom mirror. I paint my left eyelid gray with kohl – not just the eyelid but all the way to the brow. I notice that the whole left side of my face is gray with the shadow. I try to wash my face with a washcloth, but it doesn't work. Then I decide that I don't care if my husband sees it and starts asking questions.

The husband in the dream is not only her husband as an individual, but values and attitudes that the dreamer had shared with her husband and which she had begun to question.

The analysand's psyche may try to resolve these internal conflicts with reversion to the old order, with the former modes of ego-functioning and dominant complexes reasserting themselves (for example, the violent activities shown at the bottom of Plate II–3 or as intellectualizing defenses against somatic activation). The patient and therapist may have to face a fear of madness or paralyzing confusion (as shown by the three-headed white bird in the alembic in Plate II–3), one that is very different in experiential quality from the initial resistance to an encounter with the unconscious.

A dream from the same woman in analysis illustrates the fear of chaos that comes when the old order begins to be overturned:

> It is neither day nor night. My front yard is twice its usual size and is full of plants. I go outside and see two vines in bloom, next to each other but not close. I say, 'Maybe I should put in an arch and let them connect.' A middle-aged man, who speaks and looks as if he were from one or two centuries ago, comes by and stoops to look at the plants and makes comments. The scene changes, and I am a spectator. We are in Marie Antoinette's time, and a young woman is running as if she were being chased. A young man grabs her and lifts her into the stagecoach before a mob gets to her. Here and there a man on horseback rides through the city and outside the walls. He clutches a bag with gold coins and cries, 'Has anyone seen the king? Has anyone seen the queen? Where is the king? Where is the queen?' There is a mob chasing a little tan and white pig. The narrator's voice says: 'There were times when the people were so hungry that they would dismember and eat a live animal.' Although I don't see it, I know the mob has pulled a piglet apart, and I feel repulsed.

The dream begins with the dreamer in a liminal state: 'neither night nor day.' She has been experiencing a sense of growth and expansion, as represented by the size of her front yard and the plants. She considers whether to create an archway to allow two separate blooming vines to grow together. The archway would give a form for the growth and could further represent a portal into a new way of being. But the opposites are not united so easily: a man from an earlier era arrives, and there is an abrupt shift to a dangerous and frightening scene – that of the French revolution and the frenzy of a mob.

The dreamer's role is as a spectator, observing but not acting. Her dream ego is not identified with any of the characters. Just as the white bird in the alembic has three heads, we see that there are conflicting tendencies in the dreamer. One tendency is a wish to be rescued by a strange man. The hunger of the mob represents instincts that have been deprived of expression and now threaten the dreamer's ego with loss of control; the tearing apart of the pig also suggests a Dionysian frenzy. The man with the gold coins (ordinary, not sophic gold) represents her impulse to conserve what she has by a return to the old ruling order.

Although the process of analysis is fraught with peril at each stage, the work may be particularly precarious at this point. This is true especially if there has been an unconscious collusion between the therapist and the patient to avoid the long, hard, and painful labor of dealing with regressive material, including the aggressive or erotic aspects of shadow material coming into the transference.

Failure at this stage may take the form of mental instability (including the eruption of a negative transference of psychotic proportions), a severe depression, a regressive reassertion of the old way of functioning, a 'flight into health,' or a premature idealized solution (and accompanying inflation) that cannot be truly carried over into life and sustained. In the case of the latter, which is a frequent problem in analytical work, it is crucial that the patient be questioned and confronted about behavior patterns that are not in keeping with the patient's overly optimistic sense that the work is complete. It is important to stress that intimations of future developments are seen all along the way but that this does not mean that they have been truly experienced or integrated.

If the patient and analyst are able to continue the work – perhaps having almost to start over and then over again until the process can move ahead – the old one-sided adaptation may give way to new functioning, one that acknowledges a cooperative rather than hierarchical organization within the psyche.

One way to think of this stage of analysis involves Jung's concept of a complex:[99] one pole of a complex may have dominated conscious awareness, with the other (shadow) pole being acted out unconsciously or projected. Awareness of the repressed pole of the complex, while restraining the impulse toward action, will at first cause upheaval and confusion, as well as emotional pain. But if one is able to bear with the work, a more harmonious and richer way of functioning will result. This would be represented by the activities in Plate II–4, where there is a cooperative and congenial relationship between those in power and those without power. The king listens to counselors and discusses things with them, rather than expecting their obeisance or using his forces to usurp their resources or suppress their ideas. We might think of the ego and the Self as coming into a different relationship at this point.

This in turn may stimulate an up-swelling of eros, as new ways of relating are manifested internally and with other people (Plate II–5). We may see this in therapy, where the work becomes a more fully cooperative enterprise once the parental complexes and their attendant transferences are substantially resolved. Furthermore, the eros in the transference takes a more mature and related form, creating a symbolic friendship in the working alliance between analyst and patient.

The unconscious may then become available (libido freed from transference within the analysis and in life) as a source for creative inspiration in its own right (Plate II–6). A later dream from the same woman in analysis illustrates this stage:

> I am walking down the driveway, dressed in a blue and purple skirt and tunic. It is dark. I see privets on either side of the driveway, and all of the sudden I can see some of their yellow-green leaves. They are the only thing that is visible. I see glimpses of a three-quarter moon and this repeats two or three times. It felt good and mysterious in a religious way.

Recalling our discussion of Plate II–6, we can see that the dreamer is now glimpsing the light of the unconscious, as represented by the moonlight. The yellow-green leaves recall the gold highlights on leaves in many of the *Splendor Solis* images. The leaves are visible in the darkness, suggesting the *lumen naturae*. The plants in this dream are privets, which are often used for hedges. Here we see that the plants are not growing in natural profusion but are adapted for a human purpose. Hedges create a visual boundary, providing privacy, which is suggested by the word 'privet,' probably related to 'privat,' the Middle English form of 'private.' The dreamer had no idea why the moon was three-quarters full, and she did not know what this might mean in astrology. In our discussion of Plate II–3, we referred to the point at which the conscious mind has glimpsed the potential for wholeness. Here this is represented by the implied image or potential of the full moon, the implication that $4/4 = 1$ will follow $3/4$ as a natural process, just as the full moon follows the three-quarters moon.

At this stage, the person is no longer stuck in the worn-out, repetitive activities or behavior patterns that were shown in the first plate of this series, ever wishing in the transference that the analyst could solve the problems as viewed through the complexes. When the creative energies of the unconscious are freed from the personal complexes, ideally they might also be freed from any neurotically based need either to uphold or to rebel against the dominant cultural attitude.

In the final plate, the young king holds a scepter, symbolizing impersonal authority rather than a power complex.[100] This represents a state of being where the individual can mediate – but is also subject to – the greater authority of the Self and its organizing function. The king himself is subject to what the scepter represents; he does not claim that his person is the same as the authority. In the first plate of the series, Hermes – conceived as the god who understands and embodies the alchemical work – holds his scepter, the caduceus, symbolizing the dynamic interplay of the opposites, the total potential of the unconscious or collective unconscious. In the final plate, the golden scepter is held by an embodied human, albeit idealized.

A different depiction of a felt and embodied relationship to the greater wisdom of the Self is shown in Figure 46, painted by a woman in analysis. For an extended period, this woman struggled with something she could not get hold of, no matter what work she did in her analysis or in her spiritual practice. She often found some relief from creative expression but she was blocked there as well, and she was continually aware of painful, blocked energies at a physical level. She finally realized she had to bear the feelings of great inner tension and vulnerability without knowing the outcome or meaning of what she endured. After nearly two years, she made this painting, without knowing consciously what it meant or why it had to take the form it did.

A decade later, when she could view the painting more objectively, she called it, 'The Birth of a Symbol.' The human figure was her inner self, straddling some kind of primordial plant-like growth. She felt open to a primitive, unknowable influence or process that entered her body from below, passed through a channel that divided and then came together again below the inner sun at her heart chakra, then moved upward through her black-and-white striped head to become the golden growth or fountain emerging from her crown. She felt that the red marks on her hands were not so much wounds as openings to life or spirit. There is also a movement from left to right, from the three fish entering at the left to the black-and-red beaded spiral moving out of the circle at the right.

Once the woman made this painting symbolizing her inner process, she had no need to paint again for many years: she felt it represented the state in which she continued to live and, once expressed, the tension resolved and it felt like being at home. The Self, as it is represented in this painting, includes a center, the microcosm, and the macrocosm. Its wisdom is connected with Nature, even as the woman becomes more uniquely herself.

The cooperative harmony with the natural world represented in the final plate illustrates a form of human living that goes beyond the pattern of any one culture. Likewise, Jungian psychology is like a quest undertaken with religious, or rather

FIGURE 46 Birth of a Symbol. (Painting by a woman in analysis)

spiritual, feeling for the mystery to be unveiled in discovering our way to the source. While we should not, of course, minimize the importance of studying particular cultural patterns for their formative influence, the Jungian method corrects the all-too-common assumption that essential change comes only from within the cultural pattern itself.

In Jungian analysis, the patient produces the material while the analyst uses his or her interpretive skill as a participant-observer of the patient's process of self-healing. This has been contrasted to the practice of shamans, who take the active role of healer, while the patient takes an essentially passive role in the healing rituals.[101] However, we must remind ourselves that shamans work within a cultural context, a cosmology, that is shared by the patient, so that the patient's psyche is actively participating in the healing even though that may not be apparent to an outside observer. To many contemporary people, the shaman personifies the capacity to contact the healing energies of the Other World (or psychologically, the unconscious) and so we sometimes speak of 'the archetype of the shaman.'[102]

In Jungian analysis, the patient participates in the interpretation and attribution of meaning to the material he or she brings to analysis. This contrasts with the practice in classical Freudian psychoanalysis, where the analyst is considered to be a neutral, objective observer of the patient's transference neurosis and makes interpretations of the patient's material based on the theory constructed by Freud, in other words, within an already-existing framework. In the latter case, should the patient disagree with the analyst's interpretation, this is considered to be resistance on the patient's part and an indication for further interpretation of the defenses involved.

Although Jung's psychology is often called 'archetypal,' our work is also profoundly personal. Our clinical methods should not be confused with the mere intellectual analysis of mythological or cultural forms to amplify images or process in the patients' dreams. During a clinical hour, the analyst listens to the patient, interacts, and also attends to internal thoughts, emotions, and images, as well as bodily sensations that may provide information about the 'field' or the patient's unconscious state.[103] One of the challenges of analytic work is that it can call upon everything the analyst knows, and it will certainly confront him with what he doesn't know. Jung wrote:

> For since the analytical work must inevitably lead sooner or later to a fundamental discussion between 'I' and 'You' and 'You' and 'I' on a plane stripped of all human pretenses, it is very likely, indeed it is almost certain, that not only the patient but the doctor as well will find the situation 'getting under his skin.' Nobody can meddle with fire or poison without being affected in some vulnerable spot; for the true physician does not stand outside his work but is always in the thick of it.[104]

The parallels between Jungian analysis and alchemy highlight the ways in which the Jungian approach has a broader perspective than contemporary relational, interpersonal, or developmental views of analysis and yet also incorporates various aspects of these approaches. In addition to considering the quality of emotional experience within the relationship between analyst and patient, a Jungian standpoint includes the interior worlds of the patient and of the analyst, although the latter is shared only where it is judged to be therapeutically helpful. In Jungian analysis, influences beyond personal history are considered, including the dispositional, archetypal, and cultural influences on an individual's psychology. The work is not only analysis, looking back, but also synthesis, moving forward.

In the end, we must remind ourselves that however well we may analyze our patients for personality disorders or help them separate from the ill effects of disturbing parental influences in childhood, there remains the unknown source of psychic conditioning in the region of the primal Self to be tapped wherever we can find it. The process illustrated in this series is never completed once and for all: we will always have further work to do. As Jung wrote near the end of his life,

> For us the representation of the idea of the self in actual and visible form is a mere rite d'entrée, as it were a propaedeutic action and mere anticipation of its realization. The existence of a sense of inner security by no means proves that the product will be stable enough to withstand the disturbing or hostile influences of the environment. The adept had to experience again and again how unfavorable circumstances or a technical blunder or – as it seemed to him – some devilish

accident hindered the completion of this work, so that he was forced to start all over again from the very beginning. Anyone who submits his sense of inner security to analogous psychic tests will have similar experiences. More than once everything he has built will fall to pieces under the impact of reality, and he must not let this discourage him from examining, again and again, where it is that his attitude is still defective, and what are the blind spots in his psychic field of vision. Just as a lapis Philosophorum, with its miraculous powers, was never produced, so psychic wholeness will never be attained empirically, as consciousness is too narrow and too one-sided to comprehend the full inventory of the psyche. Always we shall have to begin again from the beginning. From ancient times the adept knew that he was concerned with the 'res simplex,' and the modern man too will find by experience that the work does not prosper without the greatest simplicity. But simple things are always the most difficult.[105]

THE THIRD SERIES

Introduction

BEFORE PROCEEDING WITH THE Third Series, we might ask why the *Splendor Solis* uses three different series of images to illumine the alchemical process. The symbolism of the First Series is more like the alchemy of the Middle Ages in Europe, when some alchemists really did think that they were going to make gold. Their symbolism referred to the alchemists' experiences in the laboratory, for example observations of color changes and the use of processes such as distillation or calcification. This was at first done without any awareness that something was being added from the psyche by using an image or symbol.

The medieval alchemists may appear naive if we fail to recognize the contemporary mythology surrounding twenty-first century science and technology. Scientists themselves are often convinced of their objectivity, overlooking their own philosophical, psychological, and spiritual projections, as well as the truth that scientific theories arise not only from observation but also from imagination, inspiration, and the creative application of new concepts thereby derived. In experimental psychology, too, the questions and the observations are influenced by the Zeitgeist. Perhaps the attitude in the First Series also reminds us of our training as clinicians: we learn to be aware of the moment-to-moment process with the patient by taking notes, which include qualities of affect and their expression, as well as our internal reactions and associations during the session.

The *Splendor Solis* belongs to late medieval–early Renaissance alchemy, and so even at the basic level of the First Series, the images also include features indicating that the true goal of the alchemist was to discover something about his own materiality, his own nature. In this regard, the symbolism refers to an inner experience of transformation that took place while he was working with materials in the laboratory.

The Second Series anticipates the philosophical alchemy that started in the sixteenth century and reached its zenith in the seventeenth century. The laboratory methods of the alchemists were taken up by a different Zeitgeist to create modern chemistry. Philosophical alchemy detached itself from the remaining alchemical laboratories and from the 'puffers,' who were still actively engaged in trying to change base metals into gold. As alchemy became more philosophic and therefore more speculative, its play of ideas was abstracted away from embodied mystical experience and from actual observations of matter. In the *Splendor Solis*, however, we see that its philosophy can only be appreciated when it is grounded in genuine experience (as represented by the alembics and their symbolic contents, shown in settings of ordinary human activities). This is also true of psychoanalysis from a Jungian perspective.

Viewing the Second Series, it seems as if a perspective has developed through the transformations shown in the First Series, so that experience is ready to be understood psychologically and systematized through the use of astrological symbolism. Astrology is a system of knowledge devised to explain the differences in human nature and in historical periods. When you are dealing with the elemental forces – as conveyed by the First Series – you don't know what is going to come next, but if you are operating at a more conscious level, patterns begin to emerge and events may be anticipated. This development corresponds to later stages of analysis, when the analysand is beginning to understand personal material and becomes less dependent on the analyst.

In the Second Series, the symbols themselves are being transformed in the alembic! The astrological signs and their associated patterns of behavior are more in the sphere of everyday life, which is also the province of clinical work. The interplay of images and ideas between the contents of the alembic and the surrounding scenes parallels the analyst's inner tension between two methods of analysis, the symbolic and the clinical. More and more we see the error of this dichotomy, since we are doing both all the time. You cannot work in only one way and do justice to an individual's need to develop psychic awareness.

The final series of images consists of only four pictures.[1] From a psychological point of view, the whole alchemical process is now represented by images mirroring certain fundamental states of being. The inner and outer worlds are one, but in a new way that is both more fully experienced and maintains a broader and more objective perspective.

Plate III–1 The Dark Sun

The most striking feature of this picture is the image of the sun with human features, also visible below the horizon as seen through the earth. Its golden rays fill the sky and also seem to travel through the earth to the landscape in the foreground. Above the horizon the sun is black, so that its brilliant golden rays emerge from the darkness. The presence of both light and dark in this landscape recalls the poet Robert Pinsky's description of Canto IV of Dante's *Inferno*:

> . . . a journey that gathers light from a descent into darkness, a pilgrimage of knowledge that penetrating deeper seemingly turns away from the light, which yet reappears – and yet again vanishes . . .[2]

The golden frame of this picture is filled with flowers and animals, including snails, caterpillars, butterflies, birds, and a frog. The landscape, higher in the foreground, gives way to several plains of decreasing elevation before reaching the horizon. In the foreground, delicate plants grow at the edge of a dry creek, but on the opposite bank stands the blackened stump of a dead tree, one barren branch reaching out toward the creek bed. More dead and broken trees stand on the left, surrounded by delicate green foliage. In the middle-ground, a broad green expanse rests above more distant

PLATE III–1

plains through which rivers undulate toward the horizon, where even larger trees grow. Throughout the landscape, the green growth is highlighted with gold. On the horizon is a city, its buildings tinted by the rosy light of the sun. The pale blue sky contains many pink clouds.

The darkened trees in the foreground suggest that the landscape had suffered drought or been burned, corresponding to feelings of being burned out, dried up, flat, or empty. We are also reminded of the destructive potential of analysis, particularly in its reductionistic or overly intellectualized forms. In 'Psychology of the Transference,' Jung compares the phenomenon of soul loss among so-called primitive peoples to the loss of libido in neuroses.[3] A turning-inward often precedes a new conscious attitude or change in personality. During the incubation period of such a change, a loss of available energy is commonly experienced, as if the new development has taken the energy it needs into the unconscious.

Therefore, this plate might depict either a state of incubation or depression signaling a need for change. The light of the sun has disappeared into the earth, into matter, where a kind of intelligence is at work underground, in the depths of what we usually call the unconscious. We might say that the libido has turned away from the activities of life to illumine what is buried in the ground of being.

In the painting, young plants grow from the roots of a dead tree, new life nurtured by the sun's rays after their passage through earth and water. We were prepared to absorb the meaning of this image by the depiction of the dissolution of consciousness in the unconscious in Plate I–7, where the old king was drowning under a darkened sky. In that painting, the sun and morning star shone down on a beautiful young king. Plate III–1 also symbolizes the fundamental inseparability of death and renewal in nature, including human nature, but even more fundamentally than in Plate I–7. The human expression on the face of the sun in Plate III–1 suggests a consciousness that has absorbed this reality as an inner truth.

The plant symbolism suggests healing or transformation at a very basic, cellular level, nurtured by the light of the inner sun. It also calls to mind the 'vegetative' level of the nervous system, where our psychosomatic responses arise unconsciously. The absence of humans and other animals suggests that instinctual and intellectual activities have not fully revitalized in terms of action and will. The new growth even seems to be a different kind of plant,[4] further suggesting life on a new basis. With this new attitude, illumination comes not only from outside and above but from the darkness within (*lumen naturae*).

This scene may be seen to represent a pivotal yet temporary moment, one of balance, where consciousness is both above and below.[5] But it is a dynamic moment, and a person may fall back into unconsciousness or succumb to a desiccating consciousness unnourished by the emotional and image-filled depths of the unconscious. Or she may embrace the new life, which itself will eventually run its course or outlive its usefulness. Mary Jo Spencer[6] has noted that there is something very compelling about the actual image of the dark sun looking out over a natural landscape without any signs of human presence. She has suggested that this conveys a feeling that is more like a presence behind the human condition, or even behind the elements. It is perhaps a sense of that presence that informs the capacity of a person in analysis to refrain from unconsciously pursuing familiar activities and from willful problem-solving.

Plate III–2 Children at Play

The next picture shows a spacious interior warmed by a large tile stove, with light streaming in through faceted windows. A woman is wearing the primary colors of the alchemical opus: a red dress with a black collar and a white head covering. She is seated on a bench with an infant upon her lap, while a naked toddler stands next to her, holding her skirt. A basin sits at her feet, and to her right, a white cat[7] warms itself in the corner next to the stove. An older child, dressed in blue, helps a small naked child climb onto the window seat. Nearby, a black bird, perhaps a jackdaw or European crow (a symbol of the *prima materia*), stands on the floor with its wings raised slightly, suggesting that it is in motion, either landing or taking off.[8] Two children engage in parallel play: a naked child rides a toy horse and holds a toy pinwheel, while another child, clothed in blue garments and a black cap, also plays with a pinwheel. In the foreground, apparently in a separate space, a group of children engage in cooperative play: a cushion has been made into a carriage for a young, naked child, who is drawn by two other children (reminding us of the chariots of the gods in the last series). One of these children reaches out to stroke the hair of the other. A child dressed in yellow and riding a toy horse extends a hand to the naked child on the pillow, who is supported from behind by a child dressed in blue. The golden frame surrounding the main image is decorated with flowers, berries, butterflies and other insects, as wells as birds.

The perspective of the picture leads the eye toward a doorway. Above the doorway rest two alembics containing a yellow liquid. The yellow of the alembics is *citrinatis*, a color of transition, and the text notes that,

> The principal colours are black, white and red; between these many other colours appear; a yellowish one . . . after the perfect white, and before the first red, can be seen for some time, and is therefore a perfect colour.[9]

Why two alembics? We often think of the number two as denoting something that is just coming into consciousness. The doorway opens to a dark space, which cannot be seen in its entirety. What is visible is a woman or girl carrying something, perhaps a basin, with both hands. Psychologically, the doorway might be understood as a passage to the unconscious, the unknown, with the woman being an anima figure.[10]

The mother is there with the family. We know from contemporary research in child development that the basic trust in life goes back to a good relationship to the mothering figure in the earliest years. So these children presumably have that basic trust in life. In analysis we try to address these needs or their lack through the analytic relationship, which fosters creative introversion.[11]

The text of the *Splendor Solis* states, 'Wherefore is this Art compared to the play of children, who when they play, turn undermost that which was uppermost.'[12] Children play because they can't help it: it is their nature to play with things, to play with life, not to care about achieving anything with it, but simply to play. Yet we know from therapeutic work with children that 'play' is often undertaken in a very intent way and used for psychological problem-solving or mastering an ego skill.

Just as children need play for normal psychological development, so do adults in order to continue to grow psychologically. Often people suffering from disappointments in life can hardly wait to get back to the achievement program that they left behind.

PLATE III–2

They need the advice given to them by this image: 'Just try to play, or let play go on somehow in imagination.' (Of course, the roadblocks to the capacity for play may require long therapeutic work.)

In contemporary terms, we might see this plate as suggestive of the importance of holding and play for transformation, and we might even see this room as an image of D. W. Winnicott's concept of 'transitional space:'

> the third part of the life of a human being, a part that we cannot ignore, an intermediate area of *experiencing*, to which inner reality and external life both contribute the substance of *illusion*... the ... intermediate area between the subjective and that which is objectively perceived.[13]

The number of children – ten – might be of significance. Ten is the Pythagorean Tetractus, a symbol of unity, and so may refer to the totality of an experience. Just as children completely give themselves over to their play, so should we engage in a creative process with our entire being, rather than just entertaining its possibilities. In alchemy, the *multiplicatio*, which could be performed only when the alchemical transformation had been successfully completed, was thought to progress in multiples of ten.[14]

Plate III–3 Women Washing

This picture shows a well-known alchemical symbol, women washing. A river runs through a verdant countryside. Neither its source nor its direction is visible. In the lower left, water is heated in a gold cauldron, which is surrounded by black pitchers apparently used to carry water from the river. To the right of the cauldron, a bare-headed woman dressed in black, white, and blue stands barefoot in front of a table, washing white cloth in a shallow basin. Other basins and barrels of various sizes are nearby. A black cloth or garment hangs on the broadest of these, while a tall barrel lies on its side. Two blue-hatted women stand at a table and beat fabric with mallets. One of the women wears black, white, red, and blue, while a second wears white and gold. Behind them, a woman in red wades in the stream and leans over to rinse something. To her left, a woman lifts sheets of white fabric from a basin at her feet and places them on lines to dry. Another woman comes toward her, carrying on her head a basin filled with a white substance or cloth. On both sides of the river, fabrics are spread on the grass. Two women dressed in red and white stretch a cloth between them, preparing to lay it on the grass. Across the river, to the right, a woman dressed in white and red, with a gold hat, sits on the grass and holds the end of a cloth.

Two men are part of this scene. One can be seen through a covered wooden gateway, standing in the courtyard in front of a large house or mill. The other is on the right bank of the river, just opposite the two women who are stretching the cloth between them. He appears to be pouring something on the cloth stretched out on the grass. In the background we see pathways leading to two large, domed buildings with blue-tiled, spired roofs. In the center, in the distance, there is a gate set into a wall, with an arched doorway. Beyond that a steep mountain rises to meet gold-tinged clouds. The golden frame is decorated with leaves, varied flowers, birds (including an owl), and a butterfly.

You might think that this is purely a domestic situation, as if the opus – the

165

PLATE III-3

alchemical transmutation of metals into gold and the appearance of the white bird of illumination – is reduced to women washing, something ordinary that must be done every day. The women say: 'We do this, many, many times,' which, of course, speaks directly to our work as analysts. We know how many times we have to go over the same problem. People say: 'Oh, I finally understand it for the first time.' Once is not enough and that is simply the way it is with this kind of process. Once you understand that, it seems natural instead of being a defeat.

The daily habits of life also have a saving quality: 'Just keep on with your daily routine,' is often the best advice to somebody in a state of anxiety or depression. 'Keep doing what is necessary, stay clean and keep up with your housework.' When this explanation of the symbolism of women washing was suggested to Dr. von Franz, she said: 'Oh no. It's a very mystical picture; it's not a mundane picture at all.'[15] And she was also right. Washing fabric and putting it out in the sun to dry symbolizes a combination of the *solutio* and the *solificatio*, a purification.

Later, in her lectures on alchemy, von Franz commented:

> In alchemical literature it is generally said that the great effort and trouble continues from the *nigredo* to the *albedo*; that is said to be the hard part, and afterwards everything becomes easier. The *nigredo* – the blackness, the terrible depression and state of dissolution – has to be compensated by the hard work of the alchemist and that hard work consists, among other things, in constant washing; therefore even the work of washerwomen is often mentioned in the text . . .[16]

and:

> [The instincts in a disturbed form are] the *prima materia* which has to be constantly washed and distilled . . . Here it says nine times, others say fifteen times, and some say ten years. It is really a very long process and sometimes means endlessly rehearsing the same problem in its different aspects. That is why also in alchemical texts they always allude to the fact that this part can go on for a long time and is characterized by endless repetitions – just as, unfortunately, we fall again and again into complexes which have not been worked out and have to be looked at time and again.[17]

The laying of the cloth on the ground refers to other alchemical processes, distillation and sublimation. Water on the earth evaporates into the air during the heat of the day and then in the coolness of the night, it condenses back onto the surface of the earth as dew. An alchemical text advised, 'Gather Dew in the Month of May, with a clean white Linnen Cloth spread upon the Grass.'[18] In her commentary on *Aurora Consurgens*,[19] von Franz referred to alchemical texts which advised that dew must be gathered before sunrise, before 'the sun robs it [the earth] of its dew in order to nourish itself, and then the earth is "a widow and without husband".'[20]

Alchemy has left the laboratory and finds itself in the humble, daily, tasks of life. Many spiritual disciplines use a method of mindful repetition, as in the Zen precept, 'Chop wood, carry water.' Furthermore, doing the work with awareness of its deeper significance is a participation in the miraculous transformations of Nature. This means

PLATE III–4

that 'our gold,' the philosopher's stone, or the goal of the work is something that is found again and recognized for the first time. The stone

> is familiar to all men, both young and old, is found in the country, in the village, in the town, in all things created by God; yet it is despised by all. Rich and poor handle it every day. It is cast into the street by servant maids. Children play with it. Yet no one prizes it, though, next to the human soul, it is the most beautiful and the most precious thing upon earth, and has power to pull down kings and princes. Nevertheless it is esteemed the vilest and meanest of earthly things.[21]

We sometimes wish it were possible to pass quickly and miraculously from the *nigredo* into a state of euphoria. But this is not the process symbolized in the *Splendor Solis*. The image of women washing is like saying: 'Work with nature to do it.' There is no special ability required and certainly no cause for inflation. Perhaps that is why the process is represented as women's work, with no special recognition, no public rewards.

Plate III–4 The Journey's End

In the final plate of the *Splendor Solis*, the sun shines above a muted landscape, with blackened tree stumps and delicate foliage in the foreground. A stream meanders toward a large walled city, with many spired buildings. In the near-ground, to the left, a humble house is nestled among trees.

As in the first plate of this series (III–1), the sun has decidedly human features, with contoured cheeks, furrowed brow, and eyes looking toward the left and slightly up, as if seeing – or looking for – something beyond the limits of the picture. This expression is reminiscent of the many depictions of the great healer of Greek myth, Asklepios:

> The eyes seem to look upwards and into the distance without definite aim. This . . . gives us an impression of a great inner emotion, one might almost say of suffering. This god does not stand before us in Olympian calm: he is assailed as it were by the sufferings of men, which it is his vocation to assuage. [22]

The sun's rays do not brighten the city, which is so near, nor are its lower rays visible beneath the horizon, as in Plate III–1. This image of the inner sun tells us that becoming more conscious does not result in a state of elation or bliss.

In the final series, all the royal symbols are gone – no kings, no queens, no symbols of power or prestige. These paintings were made during the Renaissance in the sixteenth century, when nations were dominated by kings, and the minds of people by the principle of kingship. Considered heretical and dangerous to invested power, alchemy insisted upon the Feminine Principle and earthbound values, expressing something that was needed by the people at that time.

These final four paintings show us that the process itself – not the origin, nor the goal – is the only expression of completion. The glorious symbolism that was so important in the earlier two series has faded, leaving us in a world of quietly evocative imagery, where ordinary life is imbued with depth and meaning.

APPENDIX

The Harley Text of Salomon Trismosin's *Splendor Solis* and Alchemical Wanderings and Adventures in Search of the Philosopher's Stone

[Note: The text of the *Splendor Solis* is in German. The Julius Kohn translation of the *Splendor Solis* in the British Library, Harley 3469, was published by Kegan Paul, Trench, Trubner & Co., in 1920. We have also indicated where, in the original illuminated manuscript, the plates appear in relation to the text. We have edited the translation and translated some Latin titles into English.]

THIS BOOK IS NAMED SPLENDOR SOLIS or *Splendor of the Sun*
AND IS DIVIDED INTO SEVEN PARTS, IN WHICH IS DESCRIBED THE
HIDDEN MYSTERY OF THE OLD PHILOSOPHERS, AS WELL AS ALL
THAT NATURE REQUIRES TO CLEARLY ACCOMPLISH THE WHOLE
WORK, INCLUDING ALL THE ADDED THINGS; AFTER WHICH NO ONE
SHALL BE ADVISED TO GRAPPLE WITH THE MYSTERY OF THE
NOBLE ART WITH HIS OWN SENSES.

I AM THE WAY AND EVEN ROAD,
WHO PASSES HERE WITHOUT A REST,
WILL FIND A GOODLY LIFE ABODE,
AND IN THE END BE EVER BLESSED.

[Plate I–1]

PREFACE

ALPHIDIUS, one of the old Philosophers, said: 'Every one who does not care for the trouble of obtaining the Philosopher's Stone, will do better in making no inquiries at all than only useless ones.' The same also says RHASES, in his book 'Light of Lights': 'Let it be said then to all, I hereby admonish them most earnestly, that none be so foolhardy to presume to understand the unknown intermixture of the elements.' For as ROSINUS says: 'All who engage in this Art, and are wanting the knowledge and perception of things, which the Philosophers have described in their books, are erring immensely.' For the Philosophers have founded this art in a natural beginning, but of a very hidden operation. Though it is evident that all corporeal things originate in and are maintained and exist of the Earth, according to Time and Influence of the Stars and Planets, as: Sun, Moon and the others, together with the four qualities of the elements, which are without intermission, moving and working therein, thereby creating every growing and procreating thing in its individual form, sex and substance, as first created at the Beginning by God, the Creator. Consequently, all metals originate in the Earth of a special and peculiar matter produced by the four properties of the four elements, which generate in their mixture the metallic force, under the influence of their respective planets.

All this is well described by the natural master ARISTOTLE, in the Fourth Book 'Meteorologicorum,' when he says, that QUICKSILVER is a matter common to all metals. But it must be known that first in Nature is the compound matter of the four elements.

In acknowledging this property of Nature, the Philosophers called their Matter MERCURIUS, or QUICKSILVER.

How this MERCURIUS takes the perfect form of Gold, Silver, or other metals through the working of Nature need not be mentioned here. The teachers of Nature's Philosophy describe it sufficiently in their books.

Upon such is based and founded the ART of the Philosopher's Stone; for it originates in Nature, thence follows a natural end in a just form, through just and natural means.

[Plate I–2]

THE FIRST TREATISE
In the following treatise we shall discourse on the origin of the stone of the wise and the art of its production.

THE Philosopher's Stone is produced by means of Greening and Growing Nature.

HALI the Philosopher says thereof: 'This Stone rises in growing, greening things.' Wherefore when the Green is reduced to its former Nature, whereby things sprout and come forth in ordained time, it must be decocted and putrefied in the way of our secret art. That by Art may be aided, what Nature decocts and putrefies, until she gives it, in due time, the proper form, and our Art but adapts and prepares the Matter as becomes Nature, for such work, and for such work provides also, with premeditated Wisdom, a suitable vessel.

For Art does not undertake to produce Gold and Silver, anew, as it cannot endow matter with its first origin, nor is it necessary to search for our Art in the places and caverns of the Earth, where minerals have their first beginning. Art goes quite another way to work and with different intention from Nature; therefore does Art also use different tools and instruments.

For that reason can Art produce extraordinary things out of the aforesaid natural beginnings, such as Nature of herself would never be able to create. For unaided Nature does not produce things whereby imperfect metals can in a moment be made perfect, but by the secrets of Our Art this can be done.

Here Nature serves Art with Matter, and Art serves Nature with suitable Instruments and method convenient for Nature to produce such new forms; and although the before-mentioned Stone can only be brought to its proper form by Art, yet the form is from Nature. For the form of every thing be it living, growing, or metallic, comes into existence by virtue of the interior force in matter – except the human soul.

But it must be borne in mind that the essential form cannot originate in matter unless it is by the effect of an accidental form, not by virtue of that form, but by virtue of another real substance, which is the Fire or some other accidental active heat.

By way of allegory, we take a hen's egg. The form of the chicken cannot take shape, without the presence and aid of accidental form, which is the intermixture of the red with the white, by virtue of the heat coming from the hatching hen. Although the egg is the hen's material, nevertheless it cannot develop either its real or accidental form, otherwise than by putrefaction, which is caused by the influence of warmth. Likewise, neither the real nor the accidental form of the Philosopher's Stone can originate in natural matter without the agency of Putrefaction or Decoction, of which we shall speak hereafter.

PUTREFACTION takes place when the natural heat of a moist body is expelled by an external heat, or else when the natural heat of the subject is destroyed by cold. For then the natural warmth leaves everything and gives room to putrefaction.

The Philosophers do not mean this kind of Putrefaction. Their Putrefaction is a moistening of dry bodies, that they may be restored to their former state of Greening and Growing. In the process of Putrefaction, moist and dry are joined together and not destroyed.

But when the moisture is quite separated from the dryness, then it is necessary to separate the dry parts that turned to ashes. This Incineration the Philosophers will also not have, but they will have their Putrefaction, which is a drying trituration[1], and calcination[2] to be done in such wise, that the natural moisture and dryness be united together, but separated and dried up from the superfluous moisture that is destructive.

[The philosopher's Putrefaction is compared to digestion:] Even as food is absorbed on entering an animal's stomach, that it may be digested and changed and afterwards supply the feeding force and moisture necessary to the existence and augmentation of Nature, and be separated of its superfluous parts. Thus everything has to be fed in its way according to its Nature as will be shown by the Philosopher's Stone.

[Plate I–3]

THE SECOND TREATISE

MATTER AND NATURE OF THE PHILOSOPHER'S STONE

MORIENUS says: You shall know that the whole work of this Art ends in two Operations hanging very close together, so that when the one is complete, the other may begin and finish, thus perfecting the whole Mastery. But as they only act on their own matter, it is necessary to give more particulars about it. GEBER says in his 'Of the Sum of Perfection,' 'that Nature produces the Metals from Mercury and Sulfur.' And to the same effect we see FERRARIUS speak in his 'Treatise on Alchemy,' in the twenty-fifth chapter, that from the beginning of the Origin of Metals, Nature also uses a slimy, heavy Water, mixed with a very peculiar white sulfuric subtle Earth, which resolves the former into a steam and vapor, raises it in the veins or crevices of the Earth, and decocts,[3] steams, and collects it together so long, till at last dryness and moisture completely unite, thereby forming the substance which we call Mercury, and which constitutes the peculiar and very first Matter of all metals. And again he treats of it in the twenty-sixth chapter as follows: 'Those who will imitate Nature, are not to use Mercury only, but Mercury mixed with Sulfur, but not the common Mercury and Sulfur but those only which Nature herself has mixed, well prepared, and decocted into a sweet fluid. In such a Mercury Nature has begun with primary action and ended in a metallic Nature, having thus done her part, leaving the rest for Art to complete her work into a perfect Philosopher's Stone.'

From the aforesaid it will be seen that he who will proceed properly in this Art shall, according to all Philosophers, begin where Nature has left off and take that Sulfur and Mercury which Nature has collected in its purest form, in which took place the immediate union, which otherwise cannot be accomplished by anybody without art.

In order to receive the force that penetrates such subtle Matter, some Alchemists calcinate Gold that they may dissolve it, and separate the elements until they reduce it to a volatile spirit or to the subtle Nature of the greasy fumes of Mercury and Sulfur; and this then is the nearest matter, that combines most closely with Gold, and receives the form of the occult Philosopher's Stone. This matter is called the Mercury of the Philosophers, about which ARISTOTLE, speaking to ALEXANDER the King, says: 'Choose for our Stone that wherewith kings are decorated and crowned.'

Though this Mercury alone is the matter and the only thing and a combination of other things, yet is this thing so manifold in its effects, and in its names, that no one can find out the true meaning from the writings of the Philosophers, and this is done for the purpose, as ROSINUS says: 'that every one may not get at it.' It is at the same time a way of producing effects and a vessel wherein all things multiply themselves, because of the adjustment of all things comprised in Nature.

For now the Philosophers say: 'Dissolve the thing, and sublimate it, and then distill it, coagulate it, make it ascend, make it descend, soak it, dry it, and ever up to an indefinite number of operations, all of which take place at the same time and in the same vessel.' ALPHIDIUS confirms this and says: 'You must know that when we dissolve we sublimate as well and calcinate without interruption.' And if our Corpus is being thrown into the Water, for the purpose of dissolution, it first turns black, then separates itself, dissolving and sublimating, it unites itself with the spirit, which is its origin and birth.

It has been compared as analogous to all things in the world, visible or invisible, possessed of a soul or not, corporeal or animal, dead or alive, mineral or vegetative; analogous to the elements and their compositions, to things hot and cold, further to all colors, all fruits, all birds, and in short to all things between Heaven and Earth, and among all these are belonging to this Art the aforesaid operations, which are explained by the Philosophers in two words 'Man and Wife,' or 'Milk and Cream.' He who does not understand these does not understand the preparation of this Art.

[Plate I–4]

THE THIRD TREATISE
Now Follows the Means Whereby the Whole Work of this mastery Is
Perfected: Explained By A Few Suitable Illustrations, Parables,
and Various Aphorisms of the Philosophers.

HERMES, a Father of Philosophy, says: 'It is indeed needed that at the End of this World, Heaven and Earth should meet and come home.' Meaning by Heaven and Earth the aforesaid two Operations; but many doubts arise, before the Work is finished. That the following Figures may be better understood we give a few Parables in illustration:

And This Is the First Parable:
GOD created the Earth plain and coarse, and very productive of Gravel, Sand, Stones, Mountains and Valleys, but through the influence of the planets, and the working of Nature, the Earth has been changed into many forms. Outside there are hard stones, high mountains and deep valleys, and strange things and colors are inside the Earth, as, for instance, Ores and their beginnings. And with such things Earth has come from the original form, in the following manner: where the Earth first began to grow large, or to expand and multiply, the constant operation of the Sun-Heat also formed in the interior of the Earth a sulfurous, vaporous, and damp heat, penetrating her through and through. This penetrating work of the Sun's heat caused in the cold and damp of the Earth, the formation of large quantities of vapor, fumes, fog, and gas, all of which grew with the length of time strong enough to follow their tendency to rise, thus causing on the Earth's surface eruptions, forming hill and dale, etc. Where there are such hills and dales, there the Earth has been matured and most perfectly mixed with heat and cold, moisture and dryness, and there the best ores may be found. But where the Earth is flat there has been no accumulation of such fumes and vapors, and there no ores will be found; whereas the uplifted part of the soil, especially such as has been slimy, loamy, and fat, and has been saturated with a moisture from on high, got soft again, forming dough-like layers one on top of the other, which in the course of time, under the influence of the Sun's heat, become more and more firm, hard, and baked; and other ground as gravel and sand, brittle and yet soft, hanging together like grapes, is too meager and dry, and has not received enough moisture, consequently it could not form itself into layers, but remained full of holes, like badly prepared pap, or like a mealy dough, which has not been watered enough; for no Earth can become stone, unless it be rich and slimy and well mixed with moisture.

After the drying up of the Water by the Sun's heat, the fat substance will keep the ground together, as otherwise it would remain brittle and fall to pieces again. That which has not become perfectly hard as yet, may become so, and turn to stone, under the constant influence of the Sun's heat and Nature, as well as the aforesaid fumes and gases originating in the properties of the elements, which are by these means still being operated upon in the interior of the Earth, and when they seize upon watery vapors with a pure, subtle earthy substance, then they form the Philosophers' Mercury;

but when they are solid and brought to a fiery, earthy, and subtle hardness, then will the Philosophers' Sulfur be the result.

About this Sulfur HERMES says: 'It will receive the powers of the highest and lowest planets, and with its force it penetrates solid things, it overcomes all matter and all precious stones.'

[Plate I–5]

The Other Parable

HERMES, the First Master of this Art, says as follows: 'The Water of the Air, which is between Heaven and Earth, is the Life of everything; for by means of its Moisture and Warmth, it is the medium between the two opposites, as Fire and Water,' and therefore it rains Water on Earth, Heaven has opened itself, and sent its Dew on Earth, making as sweet as honey, and moist. Therefore the Earth flowers and bears manifold colored blooms and fruits, and in her interior has grown a large Tree with a Silver stem, stretching itself out to the Earth's surface. On its branches have been sitting many kinds of birds, all departing at Daybreak, when the Ravenhead became white. The same tree bears three kinds of Fruit. The First are the very finest Pearls. The Second are called by Philosophers TERRA FOLIATA. The Third is the very purest Gold. This Tree gives us as well the fruit of Health; it warms what is cold, and cools what is warm; it moistens what is dry and dries what is moist; and it softens what is hard, and hardens what is soft, and is the end of the whole Art. Thereof says the Author of 'The Three Words,' 'The Three Moistures are the most precious Words of the whole Mastery.' And the same says GALENUS, when he speaks of the Herb LUNATICA or BERISSA. Its root is a Metallic Earth; it has a red stem, spotted with black, grows easily and decays easily, and gains Citrine Flowers, after three days; if it is put in Mercury, it changes itself into perfect Silver, and this again by further decoction changes into Gold, which then turns hundred parts of Mercury into the finest Gold. Of this tree speaks VIRGILIUS, in the sixth book of the AENEID, when he relates a Fable, how AENEAS and SILVIUS went to a tree, which had golden branches, and as often as one broke a branch off, another one grew in its place.

[Plate I–6]

The Third Parable

AVICENNA says in the Chapter on the MOISTURES: 'When Heat operates upon a moist body, then is blackness the first result.' For that reason have the old Philosophers declared they saw a Fog rise, and pass over the whole face of the Earth, they also saw the impetuosity of the Sea, and the streams over the face of the Earth, and how the latter became foul and stinking in the darkness. They further saw the King of the Earth sink, and heard him cry out with eager voice: 'Whoever saves me shall live and reign with me for ever in my brightness on my royal throne,' and Night enveloped all things. The day after they saw over the King an apparent Morning Star, and the Light of Day clear up the darkness, the bright Sunlight pierce through the clouds, with manifold colored rays, of brilliant brightness, and a sweet perfume from the Earth, and the Sun shining clear. Herewith was completed the Time when the King of the Earth was released and renewed, well appareled, and quite handsome, surprising with his beauty Sun and Moon. He was crowned with three costly crowns, the one of Iron, the other of Silver, and the third of pure Gold. They saw in his right hand a Scepter with Seven Stars, all of which gave a Golden Splendor, and in his left hand a golden Apple, and seated upon it a white Dove, with Wings partly silvered and partly of a golden hue, which ARISTOTLE so well spoke of when he said: 'The Destruction of one thing is the birth of another.' Meaning in this Masterly Art: 'Deprive the thing of its Destructive Moisture, and renew it with its own Essential one which will become its perfection and life.'

[Plate I–7]

The Fourth Parable
MENALDUS the Philosopher, says: 'I command all my descendants to spiritualize their bodies by DISSOLUTION, and again to materialize the spiritual things by means of a gentle decoction.' Mentioning which SENIOR speaks thus: 'The Spirit dissolves the body, and in the Dissolution extracts the Soul of the Body, and changes this body into Soul, and the Soul is changed into the Spirit, and the Spirit is again added to the Body, for thus it has stability.' Here then the body becomes spiritual by force of the Spirit. This the Philosophers give to understand in the following Signature, or Figure. They saw a man black like a Negro sticking fast in a black, dirty, and foul-smelling slime or clay; to his assistance came a young woman, beautiful in countenance and still more so in body, most handsomely adorned with many-colored dresses. And she had wings on her back, the feathers of which were equal to those of the very finest white Peacock, and the quills were adorned with fine pearls, while the feathers reflected like golden mirrors. On her head she had a crown of pure Gold, and on top of it a Silver star; around her neck she wore a necklace of fine Gold, with the most precious Ruby, which no king would be able to pay; her feet were clad with golden shoes, and from her was emanating the most splendid perfume, surpassing all aromas. She clothed the man with a purple robe, lifted him up to his brightest clearness, and took him with herself to Heaven. Therefore says SENIOR: 'It is a living thing, which no more dies, but when used gives an eternal increase.'

[Plate I–8]

The Fifth Parable
The Philosophers give to this Art two bodies, namely: Sun and Moon, which are Earth and Water, they also call them Man and Wife, and they bring forth four children, two boys, which are heat and cold, and two girls, as moisture and dryness. These are the Four Elements, constituting the QUINTESSENCE, that is the proper white MAGNESIA, wherein there is nothing false. In conclusion SENIOR remarks: 'When these five are gathered together, they form ONE substance, whereof is made the natural Stone,' while AVICENNA contends that: 'if we may get at the Fifth, we shall have arrived at the end.'

So let us understand this meaning better. The Philosophers take for example an Egg, for in this the four elements are joined together. The first or the shell is Earth, and the White is Water, but the skin between the shell and the White is Air, and separates the Earth from the Water; the Yolk is Fire, and it too is enveloped in a subtle skin, representing our subtle Air, which is more warm and subtle, as it is nearer to the Fire, and separates, the Fire from the Water. In the middle of the Yolk there is the FIFTH ELEMENT, out of which the young chicken bursts and grows.

Thus we see in an egg all the elements combined with matter to form a source of perfect Nature, just as it is necessary in this noble art.

[Plate I–9]

The Sixth Parable
ROSINOS relates of a vision he had of a man whose body was dead and yet beautiful and white like Salt. The Head had a fine Golden appearance, but was cut off the trunk, and so were all the limbs; next to him stood an ugly man of black and cruel countenance, with a bloodstained double-edged sword in his right hand, and he was the good man's murderer. In his left hand was a paper on which the following was written: 'I have killed thee, that thou mayest receive a superabundant life, but thy head I will carefully hide, that the worldly wantons may not find thee, and destroy the Earth, and the body I will bury, that it may putrefy, and grow and bear innumerable fruit.'

[Plate I–10]

The Seventh Parable
OVID the old Roman, wrote to the same end, when he mentioned an ancient Sage who desired to rejuvenate himself was told: he should allow himself to be cut to pieces and decoct to a perfect decoction, and then his limbs would reunite and again be renewed in plenty of strength.

[Plate I–11]

THE FOURTH TREATISE
OF THE MEANS BY WHICH NATURE ATTAINS HER ENDS

ARISTOTLE in the Book of Origins speaks thus: 'Sun and Man create a Man, for the Sun's force and spirit give life, and the process has to be gone through seven times, by means of the Sun's heat.'

But as the Philosophers in their work have to aid Nature with Art, so have they also to govern the heat according to the Sun, so as to create the before-mentioned Stone, which as well has to undergo seven processes. For such a work requires FIRSTLY, a heat powerful enough to soften and melt those parts of the Earth that have become thick, hard, and baked, as mentioned by SOCRATES when he says that the holes and cracks of the Earth will be opened to receive the influence of Fire and Water.

[Plate II–1]

SECONDLY: The Heat is necessary, because through its power the Earth becomes freed from darkness and blessed with light instead. In regard to which SENIOR says that heat turns every black thing white, and every white thing red. So, as Water bleaches, Fire gives off light, and also color to the subtilized Earth, which appears like a Ruby, through the tingeing Spirit she receives from the force of the Fire, thus causing SOCRATES to say that a peculiar light shall be seen in the darkness.

[Plate II–2]

THIRDLY: The Heat causes earthly things to be penetrated by a Spiritual Force, of which it is said in the 'Turba': Spiritualize the bodies and make Volatile that which is Fixed. Of which RHAZES reminds in his 'Light of Lights,' as follows: 'A heavy body cannot be made light without the help of a light body, nor can a light body be kept pressed down to the ground without the aid of a heavy body.'

[Plate II–3]

FOURTHLY: The Heat cleanses that which is unclean. It throws off the mineral impurities and bad odors and nourishes the Elixir. In mention of which HERMES advises: Separate the gross from the subtle, the Earth from the Fire. Whereof says ALPHIDIUS: The Earth can be molten and becomes Fire. Thereon says RHAZES: There are several Purifications preceding the perfect preparation, namely, Mundification and Separation.

[Plate II–4]

FIFTHLY: The Heat works elevatingly, for by its force the spirits hidden in the Earth are raised up into the Air; wherefore the Philosophers say that whosoever can bring light to a hidden thing is a Master of the Art.

The same is meant by MORIENUS, when he teaches that, 'He who can recreate the SOUL is able to see color,' and also by ALPHIDIUS saying: 'Hence it is that this Combat raises upwards, or else you shall not gain by it.'

[Plate II–5]

SIXTHLY: The Heat warms the cold Earth that while cold was half-dead. Thereof says SOCRATES: When Heat penetrates, it makes subtle all earthly things, that are of service to the matter, but come to no final form while it is acting on the matter. The Philosophers conclude on the mentioned Heats in brief words, saying: Distill seven times and you have separated the destructible moisture and it takes place as in one distillation.

[Plate II–6]

SEVENTHLY: Is the Force of the heat thus mixed with heat in the Earth, that it has made light the collected parts and resolved them so as to surpass the other elements, and therefore this heat shall be modified with the Coldness of the Moon, 'Extinguish the Fire of one thing with the Coldness of another' says CALID.

[Plate II–7]

EIGHTHLY, AUCTOR DE TRIUM VERBORUM, the author of 'The Three Words,' gives in his writings a peculiar method to govern the HEAT or the FIRE, saying:

'When the Sun is in Aries, he indicates the First Heat, or Grade of the Fire, which is weak because the heat is under the Rule of the Water, but when the Sun is in Leo, then it indicates the Second Grade, which is hotter because the great coldness of the Water being under the Rule of the Air. In the Sign of Sagittarius is the Third Grade, this being not of a burning heat, and under the Rule or Order of Rest and Pause.'

THE FIFTH TREATISE
ON THE MANIFOLD OPERATIONS OF THE WHOLE WORK IN FOUR CHAPTERS.

The First Chapter
DISSOLUTION is the FIRST Operation which has to take place in the Art of ALCHEMY, for the order of Nature requires that the CORPUS, BODY, OR MATTER, be changed into WATER which is the much spoken of MERCURY. The LIVING SILVER dissolves the adjoined pure SULFUR.

This Dissolution is nothing but a killing of the moist with the dry, in fact a PUTREFACTION, and consequently turns the MATTER black.

[Plate III–1]

The Second Chapter
The next is COAGULATION, which is turning the WATER again into the CORPUS or MATTER, meaning thereby that the SULFUR, which before was dissolved by the LIVING SILVER, absorbs the same and draws it into itself.

The Water that turned to Earth, which the Corpus has absorbed, necessarily shows other and manifold colors. For if the properties of an operating thing alter, so must the thing operated on alter.

Because in the DISSOLUTION the LIVING SILVER is active, but in the COAGULATION it is passive, operated on.

Wherefore is this Art compared to the play of children, who when they play, turn undermost that which before was uppermost.

[Plate III–2]

The Third Chapter
The Third is SUBLIMATION, distilling the before-mentioned moisture of the Earth, for if the Water is reduced into the Earth, it is evaporated into the lightness of the Air, and rises above the Earth, as an oblong cloudlet, like an egg, and this is the Spirit of the FIFTH ESSENCE, which is called the TINCTURE, ANIMA, FERMENTUM, or the OIL, and which is the very next matter to the STONE OF THE PHILOSOPHERS.

For from the Sublimation remain ashes, which by virtue of their own AIR, given to them by GOD, dissolve themselves by a moderate heat, after which Earth of a fiery Nature and property remains calcined at the bottom of the glass.

This is the proper philosophical sublimation, by means of which the perfect method is carried out. And this is why this Art is compared to Woman's Work, which consists in cooking and roasting until it is done.

[Plate III–3]

The Fourth Chapter

The fourth Chapter shows the last or fourth thing belonging to this Water which has been separated from the Earth, is again joined to the Earth. The one thing must be done with the other, if the Stone is to be made perfect.

In the reason why all natural things are put together in a body is that there may be a united composition.

In these last four Chapters is all contained wherewith the Philosophers have filled the whole world with innumerable books.

[Plate III–4]

On The Government of the Fires

If a thing is deprived of its heat, then is there no motion in it. In the order of Nature the father changes into the son, which means that the Spiritual is materialized, and the Volatile made permanent; or that Sun and Moon have come home. Of these two planets SENIOR speaks also: 'I am a hot and dry Sun, while thou, LUNA, art cold and moist, and when we shall rise in the order of our most ancient nobility, a burning light will be poured into us.' Whereby he is indicating that through the knowledge and mastery of the ancients the renewals of the moistures will be received, and Sun and Moon become transparent.

The 'Scala Philosophorum' treats of the FIRE as follows 'The Heat or Fire of the whole work is uniform, for some say that the heat of the first regimen shall be as the warmth of a brooding hen, others that it ought to be as the natural warmth of the digestion of food and nourishment of the body, while some take the heat of the Sun, when she is in the sign of ARIES, as the proper one.'

Though the stone is obtained through one operation, nevertheless has the operation of the Fire to be changed thrice. In the first operation of the work shall the heat be mild moderate and warm, till the matter turns black continually, and further till it becomes white again. This heat is compared to the heat of the Sun when he is in ARIES and begins to move towards TAURUS. When the White appears the Fire should be increased and continued until the perfect drying up or Calcination of the Stone; this heat is compared to the Sun's heat when he is in TAURUS and moving towards GEMINI. And when the stone is perfectly dried up, and calcined, the Fire has again to be made more fierce still, until the stone becomes perfectly red, and clad with a royal coat from the Fire, and this heat is compared to the summer heat, when the Sun is in LEO; that is her highest dignity, when she is in her own house. This much is enough said on the government of the FIRE.

THE FIFTH TREATISE
Second Part
On The Colors Which Appear In the Preparation of the Stone

MIRALDUS, the Philosopher, says in the 'Turba': 'It turns black twice, yellow twice, and red twice, and therefore decoct it, for in the process of DECOCTION appear many colors, and according to these is the heat changed.' And although all colors appear so are there yet but three most noticeable amongst all. The principal colors are black, white and red; between these many others appear; a yellowish one after the white, or after the first red, said by MIRALDUS, to be a perfect Color, while CONCILIATOR calls it NOT perfect, and hardly remaining on matter long enough to be visible. But the other yellowish color, which arises after the perfect white and before the first red, can be seen for some time, and is therefore a perfect color. This is the same that MIRALDUS says above, but they do not last so long as black, white, or red, which stand in the matter for four days; though black and red appear perfect a second time. But the first perfect color is the black resulting from the mildest heat.

According to Conciliator, the Whitening should take place in a mild heat, till the Black disappears. While LUCAS, the Philosopher, says in the 'Turba': 'Beware of great heat, for if you make the Fire too fierce in the beginning, then will it arise red before its time, which is useless,' for in the commencement of its government you ought to have first the black, then the white, and lastly the red.

BALDUS, the Philosopher, says in the 'Turba': 'Decoct your composition, till you see it white, and quench it in Vinegar and separate the white from the black,' for the white is a sign of approaching Fixation; it needs to be extracted from the black by means of the Fire of calcination, for the augmented heat separates the superfluous parts, leaving them but a coarse Earth under the Matter, like a coarse black ball, not capable of mixing with the pure and subtle matter of the Stone. That is what the Philosophers say: 'the red must be extracted from the white, for there is nothing superfluous in it, nor is there anything separated, but all turns perfectly red, for which purpose they order to make a stronger Fire.' Whereof PYTHAGORAS says: 'The more the colors change the stronger you must make the Fire, of which you must not be afraid. For the Matter is fixed in the White, and the species fly not from it.'

About these remarks the Philosopher Lucas: 'When our Magnesia is made white, it does not yield its species.' This may be sufficient on the Colors of the Secret Philosophic Work, now follows the Conclusion to it.

HERMES, a father of Philosophers says that, 'one should not take out the aforesaid white Magnesia until all the colors are perfect, when it will become a Water dividing itself into four other Waters, namely one to two and three to one. One third of it belongs to heat and two thirds to moisture.' These Waters are the Weights of the Philosophers.

It should further be known, that the Vine which is a Sap of the Philosophers, is extracted in the Fifth, but its Wine has to be opened in the Third, and in proper preparation.

For in Decoction it gets less, while in Trituration, it forms itself. In all this is included beginning and end. Therefore the Philosophers say that it was made perfect in SEVEN DAYS; others say in Four Days, some say in Three Times, some in Four Times, some in Ten Days, some in Forty Days, some in ONE YEAR.

'Turba' and ALPHIDIUS: In The Four Seasons of The Year, as: Spring, Summer, Autumn, and Winter, some others again say in a Day, in One Week or in One Month.

GEBER and ARISTOTLE, these Philosophers say in Three Years. All this is nothing else but one thing in another thing, for the philosophers say the Operations are manifold, and so are the times, weights and names in consequence, all of which an intelligent Artist must know well, otherwise he can produce nothing.

THE SIXTH TREATISE
ON THE PROPERTIES OF THE WHOLE WORK IN THE PREPARATION
OF THE PHILOSOPHER'S STONE

CALCINATION is put in the beginning of the Work as the Father of a Generation, and is of three kinds two of which belong to the Corpus or Matter, and the third to the Spirit. The First is a preparation of the Cold Moisture, which protects the wood from being burnt, and is the beginning of our Work. The other is a fatty moisture, which burns the wood.

The Third is an Incineration of the dry Earth, and gives a truly fixed and subtle moisture; it is little in bulk, and gives no flames, but gives a body as clear as glass. Thus the Philosophers order their Calcination to be made, and it is accomplished with AQUA PERMANENTE, or with ACETO ACCERRIMA. Such moistures are in the metals, for they are the beginning of fusion. This is proved by Hermes, when he says The Water is the beginning of all soft substances, therefore the Calcination is the indication of a destructive moisture, and of an application of a foreign fiery moist subject, from which the essentiality and life originates. For this reason it is called a fusion of the incineration, taking place with the Water of the Philosophers, which in reality is the Sublimation, or Philosophic Solution, for this changes the hard dryness

the QUINTA ESSENTIA, and separation of
parts, which got dried and compressed by
irit, which is a resolving Water, moistening
ging the introduced destructive heat into
ty of that element. Therefore it is called
coarse Earth becomes thin or subtle, and
nd the cold of this Water, and the warmth
ned into the heat of the Fire, is a reversion
A ESSENTIA of the elementary FAECES.
moisture of a very high Nature, tingeing

hich GEBER says: 'What becomes Fixed
autiful transparent substance.' For out of it
the ash extracted from ash, without which
llic Water, generated in the body, making it
cture, and a tingeing volatile spirit.
true Ablution, or cleaning of blackness
gain, to live by the introduction of a pure,
supplying the tingeing force, by means of
refaction, spoken of at the beginning of this
ng to light that which was hidden. Therefore
lemands the UTMOST SECRECY. It is the
nem in this Operation. 'Turba' says further:
nd fix that which is volatile, powder it, and
osopher's Trituration. Wherefore SENIOR
the result is as a powder. It is as well the
especially ALBERTUS MAGNUS, when he
Nature so closely as Alchemy, because of

decoction and formation. For the former takes place in fiery red and metallic waters, which have most from the form and but little from matter. It is as well the Philosophic ASSATION, or roasting, for the accidental moisture is consumed by a mild Fire and very great care is to be taken, that the spirit which dries up the body, may not escape from the body, as otherwise the operation would not be perfect. It is as well the Philosophers Distillation, or clarification; this being nothing but the uniting of a thing with its own essential moisture, and with the Coagulation the Philosophers complete the whole work.

Thereof says HERMES: that the Earth is its foster mother, by which he means that its power is complete when changed into a constant Earth capable of producing innumerable effects, as we shall see hereafter. Nothing else can yet be effected on a more natural way than this art, when followed in truth and not in form only and appearance. This SENIOR confirmed saying: 'There is no man living able to exercise this art without Nature. Yea and with such Nature as has been given us by Heaven to unite with Nature.'

THE SEVENTH TREATISE
OF THE WHOLE WORK'S MANIFOLD EFFECTS, AND WHY THE PHILOSOPHERS INTRODUCE SO MANY NAMES AND ALLEGORIES IN THIS ART OF THE PREPARATION OF THE PHILOSOPHER'S STONE

It is a common saying of the Philosophers, that whoever knows how to kill the living Silver, is a master of this art, but very great attention has to be paid to their Quicksilver, for their descriptions are very different and manifold.

SENIOR says thus: 'Our Fire is a Water. If you can give a Fire to a Fire and Mercury to Mercury, then you know enough.' He further says: 'The Soul is extracted by Putrefaction, and when nothing more of the soul remains, then have you well washed the Body, that they both again are one.' Then it is called QUINTA ESSENTIA, the Quintessence, or a Spirit, Permanent Water or Menstruum.

The 'Turba' says also: 'Take Mercury and coagulate it in the body of Magnesia, or in the Sulfur which does not burn, and dissolve it in the very strongest Vinegar; and in this Vinegar it will become neither black nor white or red, and thus it becomes a dead Quicksilver, and is of a white color, and before the approach of the Fire it becomes red.'

'Turba' speaks about it as follows: 'Lay it in Gold when it will become an elixir, that is his Tincture, and it is a beautiful Water extracted from many tinctures, it gives life and color to all whom it is given to take.' Further the 'Turba' continues: 'The Tyrian color red is the very best; after that comes a costly Purple color, and this is the true Quicksilver it brings a sweet savor, and is a genuine Tincture.' From this it is sufficiently to be seen that all Philosophers not only ascribe the beginning of the art to Quicksilver, but the Middle and perfect end as well.

HERMES, the father of Philosophers, speaks of it thus: 'I have been observing a bird called the Philosophers' ORSAN, which flies when in the Signs Of ARIES, CANCER, LIBRA, or CAPRICORN, and this bird you may receive for all eternity from true minerals and precious mountain stones. Parts shall you part, and especially that which remains after the separation, and is called of the Earth's complexion, that you see it in many colors, then will the wise men call it "CERAM SAPIENTAE" and "PLUMBUM."' In regard to this the Philosophers talk about roasting and distilling through Days of Time, according to Number and Division of the Parts, saying: 'Sublimate, rectify, fix till it sticks to the ground, further, incinerate and imbibe till it flows; make it dead and alive again; file it and break it, till the secret becomes revealed and the revealed secret, separate the Elements and unite them again, extract the Soul from the Body. Further rectify Body and Spirit; make white VENUS, deprive JUPITER of his bolt, harden SATURN, and soften MARS, make LUNA Citron-colored and solve all bodies in Water which makes them perfect.' They also teach to roast the black Sulfur till it turns red, when they distill it all they obtain white transparent Gum like the thing which is so highly praised and called LAC VIRGINIS. Then they mix the Water, which is drawn off from the Virgin Milk, and transfer it into a red golden gum and a white transparent Water, which must be left to coagulate, after which process they call it Tincture of the Wise, TINCTURA SAPIENTIAE, and a Fire to the colors, one Soul one Spirit, drawing back again to home those after wandering about far away. Further, SULFUR RUBEUM, GUMMI AUREUM, AUREUM APPARENS, CORPUS DESIDERATUM, AURUM SINGULARUM, AQUA SAPIENTIAE, especially if it possesses great whiteness. The 'Turba' says also: 'You should know that, unless you make the Gold first white, you will never be able to get it red, black and pure waters; the Crystalline will show itself from the Citron red.' Therefore says SENIOR: 'It is a peculiar thing, if you throw it over the other three already mixed up, so will it help the white over the citrine and the red, it will turn the color of Silver; after that it helps the red over the Citrine, and makes it white, over the white and red and makes it Citrine Golden colored; then it helps as well the red over the Citrine, and makes it of a white color.'

Of these things, MORIENUS speaks thus: 'Behold the perfect Citrine, and that which is altered in its Citrinity; the perfect red and the one lessened in its redness, and further the perfect black in its blackness.' Hence it is clear that the Gold of the Philosophers is different to common Gold or Silver; though some Philosophers compare it for some reasons, not only to common Gold or Silver, but even to all metals. SENIOR says: 'I am a dry and hard Iron, and nothing is like me, for I am a coagulation to the Quicksilver of the Philosophers.' 'Turba' says: 'Copper and Lead become a precious Stone of the Philosophers.' The Lead which the Philosophers call Red Lead, is a beginning of the whole work, and nothing can be done without it; therefore some say: 'From red lead make iron, or Crocum; from white lead make a white tincture, or tin, from tin make copper, from copper make white lead, from white lead make Minium [red lead], from Minium make a Tincture and you have begun the Wisdom.' Although the Philosopher says that, nothing approaches Gold so nearly as Lead, for in it is the Life and all the occult Secret; but this is not meant of common Lead.

Moreover MARCASITE,[4] of which the stinking Earth wins golden scintillations, as MORIENUS says, it is also compared to ARSENIC, AURIPIGMENT and TUTIA. Others again compare it to many things not mineral at all, as to the Four Complexions, to Teriac, to the Basilisk,[5] to blood, and such like superfluous things, among minerals to Salt, Alum, Vitriol, and other things, on account of its manifold qualities.

Above all things, ALPHIDIUS warns us thus: 'Dear Son, beware of spirits, bodies and stones which are dead, as mentioned, for in them is no way, nor would you find guidance for your purpose with them, for their force does not multiply, but comes to nothing instead, while the Salt of the Philosophers is a Tincture extracted and absorbed from the bodies of metals, like as other alkaline salts are absorbed from other bodies.'

Of this SENIOR says that at first it turns to ashes, afterwards it becomes a Salt, and at last with a great deal of labor, it becomes the Mercury of the Philosophers. But the best and noblest of all is SAL AMONIAC, as confirmed by ARISTOTLE in his book OF THE SEVEN COMMANDMENTS, where he says: 'ALMISADIR, that is SAL AMONIAC, shall serve you only, for it solves the bodies, and makes them soft and spiritual.' The same says 'Turba': 'Know that the body does not tinge itself unless the Spirit which is hidden in its interior be extracted, when it will become a Water and a body of a spiritual Nature, because the thick earthy substance cannot tinge, but the proper one is of a thin Nature, and colors the tinged spirit of a watery Nature to an Elixir, because there has been extracted a white and red fixation, of a perfect coloring, and an all penetrating Tincture, which mixed with all the metals.'

THE PERFECTION OF THE WHOLE MASTERY DEPENDS ON THESE FEW POINTS:

That the SULFUR be extracted from THE PERFECT BODIES. THEY have MARS FIXED, which Sulfur is their noblest and most subtle part, a crystalline salt, sweet and savory and a radical moisture, which, if it were to remain for a year on the Fire would always be like molten wax. Wherefore a small part exalts a large quantity of common Quicksilver into genuine Gold.

On that account, the moisture or the Water which is extracted from the metallic bodies, is called the Soul of the Stone, or Mercury, but its forces are named Spirit, when affecting things of a Sulfurous Nature; while the solid Earth is the Body, the QUINTESSENCE is the ultimate TINCTURE. All these three are a united thing of one sole root, but having manifold effects and innumerable names, which, though having all the same meaning are yet like a chain linked into one another, so that where one ends the other begins.

In the last part is to be noticed the virtues and powers of the noble Tincture, which is to its opponents like a strong tower, and of which the old Sages discovered four principal virtues. Firstly, it gives health and cures man of various diseases; Secondly, it makes perfect the metallic bodies; Thirdly, it changes all base stones into precious ones; and Fourthly, it softens every kind of glass.

Of the first the Philosophers say that if taken in a warm draught of wine or Water, it will immediately cure paralysis, dropsy, leprosy, jaundice, palpitation, colic, fever, palsy, and many other internal diseases, as well as external sores, when used as a salve. It strengthens an unhealthy stomach, takes away rheumatism and cures all mental diseases; it relieves catarrh and bad eyes, and it invigorates the heart; it brings back the faculty of hearing, and renews the teeth, restores lame limbs, it heals burns and gangrene, as well as impostumes; it can be taken or used as salve or powder, for all external injuries, fistulas, cancers, swellings.

SENIOR says that it makes the man joyous, fresh, and healthy, rejuvenates inside and outside, for it is a medicine above all other medicines Of HIPPOCRATES, GALEN, CONSTANTINE, ALEXANDER, AVICENNA, and surpasses all the learned Physicians. This medicine should as well be mixed with other ones meeting the particular disease, or with Water. About the second virtue it is written that it changes all imperfect metals into Gold, and this is evident; for everything of Silver becomes Gold in color, substance, weight and consistency, as well as in kind, fusion, softness and hardness.

Thirdly, according to what is written this medicine changes all stones into precious ones, as in jasper, White and Red Coral, Emerald, Chrysolite,[6] Sapphires, further Crystals into Garnets, Rubies and Topazes, which are much more powerful than the natural ones. It softens and fuses all base and precious stones.

And FOURTHLY, in mixing this medicine with molten glass, the latter may be cut and changed into all colors.

The rest may be learnt by experience by any skilful artist.

CONCLUSION

The most noble Art and comforter of the poor, above all natural arts, which man may ever have on Earth, the noble Alchemy, is to be esteemed as the gift of God; for it is hidden mostly in manifold proverbs, figurative sayings and parables of the old Sages.

So says the Philosopher SENIOR: 'A sensible man, if he but tries this art, will soon perceive it from the books, and get a knowledge of this art, if his mind and intellect are illuminated.'

Whosoever therefore will act wisely should search for the Wisdom of the old Philosophers, which is shown in the wit and Artfulness of the manifold parables and roundabout sayings, thus hiding the proper operations and thus rendering their unriddling difficult.

To think over these things requires a very subtle mind, and only those with suitable faculties and knowledge will find it easy and natural. But as SENIOR says: 'For those who have no natural understanding of these things, there is nothing so precious in Nature as he who possesses this Art; he is like one who had a flint from which he strikes Fire and gives to whosoever he likes, without the stone getting any smaller through it.' It is as good as giving superfluous fine Gold. This Art is also better than all commerce, Gold and Silver, and her fruits are better than the wealth of all the world. For by means of this Art, is obtained that which furthers long life, health, her youngest fruit being the true AURUM, the most powerful balm and most precious gift of God, which the old Philosophers could find in Nature with their Art.

ALCHEMICAL WANDERINGS AND ADVENTURES
IN SEARCH OF THE PHILOSOPHER'S STONE

[Translated from the *Aurum Vellus*, Rohrschach (1598) by Julius Kohn (appended to his translation of the Harley *Splendor Solis*, London, Kegan Paul, Trench, Trubner & Co., 1920).]

WHEN I was a young fellow, I came to a Miner named Flocker, who was also an Alchemist, but he kept his knowledge secret, and I could get nothing out of him. He used a Process with common Lead, adding to it a peculiar Sulphur, or Brimstone; he fixed the Lead until it became hard, then fluid, and later on soft like Wax.

Of this prepared Lead, he took 20 Loth (10 ounces), and 1 mark pure unalloyed Silver, put both materials in flux and kept the composition in fusion for half an hour. Thereupon he parted the Silver, cast it in an ingot, when half of it was Gold.

I was grieved at heart that I could not have this art, but he refused to tell his secret process.

Shortly thereafter he tumbled down a mine and no one could tell what was the artifice he had used.

As I had seen it really done by this miner, I started in the year 1473 on my travels to search out an artist in Alchemy, and where I heard of one I went to him, and in these wanderings I passed 18 months, learning all kinds of Alchemical Operations, of no great importance, but I saw the reality of some of the PARTICULAR processes, and I spent 200 Florins of my own money, nevertheless I would not give up the search. I thought of boarding with some of my friends, and took a journey to Laibach, thence to Milan, and came to a monastery. There I heard some excellent lectures and served as an assistant, for about a year.

Then I traveled about, up and down in Italy, and came to an Italian tradesman, and a Jew, who understood German. These two made English Tin look like the best fine Silver, and sold it largely. I offered to serve them. The Jew persuaded the Trader to take me as a Servant, and I had to attend the fire, when they operated with their art I was diligent, and they kept nothing from me, as I pleased them well. In this way I learnt their art, which worked with corrosive and poisonous materials, and I stopped with them fourteen weeks.

Then I journeyed with the Jew to Venice. There he sold to a Turkish merchant forty pounds of this Silver. While he was haggling with the merchant I took six Loth of the Silver, and brought it to a Goldsmith, who spoke Latin, and kept two journeymen, and I asked him to test the Silver. He directed me to an Assayer on Saint Marks' Place, who was portly and wealthy. He had three German Assay-assistants. They soon brought the Silver to the test with strong acids, and refined it on the Cupel [a porous cup used to separate precious metals from base elements]; but it did not stand the test, and all flew away in the fire. And they spoke harshly to me asking where I got the Silver. I told them I had come on purpose to have it tested, that I might know if it was real silver.

When I saw the fraud, I returned not to the Jew, and paid no more attention to their art, for I feared to get into trouble together with the Jew, through the false silver.

I then went to a College in Venice, and asked there if they could give me two meals daily while I looked for employment. The Rector told me of a Hospital where there were other Germans, and there we got sumptuous food. It was an Institution for destitute strangers, and people of all nations came there.

The next day I went to Saint Marks' Place, and one of the Assay assistants came up, and asked me where I got that Silver? Why I had it tested, and if I had any more of it? I said I had no more of that silver, and that I was glad to have got rid of it, but I had the art and I should not mind telling it to him. That pleased the Assayer, and he asked me if I could work in a Laboratory? I told him I was a Laborer travelling on purpose to work in alchemical Laboratories. That pleased him vastly, and he told me of a nobleman who kept a laboratory, and who wanted a German Assistant. I readily accepted, and he took me straight to the Chief Chemist, named Tauler, a German, and he was glad to get me. So he engaged me on the spot at a weekly wage of two crowns and board as well. He took me about six Italian miles out of Venice to a fine large mansion called Ponteleone. I never saw such Laboratory work, in all kinds of Particular Processes, and medicines, as in that place. There everything one could think of was provided and ready for use. Each workman had his own private room, and there was a special cook for the whole staff of Laboratory assistants.

The Chief Chemist gave me at once an Ore to work on, which had been sent to the nobleman, four days previously. It was a Cinnabar the Chief had covered with all kinds of dirt, just to try my knowledge, and he told me to get it done with in two days. I was kept busy, but succeeded with the Particular Process, and on testing the ingot of the fixed Mercury, the whole weighed NINE Loth, the test gave three Loth fine Gold.

That was my first work and stroke of luck. The Chief Chemist reported it to the nobleman, who came out unexpectedly, spoke to me in Latin, called me his Fortunatum, tapped me on the shoulder and gave me twenty-nine crowns. He spoke a funny kind of Latin I could hardly understand, but I was pleased with the money.

I was then put on oath not to reveal my Art to anyone. To make a long story short, everything had to be kept secret, as it should be. If someone boasts of his art, even if he has got the Truth, God's justice will not let such a one go on. Therefore be silent, even if you have the highest Tincture, but give charity.

I saw all kinds of operations at this Nobleman's Laboratory, and as the Chief Chemist favored me, he gave me all kinds of operations to do, and also mentioned, that our employer spent about 30,000 Crowns on these arts, paying cash for all manner of books in various languages, to which he gave great attention. I myself witnessed that he paid 6,000 Crowns for the Manuscript SARLAMETHON, a process for a Tincture in the Greek Language. This the nobleman had soon translated and gave me to work. I brought that process to a finish in fifteen weeks. Therewith I tinged three metals into fine Gold; and this was kept most secret.

This nobleman was gorgeous and powerful, and when once a year the Signora went out to sea, to witness the throwing of a Gem Ring into the water at the ceremony of wedding the Adriatic, our gentleman with many others of the Venetian nobility went out in his grand pleasure ship, when suddenly a hurricane arose and he with many others of the Venetian Lords and Rulers, was drowned.

The Laboratory was then shut up by the family, the men paid off, but they kept the Chief Chemist.

Then I went away from Venice, to a still better place for my purpose, where Cabalistic and Magical books in Egyptian language were entrusted to my care, these I had carefully translated into Greek, and then again retranslated into Latin. There I found and captured the Treasure of the Egyptians. I also saw what was the great Subject they worked with, and the ancient Heathen Kings used such Tinctures and have themselves operated with them, namely, Kings XOFAR, SUNSFOR, XOGAR, XOPHALAT, JULATON, XOMAN and others. All these had the great treasures of the TINCTURE and it is surprising that GOD should have revealed such Secrets to the Heathen, but they kept it very secret.

After a while I saw the fundamental principles of this art, then I began working out the Best Tincture (but they all proceed, in a most indescribable manner from the same root), when I came to the end of the Work I found such a beautiful red color as no scarlet can compare with, and such a treasure as words cannot tell, and which can be infinitely augmented. One part tinged 1,500 parts Silver into Gold. I will not tell how after manifold augmentation what quantities of Silver and other metal I tinged after the MULTIPLICATION. I was amazed.

STUDY WHAT THOU ART,
WHEREOF THOU ART A PART,
WHAT THOU KNOWEST OF THIS ART,
THIS IS REALLY WHAT THOU ART.
ALL THAT IS WITHOUT THEE
ALSO IS WITHIN,
THUS WROTE TRISMOSIN.

NOTES

References to the English translation of the Collected Works of C. G. Jung are indicated as CW by volume and paragraph number.

Foreword

1　J. Cambray, 'Synchronicity and Emergence,' *American Imago* 59/4 (2002), 409–34.

Preface

1　Jung's commentary to the *Secret of the Golden Flower* first appeared in English in 1931, and it is reprinted in CW 13.
2　The version of the *Splendor Solis* in the British Library, MS Harley 3469, is an illuminated manuscript containing twenty-two allegorical paintings and accompanying text. It is dated 1582, based upon that date appearing within two of the paintings. The text is apparently considered as unremarkable as the plates are remarkable. It was translated into English by J[ulius] K[ohn] and published as *Splendor Solis*, London, Kegan Paul, Trench, Trubner, & Co., n.d. Marie-Louise von Franz points out that it contains many passages from the *Aurora Consurgens*, ed. M.-L. von Franz, New York, Bollingen Foundation, 1966, p. 24.
3　Edward Edinger, *Anatomy of the Psyche*, Peru, IL, Open Court, 1985, p. 4.
4　The *Splendor Solis* images shown in Dr. Henderson's 1987 lecture are from the illuminated manuscript, Harley 3469, in the British Library, London.
5　The filming of this lecture was made possible by a generous grant from Georgia Johnson.
6　Michael Flanigan, the curator of San Francisco Archives for Research on Archetypal Symbolism, C. G. Jung Institute of San Francisco, generously made the copies and also provided the commentary that accompanies each image in their collection.
7　We are grateful to Ellen Garfinkle, Ph.D., who passed away after a long illness in 2001, who gave permission for us to refer to her transcription of the second half of the lecture.

Introduction

1　Foreword to the second German edition of *Alchemical Studies*, CW 13, p. 3.
2　Ibid., p. 4.

3 CW 12, ¶¶315–16.
4 CW 12, Foreword to the Swiss edition (1943), p. x.
5 CW 12, ¶¶44–331.
6 CW 13, ¶¶88.
7 Contemporary physicists and chemists often work in a different way, using machines and computers to make observations of phenomena that they cannot directly experience.
8 Foreword to 'The Psychology of the Transference,' CW 16, p. 166.
9 See, for example, 'The Archetypal Forms,' in R. Tarnas, *The Passion of the Western Mind*, New York, Ballantine Books, 1991/1993, pp. 6–12. Tarnas notes, 'Plato directs the philosopher's attention away from the external and concrete, from taking things at face value, and points "deeper" and "inward," so that one may "awaken" to a more profound level of reality' (p. 8). For additional clarification of Jung's use of the word 'archetype,' the reader is referred to his essay, 'Psychological Aspects of the Mother Archetype,' CW 9/1, ¶¶152–5. In addition to Plato, Jung cites ethnological sources: Bastian's 'elementary ideas,' the 'categories' of imagination of Hubert and Mauss, as well as Usener's 'unconscious thinking.'
10 CW 9/1, ¶151.
11 Ibid., ¶155.
12 CW 12, Foreword to the Swiss edition (1943), p. x.
13 CW 16.
14 Jung owned a copy of the 1598 Rorschach edition of *Aureum Vellus*, which contains the *Splendor Solis*. He also referred to the English translation by K[ohn] of the British Library Harley manuscript. Images from the Harley manuscript are reproduced in CW 12, ¶112, fig. 32; ¶302, fig. 95; ¶370, fig. 134; ¶484, fig. 219. Jung quotes the text in CW 12, ¶530 and CW 13, ¶153 and in CW 14, ¶¶465 and 626. In CW 13, ¶268, he refers to the image reproduced in CW 12, fig. 219.
15 Adam McLean ('Introduction' and 'Commentary' to J. Godwin's translation of S. Trismosin's *Splendor Solis*, 1991) divides the images into four series: the first four images stating the basic problem, the next seven images representing a seven-stage alchemical process, the following seven another seven-stage process, and the final four images showing 'The End of the Work.'
16 This discussion relies primarily on two histories of alchemy: John Read, *Prelude to Chemistry*, London, G. Bell & Sons, 1936, and E. J. Holmyard, *Alchemy*, New York, Dover Publications, 1957/1990.
17 J. Diamond, *Guns, Germs, and Steel*, New York and London, Norton, 1997/1999, p. 362.
18 This was the case in the Western Hemisphere, as well as in the East. Prior to contact with Europeans, meteoric iron was used by cultures in the Americas, such as the Greenland Eskimos, Mayas, and Aztecs, who had not developed tool-making from iron ore (ibid.).
19 M. Eliade, *The Forge and the Crucible*, Chicago and London, University of Chicago Press, 1956/1978, p. 25.
20 Ibid., p. 104.
21 Ibid., p. 102.
22 Ibid., p. 104.
23 Ibid., p. 51.

24 Ibid., p. 121.
25 From ch. 27, as quoted in ibid., p. 115.
26 Read, *Prelude to Chemistry*, p. 4.
27 Eliade, *Forge and Crucible*, p. 89.
28 Ibid., p. 81.
29 I. Robinet, J. F. Pas, and N. J. Girardot, *Taoist Meditation: The Mao-Shan Tradition of Great Purity*, SUNY Series in Chinese Philosophy and Culture, Buffalo, State University of New York Press, 1993.
30 *Shatapatha Brahmana*, xii. 7. 1. 7, as quoted in Eliade, *Forge and Crucible*, p. 69.
31 Read, *Prelude to Chemistry*, plate I.
32 Eliade, *Forge and Crucible*, p. 113.
33 Ibid., p. 118.
34 Ibid., p. 135.
35 See A. Mookerjee and M. Khanna, *The Tantric Way*, London, Thames & Hudson, 1977, esp. pp. 108–10.
36 Eliade, *Forge and Crucible*, p. 120. Kundalini yoga was one method or practice for this embodied transformation or alchemy.
37 M. Khanna, *Yantra: The Tantric Symbol of Cosmic Unity*, London, Thames & Hudson, 1979, p. 114.
38 Holmyard, *Alchemy*, p. 25.
39 Ibid., pp. 25–42, 60–152; Read, *Prelude to Chemistry*, pp. 1–31.
40 Read, *Prelude to Chemistry*, p. 8.
41 The following discussion is based largely on ibid., pp. 8–20.
42 Ibid., p. 9.
43 Holmyard, *Alchemy*, pp. 25–6.
44 Ibid., p. 27.
45 'The Treatise of Zosimos the Divine Concerning the Art,' III. i. 2, as quoted in C. G. Jung, 'The Visions of Zosimos' (1937/1954/1967), CW 13, ¶86.
46 Ibid.
47 Jung, 'Visions of Zosimos.'
48 Holmyard, *Alchemy*, pp. 29–31.
49 Translated by F. S. Taylor and quoted by Holmyard, *Alchemy*, p. 31.
50 Read, *Prelude to Chemistry*, p. 54.
51 Except where noted, the following discussion of Islamic alchemy is based on Holmyard, *Alchemy*, pp. 67–104.
52 Persian Christians, who declared themselves autonomous in 410 and referred to themselves as 'Chaldeans' (*The Catholic Encyclopedia*, vol. 10, Online edition, 1911/1999).
53 von Franz, *Alchemy*, op. cit., p. 108.
54 We will not focus on these processes and their psychological symbolism. We highly recommend Edward Edinger's thorough study: *Anatomy of the Psyche*, Peru, IL, Open Court, 1985.
55 Dick Davis, Introduction to Farid Ud-Din Attar, *The Conference of the Birds*, trans. Afkham Darbandi and Dick Davis, London, Penguin Books, 1984, p. 16.
56 von Franz, *Aurora Consurgens*, p. 12.
57 In: M.-L. von Franz, *Alchemy: An Introduction to the Symbolism and Psychology*, Toronto, Inner City Books, 1980, pp. 107–76.
58 W. Manchester, *A World Lit Only by Fire*, Boston, Little, Brown & Co., 1992, p. 5.

59 Peter Murray Jones, *Medieval Medicine in Illuminated Manuscripts*, London, British Library, 1998, p. 67.

60 Ibid., pp. 67–8.

61 R. Kieckhefer, *Magic in the Middle Ages*, Cambridge, Cambridge University Press, 1989/2000, p. 146.

62 The information on Albertus Magnus presented here relies on von Franz, *Aurora Consurgens*, pp. 412–21.

63 Ibid. See also von Franz's lectures on *Aurora* in her book *Alchemy*, pp. 177–272.

64 In order to understand this step, we must remind ourselves that in the Middle Ages sulfur and mercury were not the names of the elements as we use them today. Rather, they were the names of ordinary substances *as well as* the names of two basic *qualities* found in every metal. Ordinary sulfur was observed to be both yellow in color and combustible. This was thought to be so because ordinary sulfur had a great deal of the quality *sulfur* or 'sophic sulfur.' Sophic sulfur, because of its color, was thought to be the spirit of gold and, because of its combustibility, the spirit of fire. Metals that were more combustible were believed to have more sophic sulfur (i.e., the quality sulfur). The *quality* mercury referred to fusibility and fluidity, with ordinary mercury having a great deal of those qualities. Gold was thought to be composed of both fire and water, and of two 'spirits,' sulfur and mercury.

65 M.-L. von Franz, *Redemption Motifs in Fairy Tales*, Toronto, Inner City Books, 1980, p. 222.

66 Ibid.

67 Eliade, *Forge and Crucible*, pp. 47–9.

68 Ibid., p. 48.

69 Ibid., p. 49.

70 Holmyard, *Alchemy*, p. 163.

71 See: Dava Sobel, *Galileo's Daughter*, New York, Walker & Co., 1999, which describes Galileo's life and work, in addition to his relationship to his daughter.

72 C. Ginsburg, *The Cheese and the Worms*, trans. J. and A. Tedeschi, Baltimore, Johns Hopkins University Press, 1976/1980.

73 This will be discussed in the commentary on Plate I–4.

74 Holmyard, *Alchemy*, contains numerous accounts.

75 Thus Paracelsus was born at about the time the text of the *Splendor Solis* is believed to have been written. However, it seems very possible that the painter of the images in the British Library's *Splendor Solis*, dated 1582, would have known of Paracelsus' work.

76 The title page of the *Aureum Vellus* (Rorschach, 1598) makes the claim that the author of the *Splendor Solis* was Paracelsus' teacher, but we have not established the basis of this claim.

77 See for example: A. Weeks, *Paracelsus: Speculative Theory and the Crisis of the Early Reformation*, Albany, State University of New York Press, 1997.

78 Ibid., p. 165.

79 The English translation is entitled simply, 'Paracelsus,' CW 15, ¶¶1–17.

80 Ibid., ¶1.

81 Paracelsus, *Panagranum* (Sherlock's translation), quoted by Holmyard, *Alchemy*, pp. 171–2.

82 'Paracelsus as a Spiritual Phenomenon,' CW 13, ¶¶145–236 (1942/1967); 'Paracelsus the Physician,' CW 15, ¶¶18–43 (1941/1966).

83 Jung, 'Paracelsus as a Spiritual Phenomenon,' CW 13, ¶146.

84 Paracelsus, quoted in Holmyard, *Alchemy*, pp. 174–5.

85 This is based on a table in Read, *Prelude to Chemistry*, p. 27.

86 Read has pointed out that in modern literature on alchemy, mercury is often incorrectly associated with soul and sulfur incorrectly associated with spirit. (Read, *Prelude to Chemistry*, p. 297, n. 47.)

87 Tarnas, p. 156.

88 Ibid., p. 157.

89 C. W. Bynum, 'The Female Body and Religious Practice in the Later Middle Ages,' in *Fragments for a History of the Human Body*, Part One, ed., M. Feher with R. Naddaff and N. Tazi, Cambridge, MA, and London, MIT Press, 1989, p. 191.

90 Quoted in Ginsberg, *Cheese and Worms*, p. 75.

91 Ibid., pp. 71–2.

92 Quoted in Jung, 'Paracelsus as a Spiritual Phenomenon,' CW 13, ¶148.

93 'Caput de morbis somnii,' ed. Sudhoff, IX, p. 360, as quoted in Jung, 'Paracelsus as a Spiritual Phenomenon,' CW 13, footnote 6, pp. 113–14.

94 The manuscript in the British Library, Harley 3469, was translated into English by K[ohn]. His translation also includes a commentary by the translator and additional texts attributed to Trismosin.

95 von Franz, *Aurora Consurgens*, pp. 7–21.

96 Ibid., p. 24.

97 Salomon Trismosin is no doubt a name adopted by the author, in keeping with the habit of alchemists to take a name with classical associations (cf. Paracelsus, Aristotle). Salomon probably refers to the biblical Solomon, which was spelled 'Salomon' at the time. The alchemists claimed that Salomon was an alchemist and built his temple with the help of the philosopher's stone (L. Abraham, *A Dictionary of Alchemical Imagery*, Cambridge, Cambridge University Press, 1998, p. 186). The meaning of 'Trismosin' is obscure. 'Trismos' means 'grinding' in Greek and could possibly refer to the alchemist's grinding of the materials used in the laboratory, while 'tris' of course refers to the number three, which is used symbolically in a number of contexts in alchemy. Adam McLean states on his website (www.levity.com) that the author is now believed to be Ulrich Poysel, but he gives no further references or additonal information.

98 Appended to the *Splendor Solis*, trans. K[ohn]. The translation erroneously reports the date as 1498; however, it is 1598. It is also reprinted in Read, *Prelude to Chemistry*, pp. 69–74. The K[ohn] translation is reprinted in the Appendix.

99 Manchester, *World Lit Only by Fire*, p. 47.

100 Sobel, *Galileo's Daughter*.

101 Manchester, *World Lit Only by Fire*, p. 27.

102 Ibid., p. 230.

103 CW 13, ¶199.

104 Ibid.

105 CW 12, ¶23.

106 MS Germ. Fol. 42: *Splendor Solis* (1532–5). The recent translation of the *Splendor Solis* by J. Godwin (Grand Rapids, MI, Phanes Press, 1991), with an 'Introduction'

and 'Commentary' by A. McLean, contains a bibliography of *Splendor Solis* manuscripts (pp. 13–14). We have obtained and examined copies of the images from MS Germ. Fol. 42: *Splendor Solis*. One image in this series appears twice, in mirror image, suggesting that some kind of copying technique (tracing? a *camera lucida*?) was used to create them.

107 'Introduction' to J. Godwin's translation of the *Splendor Solis*, p. 9.

108 J. Godwin's recent translation is based upon manuscripts which differ from the British Library manuscript but are nearly identical to one another. They are dated 1598 and 1708, from Rorschach and Hamburg respectively. This translation is illustrated with reproductions of engravings from the 1708 Hamburg edition, which differ in many substantive features from the 1582 Harley images.

109 S. Klossowski de Rola, in a discussion of the various *Splendor Solis* manuscripts on A. McLean's website (www.alchemywebsite.com, 23 June 1999), asserts that the best illuminated paintings of the *Splendor Solis* were painted by members of the Glockendon family of Nuremberg. His research indicates that Albrecht Glockendon lived in a house called 'Das Haus beim Sonnenbad' or, 'The House near the Sun-bath.' Klossowski believes it is likely that the Harley manuscript was painted by Gabriel Glockendon. He did not document these assertions in that forum but plans to present information in a forthcoming book.

The Glockendon family had a famous workshop and produced a Prayer Book in German for Albert of Brandenburg, known as the *Glockendon Hours* (1534), which is held in the Estense Library in Modena, Italy. We have been able to view one image from this manuscript, as it appears at www.facsimile.ch/frame_werk31_d.html. This image, showing the New Testament 'Flight into Egypt' of Joseph, Mary, and the infant Christ, bears a striking stylistic resemblance to the *Splendor Solis* images.

110 This close relationship is evidenced in the *Splendor Solis* manuscript in the British Library, on one of the pages before the text proper, where an anecdote is written in pencil, in an old-fashioned script. It tells of an eighteenth-century Baron Boetcher who apprenticed himself to an apothecary in Berlin and there met an alchemist and became his apprentice. The account claims that he later invented Dresden porcelain.

111 C. de Hamel, *Scribes and Illuminators*, London, British Museum Press, 1991, pp. 57–8.

112 Ibid., p. 62.

113 Ibid.

114 Ibid.

115 There are many references to the color symbolism in alchemy in Jung's *Collected Works*. James Hillman has also written about color symbolism.

116 See, for example, J. F. Moffitt, 'Marcel DuChamp: Alchemist of the Avant-Garde,' in *The Spiritual in Art: Abstract Painting 1890–1985*, exhibition catalog, New York, Abbeville Press, 1986, pp. 257–69.

117 J. Elkins, *What Painting Is*, London and New York, Routledge, 1999. We thank Jean Kirsch for bringing this book to our attention.

118 Ibid., p. 165.

119 CW 13, ¶199.

120 CW 16, ¶358.

121 See CW 12, ¶401.

122 Joseph Henderson (*Cultural Attitudes in Psychological Perspective*, Toronto, Inner

City Books, 1984) has developed Jung's ideas to include a cultural unconscious and a typology of the individual's way of relating to culture. Andrew Samuels has written about the relationship of psyche in the context of political life (*The Political Psyche*, London, Routledge, 1993). More recently, Samuel Kimbles ('The Cultural Complex and the Myth of Invisibility,' in T. Singer (ed.), *The Vision Thing*, London, Routledge, 2000, pp. 157–69) has extended Jung's theory of complexes to include cultural complexes. This article appeared in a volume edited by Thomas Singer on the cultural and political dimensions of the psyche; Singer has also written about the underlying complexes shaping current political events ('The Cultural Complex and Archetypal Defenses of the Collective Spirit, Baby Zeus, Elian Gonzales, Constantine's Sword, and Other Holy Wars,' *San Francisco Jung Institute Library Journal* 29 (2002), 5–28). The highly creative work of these authors may offer new paradigms to the fields of political science and social history, as well as more attention in analytic work to the powerful effects of cultural attitudes and politics on the individual's psyche.

123 Jung's interest in process can be seen in a discussion on 12 March 1930, with his students in their seminar on dreams (C. G. Jung, *Seminar on Dream Analysis*, ed. W. McGuire, Bollingen Series 99, Princeton, NJ, Princeton University Press, 1984). Jung asked his students to present their 'attempts . . . to get at the composition of dreams or the melody of their motifs . . .', and during the subsequent discussion he commented, 'For the sake of completeness we should write records of all the conscious states of the dreamer during his analysis. That is a task for the future – that somebody should make a diary of whatever occurs in his conscious, and thus we would have the two sets to work with' (p. 527). Joseph Henderson's recollection of this discussion, in which he participated, will be found in our discussion of Plate II–3.

The First Series

1 When referring to a particular painting, we have designated the series by a Roman numeral and the order within the series by an Arabic numeral. Plate I–1 precedes the 'Preface' in the text.

2 Dante Alighieri, *The Inferno of Dante*, trans. R. Pinsky, New York, Farrar, Straus & Giroux, 1994, Canto XXVI, lines 16–18. Also see the Foreword by J. Freccero, pp. xv–xvi, and the note to Canto XXVI by N. Pinsky, p. 342.

3 W. Manchester, *A World Lit Only by Fire*, Boston, Little, Brown & Co., 1992, p. 24.

4 M.-L. von Franz, *Number and Time*, Northwestern University Press, 1974, p. 109. For an interesting discussion of the numbers three and six, as well as a dream of a physicist of a six-pointed star, see pp. 101–11.

5 This of course can occur at any point in treatment when the patient begins to be aware that an important aspect of his/her identity or way of functioning is not working to the benefit of the whole of the personality.

6 In 'Psychology of the Transference' Jung wrote about the symbolism of the alchemical bath and its relevance to analytic process (CW 16, ¶¶453–6).

7 For a depth psychological view of integrity, see: J. Beebe, *Integrity in Depth*, New York, Fromm International, 1995.

8 Trismosin, trans K[ohn], *Splendor Solis*, p. 17.

9 See von Franz, *Aurora Consurgens*, pp. 392–5.

10 See N. Russack, *Animal Guides in Life, Myth, and Dreams: An Analyst's Notebook*, Toronto, Inner City Books, 2002. S. Allan, *in The Shape of the Turtle: Myth, Art, and Cosmos in Early China* (Albany, State University of New York Press, 1991) explores the symbolic role of the turtle in early Chinese culture and cosmology.

11 Read, *Prelude to Chemistry*, pp. 246–51.

12 Ibid., pp. 250–4.

13 Ibid., p. 251.

14 Artists, however, were interested in nature, as shown by their sketch books and the borders of illuminated manuscripts. See Robert Bartlett (ed.), *Medieval Panorama*, Los Angeles, J. Paul Getty Museum; London, Thames & Hudson, 2001, pp. 218–19.

15 This plate follows the 'Preface' in the Harley manuscript.

16 According to Jung: thinking, feeling, sensing, and intuition. For a description of these functions in the context of introverted/extraverted attitudes, see C. G. Jung, *Psychological Types*, CW 6, ¶¶556–670. Briefly: *Thinking* 'is the psychological function which, following its own laws, brings the contents of ideation into conceptual connection with one another.... [and] may be divided into active and passive thinking' (CW 6, ¶830). *Feeling* is 'primarily a process that takes place between the ego and a given content, a process, moreover, that imparts to the content a definite value in the sense of acceptance or rejection ("like" or "dislike")' (CW 6, ¶724). *Intuition* 'mediates perceptions in an *unconscious way* ... In intuition a content presents itself whole and complete, without our being able to explain or discover how this content came into existence.... As with sensation, its contents have the character of being "given," in contrast to the "derived" or "produced" character of *thinking* and *feeling* contents' (CW 6, ¶770). *Sensation* 'is the psychological function that mediates the perception of a physical stimulus ... [and] is related not only to external stimuli but to inner ones, i.e., to changes in the internal organic processes' (CW 6, ¶792). More extensive definitions may be found in the paragraphs cited.

17 See Plate II–5.

18 Joan Halifax, *Shaman: The Wounded Healer*, London, Thames & Hudson, 1982, p. 82.

19 X. Yang, *The Golden Age of Chinese Archaeology*, New Haven and London, Yale University Press, 1999, pp. 314–15.

20 M. Eliade, *Shamanism: Archaic Techniques of Ecstasy*, Bollingen Series 76, Princeton, NJ, Princeton University Press, 1964, p. 155; ibid., p. 83.

21 CW 13, ¶259.

22 Read, *Prelude to Chemistry*, p. 27.

23 Read (ibid., p. 102) notes that, 'In exoteric alchemy, Sol and Luna denoted gold and silver; but in the esoteric literature and operations of the adepts these terms usually stood for sophic sulphur and sophic mercury respectively – or for "our sulphur" and "our mercury," as they were often called. The best source of sophic sulphur was commonly held to be gold; and thus such terms as sophic sulphur, gold of the philosophers and seed of gold are to a large extent synonymous in alchemical litera-ture. For this reason, both gold and sulphur – of the sophic kind – were identified by

the adepts with the masculine principle and represented by the symbol of Sol, which had always been associated with ordinary gold. Again, the feminine principle, sophic mercury, was linked with silver, owing to an imagined relationship between quicksilver (argent-vive) and silver (argent): the exoteric symbol of Luna was therefore transferred by the adepts to denote sophic mercury. This dual application of the symbols of Sol and Luna has given rise to much confusion of thought, not only among the original alchemists, but also among their commentators' (p. 102).

24 The symbol of a container was important to the psychoanalytic theory of Wilfred Bion (for a summary, see J. and N. Symington, *The Clinical Thinking of Wilfred Bion*, London and New York, Routledge, 1996, pp. 50–8). However, the way in which container is used in this instance has more in common with Winnicott's notion of a 'holding environment.'

25 The sword as an instrument that can divide with precision is found in many cultures. For example, in Tibetan Buddhist iconography, the sword of Manjusri symbolizes discriminating wisdom.

26 This plate follows the First Treatise, 'The Origin of the Stone of the Wise and The Art of Its Production,' in the Harley manuscript.

27 This was transcribed from examination of the original and differs in some respects from transcriptions which have been reprinted elsewhere. The transcription by K[ohn] renders as 'vino' characters which appear to this reader to look more like 'uro,' meaning to dry, burn, desiccate. However, 'vino' is used above because it makes more sense in the context of the mixing of the two fluids. In *Mysterium Coniunctionis*, Jung says that, 'wine in the form of a liquid represents the body, but as alcohol it represents spirit' (CW 14, ¶478). More scholarship will be required to clarify this point.

28 The colors of these stars are blended between the dark (black, gray) and the golden, meaning that there is a blending of these two opposites in the seven stars.

29 CW 12, ¶66. See also: M.-L. von Franz, *The Golden Ass of Apuleius*, rev. edn., Boston and London, Shambhala, 1992.

30 von Franz (ed.), *Aurora Consurgens*. The author of the Aurora was in turn paraphrasing Senior (Zadith ben Hamuel, *De chemia Senioris antiquissimi philosophi libellus*. Strasbourg, 1566, pp. 10–11).

31 *Aurora Consurgens*, p. 215.

32 Read, pp. 102–103.

33 See 'Integrity and Gender' in Beebe, *Integrity in Depth*, pp. 70–98. Beebe discusses the unpublished work of Howard Teich, who posits solar and lunar opposites, not necessarily unconscious, within each gender. This goes beyond Jung's notion of *anima* and *animus*.

34 See also Bynum, 'The Female Body and Religious Practice in the Later Middle Ages,' where she argues that Christ had a variety of features that were associated with the feminine and that women's bodies were associated with Christ's body.

35 See J. L. Henderson, *Thresholds of Initiation*, Middletown, CT, Wesleyan University Press, 1967.

36 For further discussion of Kundalini Yoga, see section on Plate II–7.

37 CW 12, ¶4.

38 This plate follows the Second Treatise, 'Matter and the Nature of the Philosopher's Stone,' in the Harley manuscript.

39 Trismosin, *Splendor Solis*, trans. K[ohn], p. 44.

40 In the 1708 Hamburg edition of the *Splendor Solis* (trans. J. Godwin, op. cit., p. 27) a crescent moon lies on the ground in front of the queen.

41 CW 12.

42 Ibid., see figs. 164 and 165, pp. 310 and 312.

43 This is the Latin as commonly used. The actual inscription reads, 'Maascheulium coagula.'

44 This again is the Latin for a common alchemical theme which is obviously implied by the actual inscription on the image, which reads, 'Viramium.'

45 Abraham, *Dictionary*, p. 211.

46 R. Patai, *The Jewish Alchemists: A History and Source Book*, Princeton, NJ, Princeton University Press, 1994, p. 183, cited in Abraham, *Dictionary*, p. 186.

47 See Abraham, *Dictionary*, p. 187.

48 See J. Culbert-Koehn, 'Analysis of Hard and Soft: Tustin's Contribution to a Jungian Study of Opposites,' *Proceedings of the California Spring Conference of Jungian Analysts and Control Stage Candidates*, C. G. Jung Institute of San Francisco, 1997, pp. 49–55.

49 CW 16, ¶¶362–3.

50 Jung encouraged Dora Kalff to look into the technique ('sandplay'), which was originally developed by Lowenfeld in London. Kalff formulated it in her own way and taught it widely. Briefly, the therapist provides a shallow tray of sand, plus water and many tiny figures of plants, animals, people, mythological figures, buildings, and objects. The patient then creates a 'world' in the sand. There are a number of books written on this subject, and an international organization of sandplay therapists publishes the *Journal of Sandplay Therapy*. For further information, see K. Bradway and B. McCoard, *Sandplay: Silent Workshop of the Psyche*, London and New York, Routledge, 1997; D. M. Kalff, *Sandplay: A Psychotherapeutic Approach to the Psyche*, Santa Monica, CA, Sigo, 1980.

51 P. Jayakar, *The Earthen Drum*, New Delhi, National Museum, n.d., p. 15.

52 This is, of course, a *trompe l'oeil*, as are all the frames.

53 C. Kerényi, *The Heroes of the Greeks*, London, Thames & Hudson, 1959, p. 351.

54 Ibid., pp. 353–4.

55 A. Roob, *Alchemy and Mysticism*, New York and London, Taschen, 1997, p. 369; G. G. Sill, *A Handbook of Symbols in Christian Art*, New York, Collier Books, 1979, p. 17.

56 J. E. Cirlot, *A Dictionary of Symbols*, New York, Barnes & Noble, 1971/1993, p. 23.

57 P. Kværne, *The Bon Religion of Tibet*, Boston, Shambhala, 1996, p. 143.

58 Quoted in ibid., p. 146.

59 Trismosin, *Splendor Solis* trans. K[ohn], pp. 22–3. For an edited version of his translation, see the Appendix.

60 T. Martin, *Ancient Greece From Prehistoric to Hellenistic Times*, New Haven and London, Yale University Press, 1996.

61 *Encyclopaedia Britannica*, 1942, vol. 7, p. 394.

62 Tarnas, *Passion of the Western Mind*, p. 73.

63 See Introduction.

64 In *Aurum Vellus*, Rorschach, 1498, and translated in the *Splendor Solis*, trans. K[ohn], p. 88.

65 CW 13, ¶118.
66 See CW 16, ¶403, for Jung's discussion of the Mercurial Fountain in the first plate of the *Rosarium Philosophorum*. This fountain has three pipes, and out of one flows the *lac virginis*.
67 CW 14, ¶4.
68 CW 12.
69 CW 12, ¶67.
70 Ibid., ¶68.
71 Ibid., ¶110.
72 Ibid., ¶112.
73 Ibid., ¶113.
74 The analyst may be tempted to discuss the transpersonal nature of the transference in order to avoid its intensity. This is a most delicate matter, and it is important that the analyst accept and value the analysand's feelings as being very real, which they are. This holding function is possible because the analyst is in turn held by the deeper perspective achieved through his or her own experience as a patient in analysis. (Jung was the first psychoanalyst to recognize the need for a training analysis for the analyst.)
75 In the Harley manuscript, the Third Treatise, 'The Means Whereby the Whole Work of this Mastery is Perfected,' consists of an introductory paragraph citing the alchemist known as Hermes followed by seven parables. This plate (I–5) follows the first parable. The plates we have numbered I–6 through I–11 follow each of the remaining six parables included in the Third Treatise, to complete the First Series.
76 Esther 1, *Revised Standard Version of the Bible*.
77 Ibid.
78 Ibid.
79 CW 9/2, ¶¶267–8.
80 CW 13, ¶119.
81 Active imagination will be discussed at more length in the commentary to Plate II–1. A collection of Jung's writings on active imagination may be found in: C. G. Jung, *Jung on Active Imagination*, ed. J. Chodorow, Princeton, NJ, Princeton University Press, 1997.
82 According to Jung, 'An image which frequently appears among the archetypal configurations of the unconscious is that of the tree or the wonder-working plant. ... If a mandala may be described as a symbol of the self seen in cross section, then the tree would represent a profile view of it: the self depicted as a process of growth' (CW 13, ¶304).
83 CW 13, ¶242.
84 The legendary founder of alchemy, an Egyptian, 'Hermes Trismegistos.'
85 Trismosin, *Splendor Solis*, trans. K[ohn], p. 28.
86 The Roman name for Persephone.
87 P. Vergilius Maro ('Virgil'), *Aeneid*, trans. T. C. Williams, Boston, Houghton Mifflin, 1910. Available on the internet at www.Perseus.org.
88 See J. Campbell, *Historical Atlas of World Mythology*, vol. 1: *The Way of the Animal Powers*, San Francisco, Harper & Row, 1983, e.g., pp. 147–51, on the bear cult.
89 M. Eliade, *Shamanism: Archaic Techniques of Ecstasy*, Bollingen Series 76, New York, Pantheon Books, 1964.

90 C. G. Jung, *Visions*, ed. Claire Douglas, Princeton, NJ, Princeton University Press, 1997, pp. 581–2.

91 CW 18, ¶1554.

92 R. Greenson, *The Technique and Practice of Psychoanalysis*, vol. 1, New York, International Universities Press, 1967, pp. 250–1.

93 Ibid., p. 250.

94 One might think of this material as being brought up by the anima or animus. Jung used the terms anima and animus to denote a specific soul-image (usually of the opposite gender), produced by the unconscious. It may be represented, for example, in a dream by an image of an individual person or by a mythological or cultural figure. Jung said that when a person is unconscious of his/her individuality, then the soul-image will be of the same sex, although this opinion has been questioned subsequently. See CW ¶¶808–11 for a brief definition and discussion of these terms.

95 In the Third Parable (see Appendix).

96 See C. G. Jung, *Mysterium Coniunctionis*, CW 14, ¶¶464–83, for amplifications of the theme of the dying king and the young king, or *puellus regius*.

97 M.-L. von Franz speaks of the Self as a self-renewing system in: *Redemption Motifs in Fairy Tales*, Toronto, Inner City Books, 1980, p. 84.

98 Trismosin, *Splendor Solis*, trans. K[ohn], p. 30.

99 This is found on the title page of *Le Tableau des Riches Inventions*, Paris, 1600. Jung owned a copy of a 1610 edition of this work, and the title page is reproduced in CW 12 as fig. 4.

100 CW 13, ¶357.

101 *Artis Auriferae* II, Basel, 1593.

102 See CW 13, ¶¶119 and 267.

103 Ibid., p. 141, footnote 39.

104 Ibid., pp. 277–8, footnote 14.

105 J. Campbell, *The Masks of God*, vol. 3: *Occidental Mythology*, Penguin Books, 1964, pp. 20–1.

106 K. Kerényi, *The Heroes of the Greeks*, London, Thames & Hudson, 1959, pp. 172–7.

107 R. Graves, *The Greek Myths*, London, Penguin Books, 1955, pp. 129–30.

108 J. Chodorow, 'Play, Imagination, and the Emotions,' North–South Conference of Jungian Analysts, 1–4 March 2001, n.p. (from a work-in-progress for the Carolyn and Ernest Fay Series in Analytical Psychology).

109 In Greek mythology, a satyr is a half-goat, half-man associated with the god Dionysus, the god of wine and orgiastic celebration of the fertility of nature. Dionysian rites included the dismemberment of a sacrificial victim. The Greek god Pan had a human torso and head but a goat's legs, horns, and ears. He was associated with woods, fields, and flocks.

110 Bynum, 'The Female Body and Religious Practice in the Later Middle Ages,' p. 174.

111 See the commentary on Plates II–4 and II–5 for further discussion of alchemical symbolism of the peacock.

112 A. Roy (ed.), *Artists' Pigments: A Handbook of Their History and Characteristics*, Washington, DC, National Gallery of Art, 1986–93, vol. 2, distributed by Oxford University Press (1993), p. 162. Cited in Elkins, *What painting Is*, p. 20.

113 The man in this painting obviously does not have black skin but lighter skin

blackened from the mud. Nevertheless, we might ask if there is a racist implication to the 'Ethiops' and the 'Ethiopian.' Ethiopian culture was much more advanced than European culture up to the time of the Renaissance, and the country has been predominantly Christian since the Middle Ages. Its possibly mythical Christian king, Prester John, was mentioned in *Mandeville's Travels* (Sir John Mandeville, ed. P. Hamelius, from the MS Cotton Titus C. XVI, British Museum, translated from the French of Jean d'Outremeuse, Early English Text Society, 1916; reprinted: Millwood, NY, Kraus Reprint, 1987, p. 199) in connection with a paradisaical land. According to Bartlett, 'Anti-black racism in the modern sense was unknown in the Middle Ages. There were not enough black people in Europe for whites to feel in any way under threat. Blacks were simply part of the human race, suffering, sinning and needing redemption like everyone else. In the later Middle Ages, there were even black saints, and one of the Magi was conventionally shown as black. On the other hand the colour black was the commonest way of signalling evil, and was very often associated with Satan, which, if it did not exactly demonize real black people, must have put them at some initial disadvantage. Executioners and torturers were often shown as black for this reason' (*Medieval Panorama*, pp. 254–5). According to von Franz, 'Ethiopia was the country whose people carried the collective projection of utter piety and religious fervour on the one hand, and on the other they were considered to be unconscious heathens. Here in alchemy the Ethiopian is often the symbol of the *nigredo*, and it is obvious what that would mean in psychological language for it is not very different from the form in which negroes still turn up nowadays in the unconscious material of white people, namely the primitive, natural man in his ambiguous wholeness. The natural man in us is the genuine man, but also the man who does not fit into conventional patterns, and who in part is very much driven by his instincts' (*Redemption Motifs in Fairy Tales*, p. 210). Also see: Marie Capitolo, 'Black and White: Retrieving Our Shadow,' *J. of Sandplay Therapy*, VI, pp. 71–86, 1997.

114 The silver was blackened by oxidation over time.

115 Dante, *Inferno*, Canto VII, lines 97–109.

116 See M.-L. von Franz, *Shadow and Evil in Fairy Tales*, rev. edn., Boston and London, Shambhala, 1995.

117 CW 7, ¶103, n. 5.

118 See 'Psychological Types' (1923), CW 6.

119 CW 16, ¶376.

120 Read, *Prelude to Chemistry*, pp. 167–8. (We will discuss fiery-water in the commentary on Plate II–1.)

121 Abraham, *Dictionary*, p. 190.

122 In 'Psychology of the Transference,' Jung discusses an image of the hermaphrodite from another famous alchemical treatise of the sixteenth century, the *Rosarium Philosophorum* (CW16 ¶¶525–37).

123 Trismosin, *Splendor Solis*, trans. K[ohn], p. 33.

124 Ibid., p. 32.

125 Hermaphroditis was the son of Hermes and Aphrodite, who became united in one body with the nymph Salmacis while bathing in a fountain.

126 von Franz, *Redemption Motifs in Fairy Tales*, p. 27.

127 Roob, *Alchemy and Mysticism*, pp. 462–3.

128 Joseph H. Henderson, 'The Four Eagle Feathers,' in *Shadow and Self*, Wilmette, IL, Chiron, 1990, p. 156.

129 Ibid.

130 Ibid., pp. 157–8. Jung also speaks of the incident in: C. G. Jung *Memories, Dreams, Reflections*, ed. A. Jaffe, New York, Vintage Books, 1965, p. 230.

131 *Pantheion* in Ancient Greece referred to a shrine for all the gods, in contrast to monotheism of the Christian epoch.

132 Graves, *Greek Myths*. In *The Great Mother* (2nd edn., Princeton, NJ, Princeton University Press, 1963) Erich Neumann states that, 'she is the Whole, containing in herself the three realms that in Greek mythology were later shared by her sons Zeus, Poseidon, and Hades' (p. 275). Later, the three aspects of the deity appeared in masculine form in Christian theology as the Trinity. In this plate, the number three also appears as the three horses and, in the main picture, in the three-storied domed building.

133 In Greek mythology, the merman Triton was the son of Poseidon and Amphitrite, a sea nymph.

134 See CW 13, ¶95, for parallels between this plate and the golden head and dismemberment in the visions of Zosimos. Jung suggested that, 'the golden head referred originally to the head of Osiris . . .' and that, 'The Greek alchemists styled themselves as "Children of the Golden Head"' (CW 12, ¶530).

135 See Mookerjee and Khanna, *Tantric Way*, Plate III, p. 83, for an image of the goddess Kali holding a sword dripping with blood and a severed head. A snake entwines her neck, and she wears a garland of severed heads and a skirt of severed arms. 'The sacrificial sword and the severed head are the symbols of dissolution and annihilation directing the Sadhaka to shed his "ego sense". The girdle of severed hands signifies one's Karma, action' (ibid., p. 85).

136 Trans. K[ohn], p. 33.

137 Neumann, *Great Mother*, p. 326.

138 See C. G. Jung, 'Aion,' CW 9/2, ¶¶72–266 for a discussion of fish symbolism.

139 Edinger, *Anatomy of the Psyche*, p. 121.

140 CW I2, ¶462.

141 Edinger, *Anatomy of the Psyche*, p. 120.

142 Cf., CW 12, p. 328, fig. 178, and Edinger, *Anatomy of the Psyche*, p. 120, fig. 5–2.

The Second Series

1 In the Harley manuscript, these seven plates correspond in the text to The Fourth Treatise: 'The Means by which Nature Attains Her Ends.'

2 For example, see M. Hansen (trans.), *The Planets and Their Children: A Blockbook of Medieval Popular Astrology*, posted on http://www.englib.cornell.edu/mhh4/planets/planets.html (1999) and W. Kenton, *Astrology: The Celestial Mirror*, New York, Thames & Hudson, 1989, figs. 28–33, 37–9, 40–1, and p. 109.

3 Read, *Prelude to Chemistry*, p. 54.

4 Trismosin, *Splendor Solis*, trans. K[ohn], p. 15.

5 Read, *Prelude to Chemistry*, p. 23.

6 CW 14, ¶1.

7 There is no contradiction in the fact that these are culturally derived images. The images cannot be archetypal in the pure sense, since an archetype is a basic pattern underlying images and behavior and cannot be directly represented. Therefore, the Greco-Roman gods and goddesses point toward certain archetypes but are within the cultural context of Western civilization.

8 Khanna, *Yantra*, p. 123.

9 CW 12, ¶34.

10 See the section on Plate I–2 for a discussion of the symbolism of the alembic and the importance of containment in psychotherapy.

11 In the engravings of the 1708 Hamburg edition, reproduced with the translation by J. Godwin, some of the flasks are open at the neck and others are closed. J. Cambray (personal communication) has suggested that these may indicate exothermic and endothermic chemical reactions.

12 CW 13, ¶345.

13 See CW 14, ¶6.

14 See D. Williams, *Deformed Discourse: The Function of the Monster in Medieval Thought and Literature*, Exeter, University of Exeter Press, 1996.

15 von Franz, *Aurora Consurgens*, p. 414.

16 See C. G. Jung, 'General Aspects of Dream Psychology' (1916/1960) and 'On the Nature of Dreams' (1945/1960), in CW 8, ¶¶443–569.

17 CW 13, ¶229.

18 See Jung's essay, 'Concerning Rebirth' (1939/1959), CW 9/1, ¶¶199–258.

19 For more discussion, see Jung's essay, 'The Psychology of the Child Archetype' (1940/1959), CW 9/1, ¶¶259–305.

20 CW 13, ¶274.

21 Roob, *Alchemy and Mysticism*, p. 407.

22 See A. Mookerjee, *Kundalini: The Arousal of the Inner Energy*, London, Thames & Hudson, 1982; and A. Mookerjee and M. Khanna, *The Tantric Way*, London, Thames & Hudson, 1977.

23 CW 12, ¶6.

24 H. Zimmer, *Myths and Symbols in Indian Art and Civilization*, ed. Joseph Campbell, Princeton, NJ, Princeton University Press, 1946/1974, pp. 70–1.

25 See Joe Cambray's Foreword to this book, where he offers his interpretation of the figures pulling the chariots.

26 Cirlot, *Dictionary of Symbols*, p. 38.

27 von Franz, *Alchemy*, p. 156.

28 M. Hansen (trans.), 'Saturn and His Children,' in Hansen, *The Planets and Their Children*.

29 Personal communication.

30 *The American Heritage Dictionary*. A. McLean has suggested that the wreath in this painting is a copying error and that there should be fire at the base of the alembic. ('Introduction' to J. Godwin's translation of the *Splendor Solis*, p. 9.)

31 CW 13, ¶257.

32 Williams, *Deformed Discourse*, p. 202.

33 See ibid., pp. 202–7.
34 S. Allan, *The Way of Water and Sprouts of Virtue*, Albany, State University of New York Press, 1997, pp. 57–61.
35 In the collection of The Hermitage, St. Petersburg.
36 CW 12, ¶4.
37 Picture 2 in 'A Study in the Process of Individuation,' CW 9.
38 Ibid., ¶533.
39 C. G. Jung, 'The Visions of Zosimos,' op. cit., ¶89.
40 E. F. Edinger, *The Mysterium Lectures*, Toronto, Inner City Books, 1995, p. 51.
41 Ibid., p. 52.
42 In Buddhist teaching, this is Second of the 'Four Reflections which Reverse the Mind': 'Everything born is impermanent and bound to die.'
43 See *Jung on Active Imagination*, for a collection of Jung's writings on active imagination. For a guidebook to using active imagination and creative expression with dreams, see J. Mellick, *The Art of Dreaming*, Berkeley, CA, Conari Press, 1996/2001.
44 CW 8, ¶¶343–442.
45 'The work must be performed "with the true and not with the fantastic imagination," . . .' (C. G. Jung, 'Religious Ideas in Alchemy,' CW 12, ¶360).
46 CW 8, ¶400.
47 Ibid., ¶401.
48 See J. Chodorow, *Dance Therapy and Depth Psychology: The Moving Imagination*, New York and London, Routledge, 1991.
49 See E. H. Eisenman, *A Dance with the Dark Angel. Shadow Play: Drama Therapy and Creative Arts Techniques*, self-published, 1995.
50 Examples of Jung's patients who painted and drew during the analyses may be found in 'A Study in the Process of Individuation' and 'Concerning Mandala Symbolism' in CW 9/1 and also in 'The Visions Seminars' recently reissued as: C. G. Jung, *Visions*, ed. Claire Douglas, Princeton, NJ, Princeton University Press, 1997.
51 P. Skar, 'The Goal as Process: Music and the Search for the Self,' *Journal of Analytical Psychology* 47 (2002), 629–38.
52 See note 49, Series I.
53 For a discussion of the symbolism of the peacock in alchemy, see the commentary on Plates II–4 and II–5.
54 Read, *Prelude to Chemistry*, p. 23.
55 C. Ginsburg, 'Clues: Roots of an Evidential Paradigm,' in *Clues, Myths, and the Historical Method*, trans. J. and A. C. Tedeschi, Baltimore, Johns Hopkins University Press, 1986/1989, p. 102.
56 Ibid., pp. 98–101.
57 Quoted in: R. Hayman, *A Life of Jung*, London, Bloomsbury, 1999, p. 242.
58 CW 13, ¶316.
59 See ibid., ¶176.
60 Ibid., p. 141, footnote 39.
61 Ginsburg, 'Freud, the Wolf-Man, and the Werewolves,' in *Clues, Myths, and the Historical Method*, pp. 146–55.

62 Dante, *Inferno*, Canto I, lines 38–45.

63 Cirlot, *Dictionary of Symbols*, p. 18.

64 Ibid., p. 281. Paracelsus was born in Scorpio, and Jung's comments in this regard are quoted in the Introduction.

65 Hansen, *The Planets and Their Children*.

66 Jung, *Seminar on Dream Analysis*, pp. 524–7.

67 For a more complete discussion, see J. L. Henderson, 'Unity of the Psyche: A Philosophy of Analysis,' in: Henderson, *Shadow and Self*, pp. 46–60.

68 See Paracelsus, *Selected Writings*, ed. J. Jacobi, trans. N. Guterman, Bollingen Series 27, New York, Pantheon Books, 1951, p. 142.

69 CW 9/1, ¶426.

70 Although *Atalanta fugiens* (1617) by Michael Maier postdates the *Splendor Solis*, it includes a comment on the role of the ibis in relation to the dragon or snake that fits well with the sequence of images in the *Splendor Solis*: 'Other animalls move upon their Feet, but Serpents, Dragons and such like Vermine use the constriction and explication of their bodyes instead of feet, and like flowing water incline themselves sometimes this way, sometimes that, as may be seen in most Rivers which run obliquely in Circuits and turn their courses like Serpents. The Philosophers therefore did not without reason call Argent Vive by the Name of a Serpent and give Serpents to Mercury, seeing that also does as it were draw its Tayle and run sometimes this way and sometimes another with a Voluble Weight. For as a Serpent moves so also does Mercury, who therefore has Wings upon his feet and Head. It is reported that in Africa there are flying Serpents which would depopulate all places if they were not destroyed by the Bird called Ibis. Wherefore Ibis is placed among the sacred Images of the Egyptians, as much for the manifest good that it does to the whole Country as for a secret reason which very few of them understand.' (H. Tilton, transcription of an English translation from the Latin in the British Library MS Sloane 3645, posted on Adam McLean's Alchemy Website.)

71 Cirlot, *Dictionary of Symbols*, p. 155.

72 C. Freeman, *The Legacy of Ancient Egypt*, Oxford, Andromeda, 1997, p. 112.

73 J. Joyce, *Portrait of the Artist as a Young Man*, London and Toronto, Heinemann Educational Books, 1964, p. 189. We thank Jean Kirsch for suggesting this quotation in relation to the image.

74 T. S. Eliot, 'Four Quartets,' in *The Complete Poems and Plays*, New York, Harcourt, Brace, 1952, QI.

75 We thank Jean Schellenberg, Ph.D. for sharing this material with us and for permitting us to reproduce her paintings. Dr. Schellenberg is a psychologist in private practice in Portola Valley, California. She uses creative expression both in her personal work and in work with her patients. She is currently writing a book on sexuality after trauma.

76 See 'A Study in the Process of Individuation' and 'Concerning Mandala Symbolism,' CW 9; and J. W. Perry, *The Self in Psychotic Process*, Dallas, TX, Spring, 1987 (including Jung's Introduction).

77 'The Unity and Trinity of Mercurius,' CW 13, ¶¶270–2:

78 von Franz, *Aurora Consurgens*, op. cit., p. 385.

79 From a 1952 interview of Jung by M. Eliade, in *C. G. Jung Speaking*, ed. W. McGuire and R. F. C. Hull, Princeton, NJ, Princeton University Press, 1977.

80 Cf., Wilfred Bion's 'pairing culture,' as described in his book *Experiences in Groups*, London, Tavistock, 1961.

81 We thank Jacques Rutzky (personal communication) for bringing this to our attention.

82 Cirlot, *Dictionary of Symbols*, p. 361.

83 M. Fordham, *Analyst–Patient Interaction: Collected Papers on Technique*, ed. S. Shamdasani, London, Routledge, 1996, p. 137.

84 Interestingly, the gestation of Jung's ideas about the self and the study of alchemy coincided with the Second World War. In 1938, after Jung had returned from his trip to India, he told his students that he was shifting his central focus away from the emphasis on familiar mythology to something more abstract, alchemy and what he called natural philosophy. His *Eranos* papers of the early 1940s, 'A Psychological Approach to the Trinity,' 'Transformation Symbolism of the Mass,' and 'The Phenomenology of the Spirit in Fairy Tales,' are works which reflect this change very well. The culmination of this phase, as theory, makes great demands on the reader's power of comprehension. Jung seemed to be studying his concept of the Self – as if it offered him a problem of higher mathematics or atomic physics – in order to learn its dynamism and internal structure. In fact, the last chapter of *Aion* in 1951 ends with, 'The Structure and Dynamics of the Self.' Here the Self is no longer the simple mythological conception of wholeness, but an abstract concept representing an intricate play of opposites. (Modified from J. L. Henderson, 'Jungian Analysis, Yesterday and Tomorrow,' a lecture given to the C. G. Jung Institute of New York in 1997.)

85 Abraham, *Dictionary*, p. 42.

86 von Franz, *Aurora Consurgens*, p. 203.

87 Ibid., p. 206.

88 Ibid., p. 15 and pp. 157–8.

89 J. Cambray (personal communication).

90 Cirlot, *Dictionary of Symbols*, p. 37.

91 Trismosin, *Splendor Solis*, trans. K[ohn], pp. 17–18.

92 Edinger, *Anatomy of the Psyche*, op. cit., p. 8.

93 E. Neumann, 'Mystical Man,' *Eranos* 6, p. 408.

94 Psychologically, this would be a numinous symbol mediating the conscious connection to the greater wisdom of the Self and Nature.

95 D. N. Sherwood, personal observations, unpublished research, and personal communications from Pansy Hawkwing.

96 Those with further interest in this topic may wish to consult: C. G. Jung, *The Psychology of Kundalini Yoga: Notes of the Seminar Given in 1932 by C. G. Jung*, ed. S. Shamdasani, Princeton, NJ, Princeton University Press, 1996.

97 We shall encounter the image of women washing again in the next series (Plate III–3).

98 J. Bernstein, 'Listening in the Borderland: Discriminating the Pathological from the Sacred,' *Salt Journal* 2/2 (January/February 2000), 13–21; and C. G. Jung, *The Earth Has a Soul: The Nature Writings of C. G. Jung*, ed. M. Sabini, Berkeley, CA, North Atlantic Books, 2002.

99 See D. F. Sandner and J. Beebe, 'Psychopathology and Analysis,' in M. Stein (ed.), *Jungian Analysis*, Boulder and London, Shambhala, 1984, pp. 294–334.

100 von Franz, *Redemption Motifs in Fairytales*, p. 27.
101 Sandner, *Navajo Symbols of Healing*.
102 Sandner, 'Analytical Psychology and Shamanism'; P. Damery, 'Reflections on the Archetype of Shamanism and Implications in the Healing Professions,' *San Francisco Jung Institute Library Journal* 20 (2001), 45–58; and S. B. Hermann, 'Donald Sandner, The Shamanic Archetype,' *San Francisco Jung Institute Library Journal* 21 (2002), 23–42.
103 See Joe Cambray's Foreword to this book for an example.
104 CW 12, ¶5.
105 CW 14, ¶759.

The Third Series

1 In the Harley manuscript, the plates in this series correspond in the text to the Fifth Treatise, entitled, 'The Manifold Operations of the Whole Work.'
2 Dante, *Inferno*, p. 311.
3 CW 16, ¶373.
4 P. Damery (personal communication) has suggested that the new plants are better adapted to the bright sunlight of higher altitudes.
5 A. McLean has interpreted this image as a dissolution of 'the border between the conscious and unconscious . . . The conscious, radiant part of the soul has entered into the unconscious realm, which itself, now like a dark Sun, makes its forces felt in the conscious sphere' ('Commentary', to *Splendor Solis*, trans. J. Godwin, p. 110).
6 Comments made at a lecture by Dr. Henderson on the *Splendor Solis*, San Francisco, 1987.
7 According to Read, 'A particularly intriguing association was that of the cat with Luna, or sophic mercury, because the pupil of a cat's eye was said to expand when the moon was waxing and to contract when it was waning' (*Prelude to Chemistry*, p. 103).
8 It is generally thought that for the alchemists, the crow signified black or putrefying matter, but we might also think of the crow, a bird and a carrion eater, as representing a spiritual readiness to digest the putrefying matter.
9 Trismosin, *Splendor Solis*, trans. K[ohn], p. 65.
10 Jung wrote, 'The inner personality is the way one behaves in relation to one's inner psychic processes; it is the inner attitude, the characteristic face, that is turned toward the unconscious. I call the outer attitude, the outward face, the *persona*; the inner attitude, the inward face, I call the *anima*' (CW 6, ¶803).
11 The importance of containment in the analytic process is discussed with regard to Plate I–2.
12 Trismosin, *Splendor Solis*, trans. K[ohn], p. 39.
13 D. W. Winnicott, 'Transitional Objects and Transitional Phenomena' (1951), reprinted in D. W. Winnicott, *Through Paediatrics to Psycho-Analysis*, New York, Basic Books, 1975, pp. 230–1.
14 von Franz, *Aurora Consurgens*, p. 386.

15 Personal recollection, J. L. Henderson.
16 von Franz, *Alchemy*, p. 220.
17 Ibid.
18 Quoted in Read, *Prelude to Chemistry*, p. 157.
19 von Franz, *Aurora Consurgens*, p. 206.
20 von Franz concluded that, 'the east or dawn was correlated not only with the *rubedo* (blood and life) but also with the feminine, white, "dewy" substance fertilized by the spirit' (*Aurora Consurgens*, p. 206). However, dew was also associated with the mercurial fiery-water, or spirit, and so can be seen to correspond to the masculine spiritual substance which fertilizes the earth (Roob, *Alchemy and Mysticism*, p. 47).
21 From *Gloria Mundi*, dated 1526, quoted in Read, *Prelude to Chemistry* p. 130.
22 Wolter, as quoted in K. Kerényi, *Asklepios: Archetypal Image of the Physician's Existence*, trans. R. Manheim, Bollingen Series 65/3, New York and London, Pantheon 1959 (originally published in German as *Der Göttliche Arzt*, 1947), pp. 22–3.

Appendix

1 A process of rubbing, grinding, or crushing into small particles
2 A process of heating a substance to a high temperature below its melting or fusing point, causing the loss of moisture, reduction, or oxidation and the decomposition of carbonates and other compounds.
3 Makes concentrated by boiling.
4 A mineral with the same composition as pyrite, or 'fools' gold,' but differing in crystal structure.
5 See our discussion of Plate I–4 regarding the symbolism of the basilisk.
6 A mineral silicate of iron and magnesium found in igneous and metamorphic rocks.

BIBLIOGRAPHY

Abraham, L. *A Dictionary of Alchemical Imagery*, Cambridge, Cambridge University Press, 1998.

Allan, S. *The Shape of the Turtle: Myth, Art, and Cosmos in Early China*, Albany, State University of New York Press, 1991.

Allan, S. *The Way of Water and Sprouts of Virtue*, Albany, State University of New York Press, 1997.

Artis Auriferae II, Basel, 1593.

Bartlett, R. (ed.) *Medieval Panorama*, Los Angeles, The J. Paul Getty Museum; London, Thames & Hudson, 2001.

Beebe, J. *Integrity in Depth*, New York, Fromm International, 1995.

Bernstein, J. 'Listening in the Borderland: Discriminating the Pathological from the Sacred,' *Salt Journal* 2/2 (January/February 2000), 13–21.

Bion, W. *Experiences in Groups*, London, Tavistock, 1961.

Bradway, K. and B. McCoard, *Sandplay: Silent Workshop of the Psyche*, London and New York, Routledge, 1997.

Bynum, C. W. 'The Female Body and Religious Practice in the Later Middle Ages,' in M. Feher with R. Naddaff and N. Tazi (eds.), *Fragments for a History of the Human Body*, Cambridge, MA, and London, MIT Press, 1989, Part One, pp. 160–219.

Campbell, J. *The Masks of God*, vol. 3: *Occidental Mythology*, Harmondsworth, Penguin Books, 1964.

Campbell, J. *Historical Atlas of World Mythology*, vol. 1: *The Way of the Animal Powers*, San Francisco, Harper & Row, 1983.

Chodorow, J. *Dance Therapy and Depth Psychology: The Moving Imagination*, New York and London, Routledge, 1991.

Chodorow, J. 'Play, Imagination, and the Emotions,' *North–South Conference of Jungian Analysts*, 1–4 March 2001, n.p. (from a work-in-progress for the Carolyn and Ernest Fay Series in Analytical Psychology).

Cirlot, J. E. *A Dictionary of Symbols*, New York, Barnes & Noble, 1971/1993.

Culbert-Koehn, J. 'Analysis of Hard and Soft: Tustin's Contribution to a Jungian Study of Opposites,' *Proceedings of the California Spring Conference of Jungian Analysts and Control Stage Candidates*, C. G. Jung Institute of San Francisco, 1997, pp. 49–55.

Damery, P. 'Reflections on the Archetype of Shamanism and Implications in the Healing Professions,' *San Francisco Jung Institute Library Journal* 20 (2001), 45–58.

Dante Alighieri, *The Inferno of Dante*, trans. R. Pinsky, New York, Farrar, Straus & Giroux, 1994.

Davis, D. Introduction to Farid Ud-Din Attar, *The Conference of the Birds*, trans. Afkham Darbandi and Dick Davis, London, Penguin Books, 1984.

Diamond, J. *Guns, Germs, and Steel*, New York and London, Norton, 1997/1999.

Edinger, E. F. *Anatomy of the Psyche*, Peru, IL, Open Court, 1985.

Edinger, E. F. *The Mysterium Lectures*, Toronto, Inner City Books, 1995.

Eisenman, E. H. *A Dance with the Dark Angel: Shadow Play, Drama Therapy and Creative Arts Techniques*, self-published, 1995.

Eliade, M. *The Forge and the Crucible*, Chicago and London, University of Chicago Press, 1956/1978.

Eliade, M. *Shamanism: Archaic Techniques of Ecstasy*, Bollingen Series 76, New York: Pantheon Books, 1964.

Elkins, J. *What Painting Is*, London and New York, Routledge, 1999.

Eliot, T. S. 'Four Quartets,' in *The Complete Poems and Plays*, New York, Harcourt, Brace, 1952.

Fordham, M. *Analyst–Patient Interaction: Collected Papers on Technique*, ed. S. Shamdasani, London, Routledge, 1996.

Freeman, C. *The Legacy of Ancient Egypt*, Oxford, Andromeda, 1997.

Ginsburg, C. *The Cheese and the Worms*, trans. J. and A. Tedeschi, Baltimore, Johns Hopkins University Press, 1976/1980.

Ginsburg, C. *Clues, Myths, and the Historical Method*, trans. J. and A. Tedeschi, Baltimore, Johns Hopkins University Press, 1986/1989.

Graves, R. *The Greek Myths*, London, Penguin Books, 1955.

Greenson, R. *The Technique and Practice of Psychoanalysis*, vol. 1, New York, International Universities Press, 1967.

Halifax, J. *Shaman: The wounded healer*, London, Thames & Hudson, 1982.

de Hamel, C. *Scribes and Illuminators*, London, British Museum Press, 1991.

Hansen, M. (trans.) *The Planets and Their Children: A Blockbook of Medieval Popular Astrology*, www.englib.cornell.edu/mhh4/planets/planets.html, 1999.

Hayman, R. *A Life of Jung*, London, Bloomsbury, 1999.

Hermann, S. B. 'Donald Sandner, the Shamanic Archetype,' *San Francisco Jung Institute Library Journal* 21 (2002), 23–42.

Henderson, J. L. *Thresholds of Initiation*, Middletown, CT, Wesleyan University Press, 1967.

Henderson, J. L. *Cultural Attitudes in Psychological Perspective*, Toronto, Inner City Books, 1984.

Henderson, J. L. *Shadow and Self*, Wilmette, IL, Chiron, 1990.

Holmyard, E. J. *Alchemy*, New York, Dover Publications, 1957/1990.

Jayakar, P. *The Earthen Drum*, New Delhi, National Museum, n.d.

Jones, P. M. *Medieval Medicine in Illuminated Manuscripts*, London, British Library, 1998.

Joyce, J. *Portrait of the Artist as a Young Man*, London and Toronto, Heinemann Educational Books, 1964.

Jung, C. G. *Collected Works* (CW) by volume and paragraph number, ed. H. Read, M. Fordham, G. Adler, and W. McGuire, trans. in the main by R. Hull, London, Routledge & Kegan Paul; Princeton, NJ, Princeton University Press.

Jung, C. G. *Memories, Dreams, Reflections*, ed. A. Jaffe, New York, Vintage Books, 1965.

Jung, C. G. *C. G. Jung Speaking*, ed. W. McGuire and R. F. C. Hull, Princeton, NJ, Princeton University Press, 1977.

Jung, C. G. *Seminar on Dream Analysis*, ed. W. McGuire, Bollingen Series 99, Princeton, NJ, Princeton University Press, 1984.

Jung, C. G. *The Psychology of Kundalini Yoga: Notes of the Seminar Given in 1932 by C. G. Jung*, ed. S. Shamdasani, Princeton, NJ, Princeton University Press, 1996.

Jung, C. G. *Visions*, ed. C. Douglas, Princeton, NJ, Princeton University Press, 1997.

Jung, C. G. *Jung on Active Imagination*, ed. J. Chodorow, Princeton, NJ, Princeton University Press, 1997.

Jung, C. G. *The Earth Has a Soul, The Nature Writings of C. G. Jung*, ed. M. Sabini, Berkeley, CA, North Atlantic Books, 2002.

Kalff, D. M. *Sandplay: A Psychotherapeutic Approach to the Psyche*, Santa Monica, CA, Sigo, 1980.

Kandinsky, W. *Concerning the Spiritual in Art*, New York, Dover Publications, 1914/1977.

Kenton, W. *Astrology: The Celestial Mirror*, London and New York, Thames & Hudson, 1989.

Kerényi, K. *Asklepios: Archetypal Image of the Physician's Existence*, trans. Ralph Manheim, Bollingen Series 65.3, New York and London, Pantheon, 1959. Originally published in German as *Der Göttliche Arzt*, 1947.

Kerényi, K. *The Heroes of the Greeks*, London, Thames & Hudson, 1959.

Khanna, M. *Yantra: The Tantric Symbol of Cosmic Unity*, London, Thames & Hudson, 1979.

Kieckhefer, R. *Magic in the Middle Ages*, Cambridge, Cambridge University Press, 1989/2000.

Kimbles, S. L. 'The Cultural Complex and the Myth of Invisibility,' in T. Singer (ed.), *The Vision Thing*, London, Routledge, 2000, pp. 157–69.

Kværne, P. *The Bon Religion of Tibet*, Boston, Shambala, 1996.

Manchester, W. *A World Lit Only by Fire*, Boston, Little, Brown & Co., 1992.

Mandeville, J. *Mandeville's Travels*, ed. P. Hamelius, from the MS. Cotton Titus C. XVI, British Museum, translated from the French of Jean d'Outremeuse and published by the Early English Text Society, 1916; Millwood, NY, Kraus Reprint, 1987.

Martin, T. *Ancient Greece From Prehistoric to Hellenistic Times*, New Haven and London, Yale University Press, 1996.

McLean, A. 'Introduction' and 'Commentary' to J. Godwin's translation of S. Trismosin's *Splendor Solis*, Grand Rapids, MI, Phanes 1991.

McLean, A. (ed.) www.alchemywebsite.com. Excellent source of information by the scholar of alchemy, Adam McLean.

Mellick, J. *The Art of Dreaming*, Berkeley, CA, Conari Press, 1996/2001.

Moffitt, J. F. 'Marcel DuChamp: Alchemist of the Avant-Garde,' in *The Spiritual in Art: Abstract Painting 1890–1985*, exhibition catalog, New York, Abbeville Press, 1986, pp. 257–69.

Mookerjee, A. *Kundalini: The Arousal of the Inner Energy*, London, Thames & Hudson, 1982.

Mookerjee, A. and M. Khanna, *The Tantric Way*, London, Thames & Hudson, 1977.

Neumann, E. *The Great Mother*, trans. R. Manheim. Princeton, NJ, Princeton University Press, 1955/1963.

Neumann, E. 'Mystical Man,' *Eranos* 6, Bollingen Series 30, Princeton, NJ, and London, Princeton University Press, 1968.

Paracelsus, *Paracelsus, Selected Writings*, ed. J. Jacobi, trans. N. Guterman, New York, Pantheon, 1951.

Perry, J. W. *The Self in Psychotic Process*, Dallas, TX, Spring, 1987.

Read, J. *Prelude to Chemistry*, London, G. Bell & Sons, 1936.

Robinet, I., J. F. Pas and N. J. Girardot, *Taoist Meditation: The Mao-Shan Tradition of Great Purity*, Suny Series in Chinese Philosophy and Culture, Buffalo, State University of New York Press, 1993.

Roob, A. *Alchemy and Mysticism*, New York and London, Taschen, 1997.

Russack, N. *Animal Guides in Life, Myth, and Dreams: An Analyst's Notebook*, Toronto, Inner City Books, 2002.

Rutter, V. B. *Woman Changing Woman: Feminine Psychology Re-Conceived through Myth and Experience*, San Francisco, HarperCollins, 1993/1994.

Samuels, A. *The Political Psyche*, London, Routledge, 1993.

Sandner, D. *Navajo Symbols of Healing*, Rochester, VT, Healing Arts Press, 1979.

Sandner, D. 'Analytical Psychology and Shamanism,' D. Sandner, and S. H. Wong (eds.), *The Sacred Heritage: The Influence of Shamanism on Analytical Psychology*, New York and London, Routledge, 1997, pp. 3–11.

Sandner, D. and J. Beebe, 'Psychopathology and Analysis,' in M. Stein (ed.), *Jungian Analysis*, Boulder, CO, and London, Shambhala, 1984, pp. 294–334.

Singer, T. (ed.), *The Vision Thing*, London, Routledge, 2000.

Singer, T. 'The Cultural Complex and Archetypal Defenses of the Collective Spirit, Baby Zeus, Elian Gonzales, Constantine's Sword, and Other Holy Wars,' *San Francisco Jung Institute Library Journal* 29 (2002), 5–28.

Sill, G. G. *A Handbook of Symbols in Christian Art*, New York, Collier Books, 1979.

Skar, P. 'The Goal as Process: Music and the Search for the Self,' *Journal of Analytical Psychology* 47 (2002), 629–38.

Sobel, D. *Galileo's Daughter*, New York, Walker & Co., 1999.

Symington, J. and N. *The Clinical Thinking of Wilfred Bion*, London and New York, Routledge, 1996.

Tarnas, R. *The Passion of the Western Mind*, New York, Ballantine Books, 1991/1993.

Trismosin, S. *Splendor Solis*, illuminated manuscript, MS Germ. Fol. 42, Berlin, Staatsbibliothek Preussischer Kulturbesitz, *c.*1532–5.

Trismosin, S. *Splendor Solis*, illuminated manuscript, MS Harley 3469, London, British Library, 1582.

Trismosin, S. *Splendor Solis*, printed with engravings, in *Aureum Vellus, oder Guldin Schatz und Kunstkammer*, Hamburg, 1708.

Trismosin, S. *Splendor Solis*, MS Harley 3469 (1582), trans. J. K[ohn], London, Kegan Paul, Trench, Trubner, & Co., n.d., *c.*1920.

Trismosin, S. *Splendor Solis* (1598 and 1708), trans. J. Godwin, Grand Rapids, MI, Phanes Press, 1991.

von Franz, M.-L. (ed.) *Aurora Consurgens*, New York, Bollingen Foundation, 1966.

von Franz, M.-L. *Number and Time*, Northwestern University Press, 1974.

von Franz, M.-L. *Alchemy: An Introduction to the Symbolism and the Psychology*, Toronto, Inner City Books, 1959/1980.

von Franz, M.-L. *Redemption Motifs in Fairy Tales*, Toronto, Inner City Books, 1980.

von Franz, M.-L. *The Golden Ass of Apuleius*, rev. edn., Boston and London, Shambhala, 1992.

von Franz, M.-L. *Shadow and Evil in Fairy Tales*, rev. edn., Boston and London, Shambhala, 1995.

Virgil (P. V. Maro), *Aeneid*, trans. Theodore C. Williams, Boston, Houghton Mifflin, 1910. Available on the internet at www.Perseus.org.

Weeks, A. *Paracelsus, Speculative Theory and the Crisis of the Early Reformation*, Albany, State University of New York Press, 1997.

Williams, D. *Deformed Discourse: The Function of the Monster in Medieval Thought and Literature*, Exeter, University of Exeter Press, 1996.

Winnicott, D. W. 'Transitional Objects and Transitional Phenomena' (1951), in *Through Paediatrics to Psycho-Analysis*, New York, Basic Books, 1975.

Yang, X. *The Golden Age of Chinese Archaeology*, New Haven and London, Yale University Press, 1999.

Zimmer, H. *Myths and Symbols in Indian Art and Civilization*, ed. J. Campbell, Princeton, NJ, Princeton University Press, 1946/1974.

INDEX

A NOTE FROM THE LIFE BALANCE INSTITUTE

The Life Balance Institute offers programs for successful individuals who have arrived at the point in which they are ready to address what is sometimes referred to as second half of life issues; what C. G. Jung referred to as 'reconciling the opposites.' Underlying all programs is a value-based approach to conducting a strategic analysis of an individual's life. Images, symbols, and myths are an essential part of the process for most participants.

I was in analysis with Dr. Henderson in the years immediately preceding the formation of the Life Balance Institute. In part, it was the skills and insights that I gained from his wisdom that became the groundwork for the founding of the Institute. I remember vividly the time frame in which Dr. Henderson worked with me, utilizing the images from the *Splendor Solis*. These images contributed an understanding of the possibility of transformation that words could not. It is a pleasure to participate in the sharing of Dr. Henderson's work with others.

We are honored to present our first Life Balance publishing award to Dr. Joseph Henderson and to provide a grant for *Transformation of the Psyche: The Symbolic Alchemy of the* Splendor Solis.

Phillip Moffitt
Founder and President
Life Balance Institute
Tiburon, California